The Economics of Mon

In this book, a historical analysis of the precedents of the euro is examined within the context of the current issues affecting the eurozone and the long-term effects of the institutional changes implemented since 2010.

The book begins by placing the eurozone challenges in the historical context of previous monetary unions, drawing on the experience of the gold standard. It then specifically focuses on the problems arising from the running of permanent trade imbalances within the eurozone. The authors explore the advantages and disadvantages of being a member of the eurozone and attempt to measure the optimality of a currency area by the calculation of an index on internal macroeconomic asymmetries. They address the proposals recently made in favour of a fiscal union in the eurozone, including the economic and political feasibility of fiscal transfers in the eurozone. The final two chapters discuss whether the monetary union is in fact more than just that, and whether it will lead inevitably to some form of political union if it is to survive.

With chapters by leading experts from both Europe and the UK, this book will appeal to students in economics, finance, politics, EU integration and European studies, as well as academics and professional economists doing research in EU integration, the eurozone, monetary history and monetary and banking unions in Europe, the UK and elsewhere.

Juan E. Castañeda is Director of the Institute of International Monetary Research and a Senior Lecturer in Economics at the University of Buckingham. He has worked with the European Parliament's Committee of Economic and Monetary Affairs and has been an Honorary Senior Visiting Fellow in Cass Business School, visiting researcher at the Centre of Monetary and Financial Alternatives at Cato, and lecturer at UNED University in Madrid. He is a member of the IEA's Shadow Monetary Policy Committee.

Alessandro Roselli is a visiting fellow at Cass Business School, City University, London and at the University of Buckingham, UK. He has spent most of his career at the central Bank of Italy and has been A.C. Jemolo fellow at Nuffield College, University of Oxford. He has written extensively on banking, finance and economic history.

Geoffrey E. Wood is Professor in Monetary Economics, University of Buckingham and Emeritus Professor in Economics, Cass Business School. He has lectured in economics at the University of Warwick and in banking and finance at City University, London, where he has been Professor since 1986. He worked at the Bank of England as Economist, and later as Special Adviser on Financial Stability.

Routledge Studies in the European Economy

Central and Eastern Europe in the EU
Challenges and Perspectives Under Crisis Conditions
Edited by Christian Schweiger and Anna Visvizi

Greek Employment Relations in Crisis
Problems, Challenges and Prospects
Edited by Horen Voskeritsian, Panos Kapotas and Christina Niforou

Centrally Planned Economies
Theory and Practice in Socialist Czechoslovakia
Edited by Libor Žídek

SME Finance and the Economic Crisis
The Case of Greece
Alina Hyz

Russian Trade Policy
Achievements, Challenges and Prospects
Edited by Sergei Sutyrin, Olga Y. Trofimenko and Alexandra Koval

Digital Transformation and Public Services
Societal Impacts in Sweden and Beyond
Edited by Anthony Larsson and Robin Teigland

Economic Policy, Crisis and Innovation
Beyond Austerity in Europe
Edited by Maria Cristina Marcuzzo, Antonella Palumbo and Paola Villa

The Economics of Monetary Unions
Past Experiences and the Eurozone
Edited by Juan E. Castañeda, Alessandro Roselli and Geoffrey E. Wood

For more information about this series, please visit: www.routledge.com/series/ SE0431

The Economics of Monetary Unions

Past Experiences and the Eurozone

**Edited by Juan E. Castañeda,
Alessandro Roselli and
Geoffrey E. Wood**

Routledge
Taylor & Francis Group

LONDON AND NEW YORK

First published 2020 by Routledge

2 Park Square, Milton Park, Abingdon, Oxon OX14 4RN
605 Third Avenue, New York, NY 10017

Routledge is an imprint of the Taylor & Francis Group, an informa business

First issued in paperback 2021

British Library Cataloguing-in-Publication Data
A catalogue record for this book is available from the British Library

Library of Congress Cataloging-in-Publication Data
Names: Castañeda, Juan E., editor. | Roselli, Alessandro, editor. | Wood, Geoffrey E., 1945– editor.
Title: The economics of monetary unions : past experiences and the Eurozone / edited by Juan E. Castañeda, Alessandro Roselli and Geoffrey E. Wood.
Description: 1 Edition. | New York : Routledge, 2020. | Series: Routledge studies in the European economy | Includes bibliographical references and index.
Identifiers: LCCN 2019049389 (print) | LCCN 2019049390 (ebook)
Subjects: LCSH: Monetary unions—Europe. | Eurozone. | Monetary policy—Europe. | Europe—Economic conditions—21st century. | Europe—Politics and government—21st century.
Classification: LCC HG925 .E356 2020 (print) | LCC HG925 (ebook) | DDC 332.4/5094—dc23
LC record available at https://lccn.loc.gov/2019049389
LC ebook record available at https://lccn.loc.gov/2019049390

ISBN: 978-0-367-34786-4 (hbk)
ISBN: 978-1-03-217307-8 (pbk)
DOI: 10.4324/9780429327964

Typeset in Times New Roman
by Apex CoVantage, LLC

Contents

Figures

Tables

Contributors

Guillaume Bazot is Maître de Conférences at Université Paris VIII. He earned a PhD (2011) from the EHESS and was a post-doctoral fellow at the Paris School of Economics (2012–2014). His research is related to monetary policy and financial macroeconomics in historical perspective.

Juan E. Castañeda has been Director of the Institute of International Monetary Research since 2016. A Doctor of Economics since 2003 (UAM, Madrid) and lecturer in Economics at the University of Buckingham since 2012, Castañeda has experience working and researching in monetary policy and central banking. He has worked with the European Parliament's Committee of Economic and Monetary Affairs and submitted written evidence for a UK Parliament report on the euro. He has been an Honorary Senior Visiting Fellow in the faculty of finance (Cass Business School) and a visiting researcher at Cass Business School and the Centre of Monetary and Financial Alternatives at Cato, and lecturer at UNED University in Madrid. He is the review editor of *Economic Affairs* and has been a columnist of *Expansion* and of several online papers and sites. In 2017, he was appointed as "External Expert" in Economics of COST, the European Cooperation in Science and Technology Agency, and since September 2018 he has also been a member of the Institute of Economic Affairs' Shadow Monetary Policy Committee.

Lorenzo Codogno is the founder and chief economist of his consulting vehicle, Lorenzo Codogno Macro Advisors Ltd, and Visiting Professor in Practice at the European Institute of the London School of Economics. Between May 2006 and February 2015, he was the chief economist and director general at the Treasury Department of the Italian Ministry of Economy and Finance in charge of the economic analysis and planning directorate, with responsibility for macroeconomic forecasts, analysis on the Italian/international economy and domestic/international monetary and financial issues. Throughout this period, he was also head of the Italian delegation at the Economic Policy Committee of the European Union, which he chaired from January 2010 to December 2011, thus attending Ecofin/Eurogroup meetings with Ministers. At the OECD, he headed the Italian delegation at the Economic Policy Committee, the Economic and Development Review Committee and the Working Party 1, which he chaired from January

2013 to February 2015. He joined the Ministry from Bank of America, where he was the managing director, senior economist, and co-head of European Economics based in London over the previous eleven years. Before that, he worked in the research department of Unicredit. He studied at the University of Padua in Italy and has a master's degree from Syracuse University, Syracuse, New York.

Tim Congdon is Chairman and Founder of the Institute of International Monetary Research. He advised the UK's 1979–1997 Conservative government on economic policy, serving as a member of the Treasury Panel (the so-called wise men, or wise persons when a lady had been appointed) from 1992 to 1997. He is usually regarded as the UK's leading exponent of the "monetarist" school of thought, and was influential in the late 1970s and early 1980s in the defence of "Thatcherite monetarism". After starting his career as a journalist on *The Times*, he became an economist in the City of London in 1976. He founded the research consultancy, Lombard Street Research, in 1989, which he left in 2005. Five significant works have appeared since then. In 2005, he published a long pamphlet, *Money and Asset Prices in Boom and Bust*, and in 2009, he published a critique of the Bank of England's conduct in the Northern Rock affair called *Central Banking in a Free Society*. In 2007, a collection of essays on *Keynes, the Keynesians and Monetarism* appeared in the UK, in 2011 another collection with the title *Money in a Free Society* was published by Encounter Books in New York, and in 2017 he edited a volume on the monetary causes of the global financial crisis, *Money in the Great Recession*, published by Edward Elgar.

Frank Decker is an honorary associate at the University of Sydney Law School. He holds a Dr. rer. pol. in Economics from the University of Bremen, a Master of Applied Finance (MAppFin) from Macquarie University Sydney and a Dr. rer. nat. in Theoretical Physics from the Free University of Berlin. He works internationally as a strategy consultant. Decker's academic work has focused on monetary theory and the economic role and impact of property rights. Publications include several articles, books and entries in reference works on the property theory of money. He has also worked extensively on the monetary history of Australia and New Zealand.

Simeng He (CEO of MinimalismFun) finished her PhD of Economics and Finance at the University of Buckingham. She was a visiting lecturer for the Business School (University of Buckingham) and enjoyed a research internship at the Institute of International Monetary Analysis on macroeconomic data analysis. She is now working to bring minimalism into personal finance and life style of young professionals.

Lars Jonung has been a professor emeritus at the Knut Wicksell Centre for Financial Studies, Department of Economics, Lund University, Sweden, since 2010. He served as chairman of the Swedish Fiscal Policy Council from 2012 to 2013. He was Research Advisor at DG ECFIN, European Commission, Brussels, 2000–2010, working on European macroeconomic issues. Prior to moving to Brussels, he was a professor of economics at the Stockholm School of Economics,

Stockholm. Jonung served as the chief economic adviser to Prime Minister Carl Bildt from 1992 to 1994. His research covers monetary and fiscal policy, inflationary expectations, the euro, the economics of European integration and the history of Swedish economic thought. Recently he has published work jointly with Fredrik NG Andersson on the inflation targeting regime of the Riksbank. He is the author of several books and articles in English and Swedish. He holds a PhD in Economics from the University of California, Los Angeles (1975).

Donato Masciandaro is Full Professor of Economics at Bocconi University since 2001. Since 2005 he has held the Chair in Economics of Financial Regulation at Bocconi University, Milan, where since 2018 he has also been Director of the Baffi Carefin Centre for Applied Research on International Markets, Banking, Finance and Regulation. He has been Member of the Management Board and Honorary Treasurer of the SUERF (Sociètè Universitarie Europèenne de Recherches Financières) since 2011. He is Associate Editor of the *Journal of Financial Stability* since 2010 and of the *Italian Economic Journal* since 2016. His research focuses on monetary policy, financial regulation and illegal financial markets.

Eric Monnet is Director of Studies at the EHESS and Full Professor of economic history at the Paris School of Economics. A research fellow at the CEPR, he previously worked as a researcher at the Bank of France and was affiliated to the think tank Bruegel. He has published extensively on the history of central banking and the international monetary system in the 19th and 20th centuries. He is the author of *Controlling Credit: Central Banking and the Planned Economy in Postwar France, 1948–1973*, Cambridge University Press (2018).

Matthias Morys is Senior Lecturer in the Department of Economics at the University of York (UK). He earned a PhD (2006) from the London School of Economics and worked as a postdoctoral research fellow at the University of Oxford (2005–2008) prior to coming to York. His research interests include monetary and financial history of the 19th and 20th centuries, globalisation in historical perspective and the economic history of Central, East and South-East Europe. Matthias Morys acted as an academic advisor to the South-East European central banks in their 2006–2014 project to collect, systematise and publish their monetary history data from the 19th century to World War II.

Davide Romelli has been Assistant Professor of Economics at Trinity College Dublin since 2016. He holds a PhD in Economics from ESSEC Business School and THEMA-University of Cergy-Pontoise. He is Director of IM-TCD (Trinity College Dublin's International Macroeconomics Research Unit), SUERF Research Affiliate and Fellow of the Baffi Carefin Centre for Applied Research on International Markets, Banking, Finance and Regulation. His research focuses on international finance and macroeconomics, central banking and financial supervision.

Alessandro Roselli is a visiting fellow at Cass Business School, City University, London, and at the University of Buckingham, UK. He has spent most of his career at the Central Bank of Italy and has been A.C. Jemolo Fellow at Nuffield College, University of Oxford. He has written extensively on banking, finance and economic history. His most recent books include *Financial Structures and Regulations: A Comparison of Crises in the UK, USA and Italy* and *Money and Trade Wars in Interwar Europe*, both published by Palgrave Macmillan.

Felix Roth has been Senior Research Fellow at the Chair for International Economics at the University of Hamburg since 2017, where he currently is finalizing his German Habilitation in economics. He studied sociology, economics and European law at Nancy2 and the University of Munich, from which he received his diploma in sociology in 2003. His doctoral thesis in economics was jointly supervised by the London School of Economics and the University of Göttingen, from which he received his PhD in Economics in 2007. His academic research is focused on the relationship between intangible capital and productivity growth, as well as on the determinants of public support for the euro. He has published in *Journal of Common Market Studies, Review of Income and Wealth, Kyklos* and *Journal of European Integration*, as well as monographs and contributions to collected volumes. He has about ten years of experience of working on EU issues as an expert for DG RTD and JRC, as 2014/15 DG ECFIN Research Fellow, and as a research fellow at the Centre for European Policy Studies in Brussels.

Uwe Schollmeyer studied economics at the University of Bayreuth and worked as a research assistant at the Economics Department of the Justus Liebig University Giessen. In addition, he lectured economics and business administration at a number of other education and training institutions. In 2007 he entered the Bundesbank and worked in the Payment and Settlement Systems Department. His first responsibility was the oversight and analysis of CLS, CPSS and business continuity matters. Afterwards he conducted qualitative and quantitative payment analyses and wrote on the macroeconomic role of cashless payments. Since 2012 he has been a member of the academic staff as senior lecturer at the Deutsche Bundesbank University of Applied Sciences in Hachenburg. His main areas of teaching include cash, payment and securities settlement systems, financial market infrastructures, liquidity and financial stability, as well as general economics.

Pedro Schwartz is Rafael del Pino Professor in the Department of Economics at Camilo José Cela University in Madrid. He has been a visiting lecturer at the University of Buckingham in the UK (2014–2018). From September 2014 to September 2016 he was President of the Mont Pèlerin Society, of which he has been a member since 1978. He is a Bachelor and Doctor in Laws of the Universidad Complutense de Madrid, and a Master of Economics and a PhD in Political Thought at the London School of Economics. As a member of the Intelligence Department of the Bank of Spain, he directed the History Division specialising in monetary history. At the four Spanish universities where he has taught he was a professor of the history of economic thought. He belongs to the board of the Spanish think tank Pro Civismo and to the Academic Advisory Board of the Institute of Economic Affairs in London; he is also a member of the Liberales Institut Zürich and of the European Centre of Austrian Economics at Liechtenstein. In the US, he is Adjunct Scholar of the Cato Institute. He is also an academician of the Real Academia de Ciencias Morales y Políticas of Spain. He helped introduce the Santander Universidades Programme in the UK.

Dimitrios P. Tsomocos is Professor of Financial Economics at Saïd Business School and Fellow in Management at St Edmund Hall, University of Oxford. He co-developed the Goodhart – Tsomocos model of financial fragility in 2003 while working at the Bank of England. The impact has been significant, and more than ten central banks have calibrated the model, including the Bank of Bulgaria, Bank of Colombia, Bank of England and the Bank of Korea. In 2011, Tsomocos provided testimony to House of Lords for the Economic and Financial Affairs and International Trade Sub Committee's report, "The future of economic governance in the EU". He holds a BA, MA, MPhil, and a PhD from Yale University. More information can be found at www.tsomocos.org.

Paul van den Noord spent the bulk of his career at the OECD in Paris, first as a senior economist from 1989 to 2007 and next as a counsellor in the Chief Economist's Office from 2010 to 2013. In the latter capacity he has been OECD Delegate to the G20 and in the former capacity the OECD Secretary at the G10. From 2007 to 2010 he was seconded to the European Commission in Brussels where he acted as Economic Advisor in DG ECFIN. More recently, from 2013 to 2017, van den Noord worked at Autonomy Capital, a global-macro hedge fund in London and Geneva. He was also Associate Fellow at Chatham House in London from 2013 to 2017 and was Visiting Professor at the College of Europe in Bruges from 2014 to 2018. He started his career as a research fellow at the Foundation for Economic Research (SEO) in Amsterdam (1979–1989) and as a lecturer at the University of Amsterdam (1983–1985), where he holds a PhD. He has published extensively in the areas of fiscal policy, monetary policy, housing markets and the political economy of Monetary Union in Europe.

Roland Vaubel is Professor Emeritus of Economics (Political Economy) at the University of Mannheim, Germany. He received a BA in Philosophy, Politics and Economics from the University of Oxford, an MA from Columbia University, New York, and a doctorate from the University of Kiel, Germany. He has been Professor of Economics at Erasmus University Rotterdam and has taught at the University of Chicago (Graduate School of Business) as Visiting Professor of International Economics. He is a member of the Advisory Council to the German Federal Ministry of Economics and of the Academic Advisory Council of the Institute of Economic Affairs, London. He is a member of the editorial boards of the *European Journal of Political Economy*, *Constitutional Political Economy*, the *Review of International Organizations* and *Cato Journal*.

Xuan Wang is a PhD (DPhil) candidate in Financial Economics at the Saïd Business School, University of Oxford. Wang is a Clarendon Scholar and a member of Exeter College. Prior to his doctoral studies, Wang obtained an MPhil in Economics with Distinction from the University of Oxford and worked at the Bank of England as a full-time economist. His recent work includes "When Do Currency Unions Benefit from Default?" and studying financial stability and endogenous liquidity at the low interest rate environment. During his doctoral studies, Wang has been a College Lecturer in Economics at Magdalen College, Oxford, teaching microeconomics, macroeconomics and quantitative economics to undergraduate students studying philosophy, politics and economics. In 2018, he co-organised the Inaugural Oxford Saïd Macro-Finance Workshop, and in 2019, he co-organised the Oxford NuCamp-Saïd Macro-Finance Conference on Money, Credit, and Financial Stability. More information about Wang's work can be found at https://sites.google.com/view/xuan-wang.

Geoffrey E. Wood is Professor in Monetary Economics, University of Buckingham, and Emeritus Professor in Economics, Cass Business School. He has lectured in economics at the University of Warwick and in banking and finance at City University, London, where he has been Professor since 1986. He worked at the Bank of England as Economist, and later as Special Adviser on Financial Stability. He was also Visiting Scholar at the Federal Bank of St Louis. He has acted as an economic adviser to various firms and organisations, including W. Greenwell & Co., Buckmaster & Moore, the Union Discount Company of London, the New Zealand Treasury and the Bank of Finland. Visiting professorships have taken him to universities around the world: South Carolina, Harvard, London, Athens and Oxford. Since 1991 he has been a trustee of the Wincott Foundation. He is the author, co-author or editor of over 20 books, and he has published over 50 papers in academic journals, as well as doing a good amount of written and broadcast journalism. Recent books co-edited with F.H. Capie include *The Development of Monetary Theory in the 1920s and 1930s* (1999), *Policy Makers on Policy* (2001), *Monetary Unions: Theory, History, Public Choice* (2003), *The Lender of Last Resort* (2007), with David Mayes *The Structure of Financial Regulation* (2007) and with David Mayes and Juan E. Castañeda *European Banking Union: Prospects and Challenges* (2016).

Preface

The papers in this volume were first presented and discussed at a conference held at the University of Buckingham. We are very grateful to the University, and also to the Institute of International Monetary Research, for generous financial support. The University also very kindly let us inaugurate with our conference the main lecture theatre in the then newly completed Vinson Building. Using the theatre was a delight.

Of course, no conference runs without substantial administrative assistance. The Institute of International Monetary Research used its printing and distribution facilities to print and distribute the programme and the papers for the conference. And the overall organisation of the whole event was managed by Gail Grimston, the Institute's administrator. Without her management the conference might not have run, and certainly would not have run as well as it so manifestly did. Her work was invaluable, and we are very grateful to her.

Abbreviations

ANFA	Agreement on Net Financial Assets
ANZUKMU	Australia, New Zealand and the United Kingdom Monetary Union
APP	Asset Purchase Programme (Eurosystem)
AR	Apprehension Ratio
BCEAO	West African Economic and Monetary Union
BdL	Bank deutscher Länder
BEAC	Central African Economic and Monetary Community
BESP	Banking Electronic Speedy Payment (Russia)
BIS	Bank for International Settlements
BOJ-Net FTS	Bank of Japan Financial Network System – Funds Transfer System
BPE	Behavioural Political Economics
CA	Current Account
CCP	Central Counterparty
CDU	Christian Democratic Union party
CHATS	Clearing House Automated Transfer System (Hong Kong)
CHIPS	Clearing House Interbank Payments System (US)
CSU	Christian Social Union party
CLS	Continuous Linked Settlement
CPMI	Committee for Payments and Market Infrastructures
CPSS	Committee on Payment and Settlement Systems
CR	Coverage Ratio
DLT	Distributed Ledger Technology
DOLS	Dynamic Ordinary Least Squares
EA	European Area
EAF	Elektronische Abrechnung Frankfurt, later Euro Access Frankfurt (Germany)
EB	Eurobarometer
EBA	European Banking Association
ECB	European Central Bank
ECCB	Eastern Caribbean Currency Union
ECHO	Exchange Clearing House Limited
EDIS	European Deposit Insurance Scheme
EISF	European Investment Stabilisation Function

ELA	Emergency Liquidity Assistance
ELS	Elektronischer Schalter, later Euro Link System (Germany)
EMF	European Monetary Fund
EMS	European Monetary System
EMU	European Monetary Union
ERM	European Exchange Rate Mechanism
ESM	European Stability Mechanism
EU	European Union
EUISF	European Unemployment Insurance Fund
FDIC	Federal Deposit Insurance Corporation
FE-DFGLS	Fixed Effect Dynamic Feasible General Least Squares
FGLS	Feasible General Least Squares
FX	Foreign Exchange
FXYCS	Foreign Exchange Yen Clearing System
GDP	Gross Domestic Product
GEI	General Equilibrium with Incomplete markets
HICP	Harmonised Index of Consumer Prices
HKD	Hong Kong dollar
HKMA	Hong Kong Monetary Authority
IBRD	International Bank for Reconstruction and Development
IIP	International Investment Position
IMF	International Monetary Fund
IOSCO	International Organization of Securities Commissions
ISA	Interdistrict Settlement Accounts (US)
LMU	Latin Monetary Union
LOLR	Lender of Last Resort
LTRO	Long Term Refinancing Operations
LVPS	Large-Value Payment System
LVTS	Large-Value Transfer System (Canada)
MB	Monetary Base
MC	Markets Committee
MIP	Macroeconomic Imbalance Procedure
MS	Member States
MT	Medium Term
NCB	National Central Bank
NPL	Non-Performing Loans
NSD	National Settlement Depository (Russia)
NSDAP	National Socialist German Workers' Party
OCA	Optimal Currency Area
OMT	Outright Monetary Transactions
PNS	Paris Net Settlement (France)
POPS	Pankkien On-line Pikasiirrot ja Sekit-järjestelmä (Finland)
R	Reserves
SIC	Swiss Interbank Clearing
SIX	Swiss Exchange

SMU	Scandinavian Monetary Union
SRF	Single Resolution Fund
SSM	Single Supervisory Mechanism
ST	Short Term
TARGET2	Trans-European Automated Real-time Gross settlement Express Transfer System 2
TFEU	Treaty on the Functioning of the European Union
TLTRO	Targeted Longer Term Refinancing Operations
UK	United Kingdom of Great Britain and Northern Ireland
US	United States of America
USSR	Union of Soviet Socialist Republics
WWI	World War I
WWII	World War II
ZLB	Zero Lower Bound

1 Introduction

*Juan E. Castañeda, Alessandro Roselli
and Geoffrey E. Wood*

The creation of the euro divided economists. Some thought it would have major favourable effects, promoting trade and growth across the eurozone. Others thought it a bad idea, inevitably damaging to the diverse economies of the eurozone. And there were some who thought it desirable in principle, but a good idea needing work to achieve anything like its full possibilities. In particular, fiscal union and even political union were seen to be necessary to complete the monetary union.

The creation of the euro can be thus seen from a double perspective. The economic perspective, that it followed previous unsuccessful attempts by European countries to stabilize the exchange rates of their currencies, through a coordination of their economic policies, within the floating rates regime that had prevailed after the Bretton Woods system's collapse. Alternately, from a political perspective, as a monetary arrangement that would promote political union in Europe in response to what seemed a series of never-ending wars.

The year 1992 saw the failure of the Exchange Rate Mechanism (ERM), the last of those attempts to stabilize the exchange rates of European currencies, which prompted Milton Friedman's appropriate comment, titled "Déjà vu?": "How many more fiascos will it take before responsible people . . . are finally convinced that a system of pegged exchange rates is not a satisfactory financial arrangement for a group of large countries with independent political systems and independent national policies?"[1]

The second perspective, with its broadly political background, brings us to the French–German bargain of the unification of Germany within a unified Europe. In the same year as the ERM's failure, 1992, the Maastricht Treaty was signed by the European Council to create a single market and a monetary union, by introducing the euro at the end of a convergence period.[2]

An interesting perspective on these two views is provided in Chapters 13–16 of *Living the Cold War* (2017), in which Christopher Mallaby gives an account of his years as British Ambassador to West Germany (as it was when he started in post there).

> In many public speeches I made in Germany, European affairs were a frequent theme. When the Maastricht agreement was being negotiated, I thought that the British objections to a European single currency were unanswerable. How could it be sensible to have a single currency with one interest rate and one

exchange rate for countries with different levels of development and rates of growth? . . . Business audiences understood my strictures, but some others, including politicians enthusiastic about the EU, did not want to know about economic objections; they wanted the single currency because they wanted progress in building a united Europe.

(p. 189)

He then goes on:

At this time the Federal Government had doubts about the single currency and the Bundesbank was dead against it. Mitterand (President of France, 1981 to 1995) later persuaded Kohl (Chancellor of Germany, 1982 to 1993) to commit to it in return for French agreement to German reunification.

Kohl was the more susceptible to this pressure because he had realised there was need for total economic transformation in East Germany as soon as possible to prevent economic collapse, and he believed the then government of East Germany was not competent to carry that out. Further, he feared that Gorbachev's position in the USSR was not secure, and wanted reunification to be achieved as rapidly as possible lest someone hostile to reunification replace Gorbachev (p. 225).[3]

The issue of whether the eurozone can be seen as an optimum currency area is an economic question, but it should not be forgotten that there is another perspective, a political one that for better or worse has accompanied the launch of the euro since its very inception.[4]

Robert Mundell published two papers on monetary unions, one providing support to the first view and one to the second (1961 and 1973). His two papers are part of the literature on "optimum currency areas", which many scholars have sought to apply to study of the euro. This literature is recent in its origins. The question of whether the chosen domain of a currency is optimal, or at least sensible, is important. In this regard, Peter Kenen argued that a fiscal redistribution scheme should take the place of any missing exchange rate flexibility.[5] But nonetheless the optimal area currency concept developed relatively recently. Bennett McCallum (2003, p. 8) advances an explanation:

The optimal currency area concept was introduced, as is well known, by Mundell (1961). Despite appearances, the foregoing should be regarded as a striking statement because it is surprising that such a basic idea would not have been developed previously.

McCallum (2003, p. 10) explains this late development as follows:

Prior to the 1950s, the predominant position among international and monetary economists was that some metallic monetary standard should be adopted by all countries. The most common position was that the *same* monetary standard, typically the gold standard, should prevail everywhere.[6]

This orthodoxy was, McCallum suggests, ended by the publication of Friedman's "The Case for Flexible Exchange Rates" together with other papers in favour of floating, such as Lutz (1954), Sohmen (1957) and Yeager (1959). In combination with acceptance of the belief that monetary policy could be used to offset temporary adverse demand shocks, there was clearly now a case for floating exchange rates as well as for the other extreme, a single worldwide currency. Hence, McCallum argues, since the concept of a monetary area other than the whole world was now of interest, economic arguments were relevant in discussion of the creation of the euro.[7] Did the euro area at least approximate to an optimum currency area (OCA)?

There can be few doubts that, at its beginning, it could not be considered as having the features of an optimum currency area, given the huge economic and social discrepancies existing between its potential members. The issue is therefore not so much to ask whether an OCA was already there, but to question whether the necessary steps towards it have been, or are going to be, taken. As observed by Capie and Wood (2002) whether the eurozone becomes as an optimum currency area is, eventually, an issue of political feasibility.

Another important issue affecting any type of fixed exchange rate system, and the eurozone is an example of it as member states have irrevocably fixed the exchange rate of their national currencies to the euro, is the issue of preserving symmetry in the running of a monetary union. The main difficulty is perhaps that any movement towards making the eurozone a more optimal currency area and indeed more symmetric has to proceed through two different economic philosophies:[8] a "northern vision" mainly based on the application of rigorous and consistent rules (mostly focussed on "supply side" measures) versus a "southern vision" that favours more flexibility in the application of the rules and more room to exert discretion; the former mostly relying on preserving price stability as the ultimate policy goal, the latter on "demand management policies" that focus more on stabilisation policies.

But relevant or not to its creation, economics is relevant to evaluating its performance, and in considering how that performance could be improved. At the same time, politics cannot be neglected; they, after all, influence what is done at least as much (certainly in the short term) as economics. That need for joint economic and political consideration brings us to the contents of this volume, a set of papers given initially at the University of Buckingham in 2019, in a conference co-hosted by the Institute of International Monetary Research. This introduction first surveys these papers, and then concludes by seeing what themes emerge from them.

The papers themselves are in five groups. This review of them starts with the papers that contain pure historical comparison, drawing on the experience of the gold standard. These two are then followed by two papers that consider the inevitable financial imbalances within a monetary union, and their possible financial consequences – a difficulty increased by the imbalances being between countries each with their own fiscal policies, in contrast to the handling of imbalances within a monetary union such as the US.[9] Discussion of imbalances of course starts discussion of threats to the union's survival. The next section, "When may unions fail?", considers some of those, and leads to a discussion of political factors which may affect the survival of a union, to possible debt market operations which can help survival, and in the last paper of this section to plans which fall short of full fiscal union but go sufficiently far towards it to stabilise the union. The final two papers discuss whether the monetary union is in fact more than just a monetary union, and whether it will lead inevitably to some form of political union if it is to survive.

1 The papers

1.1 Lessons from previous currency and monetary unions

The first two papers constitute attempts to learn from a previous union, the gold standard.[10] The authors of the first paper (Guillaume Bazot, Eric Monnet and Matthias Morys) remark on similarities between the eurozone and the gold standard: fixed exchange rates and free capital movements, with a consequent lack of autonomous monetary policies. However, under the gold standard these conditions did not prevent central banks from acting as a buffer to preserve financial stability, a role carried out today by the European Central Bank (ECB) through a range of measures.

Central banks *avoided* symmetrical behaviour through managing their balance sheets, and sometimes using international loans. They reacted to asymmetric shocks, offsetting them by producing negative correlation between the domestic and foreign components of the balance sheet, and by restrictions to banknotes' convertibility into gold (a form of capital control). The gold standard "rules of the game" – gold convertibility, changes in the money supply in the same direction as changes in the international reserves – were not rigidly followed.

The effects of these policies are measured by observing the central banks' reaction to changes in the discount rate of the Bank of England, the system's pivot.[11] In particular, the core countries (Germany, France) adopted systematic sterilization policies, opposite to what the rules of the game would have suggested (for instance, by expanding the domestic "portfolio" in case of contraction of the foreign reserves), in this way stabilizing the money supply; while peripheral countries (such as Italy) relied on capital controls through convertibility restrictions (again, not following the rules of the game). In addition, as mentioned earlier, central bank cooperation acted through international loans (as that of the Banque de France to the Bank of England during the Barings crisis of 1890). This flexibility can explain the stability of the classical – pre-WWI – gold standard.

In today's eurozone, the ECB uses versions of these operations to maintain financial stability, countering a very asymmetric distribution of loans and trying to stabilize interest rates, through macroprudential measures such as long-term refinancing operations or Emergency Liquidity Assistance, or – as a last resort – temporary capital controls. All measures, however, that cannot solve chronic current account imbalances. The authors conclude that lessons have plainly been learned from the gold standard, but that whether they are sufficient is for discussion.

The next paper, by Juan E. Castañeda, Alessandro Roselli and Simeng He, further pursues comparisons with the gold standard. The recent (2010–2012) crisis in the eurozone has revived discussions on the adoption of policies symmetric between creditors and debtors and aimed at preventing fundamental disequilibria within systems characterized by fixed exchange rates among different currencies, or in a monetary union where a single currency has replaced the system's national currencies, as in the case of the eurozone itself. In monetary history this debate has often been focussed on previous systems having these features, and in particular on the working of the gold standard: on whether its members pursued, in fact and to what extent, symmetric policies to preserve the system's stability. In this paper the authors briefly survey the features of international monetary systems that have in common symmetry as a balancing factor, and then explore the meaning and consequences of asymmetric monetary policies under the gold standard. They offer a new measure of asymmetry in the running of the gold standard for the biggest five European economies in the pre-WWI period (UK, Italy, France, Germany and Spain) and use this measure to draw policy implications deriving from the gold standard constraints. Did central banks act symmetrically? The results show that the UK was the country which followed most closely the symmetry rule of the game; at the other extreme was Italy. The common pattern of behaviour was an under-issue of currency (minimal, in the case of Britain).

Was policy affected by the observance of the legal conversion ratio, or were there other criteria? Italy, Germany France and Spain seemed to have paid attention to the deviations of the coverage ratio from a (high) safety ratio in order to maintain convertibility. Achieving a safety ratio of 35% seemed to have been taken as a pre-condition to be able to abide by symmetry in the running of the gold standard.

These two chapters, and other work using comparisons with the gold standard, are the bedrock of work on the euro, for the gold standard is the clearest previous example of several countries agreeing to use a common money, and one issued by none of them individually, but rather by all collectively.

1.2 *Financing imbalances in a single monetary area. An assessment of Target2*

In Chapter 4 Uwe Schollmeyer addresses one of the most contentious issues affecting the eurozone in the last few years, one which has received an increased attention in the financial media and particularly in Germany: the accumulation of TARGET2 (im)balances across national central banks in the eurozone, with the Bundesbank holding the largest creditor position, and Banca d'Italia and Banco de España the largest debtor positions.

Schollmeyer offers a novel perspective on this question by analysing the TARGET2 payment system *"from an integrated central banking perspective"* (Schollmeyer's italics), as well as by assessing its alternatives. In doing so, he shows the intrinsic link between TARGET2 balances and the way in which the monetary policy of the ECB is implemented, drawing our attention to the effects of the running of the ECB's Asset Purchase Programme (2015–2018) in the accumulation of TARGET2 balances in recent years. Schollmeyer not only (briefly) discusses how TARGET2 works but also compares it with other large payment systems in other jurisdictions across the world, such as that of the US. This makes it easier to assess the advantages and disadvantages of TARGET2 in light of the alternative systems operating in other monetary unions.

In assessing the alternatives to TARGET2 (such as a more centralised euro-system, the settlement of the balances in a different currency or the privatisation of money creation) Schollmeyer is quite sceptical about them all; in his view, it is the unique decentralised money creation architecture of the eurosystem in a multinational monetary area which very much restricts the ability to change the current system. As he concludes the chapter, "any of the discussed alternatives shows major problems that would potentially be much worse than accumulating TARGET2 balances in the eurosystem's NCBs. In the end the basic insight that a claim against a central bank is the least risky asset in our fiat money system still holds true".

Payment imbalances are also a central topic in Frank Decker's analysis of the eurosystem in Chapter 5. Decker's approach is using the analytical tool of "credit mechanics" to decode the underlying workings of monetary unions in general, which he then applies to the eurosystem. Credit mechanics expresses the formal relations that must hold between bank creditor and debtor accounts in any monetary system, be it a domestic system or an international monetary union.

According to this approach, each monetary union relies on an underlying stabilising agreement that must deal with the occurrence and settlement of inter-bank balances. A monetary union can only be sustained if surplus banks advance credit to deficit banks or if deficit banks offer acceptable assets to settle their debts. In a typical domestic setting, deficit banks provide eligible assets (as a last resort, central bank liabilities) to their counterparties in order to periodically settle their balances and stay solvent. The solvency risk of a deficit bank is in the end the disciplining element, which keeps deposit liabilities of different domestic banks at par. An international monetary union is similarly created. However, a member country will exit the union if balances cannot be settled and par-clearing can no longer be maintained.

After a survey of historical examples of successful international unions, the working of the "credit mechanics" is examined in reference to the eurosystem. Decker reminds us that there were three principle design choices for the European Monetary Union. Specifically, he argues that a successful union could have been established based on independent national central banks without an ECB. Decker argues that the actual design chosen for the eurosystem represents one of the weaker choices available. Despite the no-bail out Treaty provisions and the retention of national central banks (NCBs), the eurosystem design is underpinned by unlimited and unsecured inter-central bank credit. Note and deposit liabilities are created by nationally distinct institutions and therefore, in Decker's view, represent distinct moneys, denominated in the same ideal unit (the euro), that are held at par through the technical procedure of the inter-bank clearing system TARGET2, which permits unlimited and uncollateralized credit facilities among NCBs via the ECB. Settlement is not required other than on exiting the eurosystem. As a consequence, NCB assets have been mutualized, in a sort of monetary transfer union, being not aligned with the fact that NCBs are not ECB branches and that a fiscal and political union has not yet been achieved. Decker argues that the wide-ranging loss of monetary sovereignty and the implied unlimited support given to deficit-NCBs has for a long time been concealed by the seemingly technical nature of the TARGET2 payment system.

Decker then turns to reform proposals. He argues that incremental reforms such as the periodic settlement of TARGET2 balances based on the US model are unlikely to be effective due to the strong influence of deficit-NCBs in the ECB Governing Council. He therefore argues that more wide-ranging reforms must be envisaged. He broadly classifies these into proposals favouring state ordering and private ordering. The recent development path has been towards state ordering, as is reflected in the large eurosystem government security holdings. Decker argues that European central banking must return to a narrow mandate consistent with private ordering principles – where a central bank is more a bankers' bank than a monetary authority. This implies a narrow focus on the creation of sound "property-based" money by refinancing assets in low risk operations at market interest rates and a minimum of outright government debt holdings, a model that underpinned the success of the Bundesbank and the Swiss National Bank in the 1980s.

On this basis, a scheme for a European Monetary Union with a single central bank and the demotion of NCBs into mere ECB branches could be devised. However, Decker argues that a successful single institution would require a strong European treasury and a European tax to underpin its last resort lending function. This would be inconsistent with the current state of European political and fiscal integration. A further option would be a federation of separate national central banks, issuing euro-denominated notes and deposits, which are mutually accepted at par. Their monetary policies would be independent but interlinked with their par-clearing obligation. Settlement of inter-bank balances should be made periodically with good-quality assets; countries would be free to exit and re-enter the union. Under such a scheme the ECB would no longer be required.

1.3 When may unions fail?

Masciandaro and Romelli describe the essential features of the European Monetary Union (EMU), then consider EMU on the basis of standard optimal currency area (OCA) theory, and revisit this theory by applying a different instrument of analysis, the behavioural political economy approach, which aims at evaluating the optimality of a currency union from the perspective of citizens and policymakers' preferences.

EMU is characterized by a single currency and a delegation, by the member states, of monetary policy to a supranational institution, the European System of Central Banks. From that delegation medium- to long-term benefits are expected. OCA theory, as formalized in the 1960s and used as the basis for evaluating, over the last decades, the viability and desirability of the European monetary integration, shows – in terms of a cost–benefit analysis – that the rationale of a single currency is that it decreases monetary transaction costs, thus favouring transactions within the union, and also assists the mobility of factors of production. Those benefits are higher when market integration is greater and markets are more efficient. They are to be compared to the short-term costs of inability to react to macroeconomic shocks or to address business-cycle problems at a national level. Losses are higher when supranational stabilization policies, as distinct from the monetary policy of the union, are missing or in some way defective.

The authors observe that EMU has so far shown convergence of inflation and interest rates over the eurozone; trade has been modestly boosted, but a convergence of per-capita income towards a higher level of output has not occurred. Overall, the standard OCA approach does not provide a firm answer: benefits have been more evident in countries that have been able to increase productivity, while "peripheral" countries continue experiencing financial instability and debt-related problems.

The behavioural political economy approach, and more specifically the "prospect approach", tries to evaluate a currency union from the perspective of citizens and policymakers' preferences, where the latter try to maximize consensus among the former. This approach relies mainly on two criteria: the "reference point (or status quo) dependence" and the "loss aversion relative to that point". The first makes it possible to evaluate benefits and losses perceived by citizens: the expected monetary stability benefits and expected sovereignty losses are evaluated in relation to that reference point, and it shows a diminishing sensitivity over time. The second shows that people tend to give more weight to losses than to equivalent gains. The individual perceived gains and losses are captured by parameters, which give a measure of (in the EMU case) Europhilia or Europhobia. The mathematical framework used by the authors allows one to follow the evolution of individuals' attitudes to EMU as a function of the expected benefits and losses. Any shock that changes the perceived costs and benefits will change also the optimal Europhilia. This framework allows a better understanding of the dynamics of EMU support, beyond what the Eurobarometer surveys show, i.e. it tries to explain why the perception of EMU – the degree of euro support – has changed over time in specific member countries.

For Italy, a strong decrease in Europhilia over 25 years (1993–2018) is due to the fact that a falling inflation has a diminishing "endowment" effect – that is, the perceived gain is fading with the passage of time – while a negative output trend, the perceived loss, makes people complain about the lack of sovereignty.

Juan E. Castañeda and Pedro Schwartz point out that the traditional optimal currency union literature offers the rationale for the adoption of a single currency but it does not provide specific indicators or values to assess how near a single currency may be to optimality. In their paper they propose and calculate an overall index of macroeconomic integration in a currency area, as well as several sub-indices. They have calculated such metrics for the eurozone and have observed that internal asymmetries (1) grew from the very launch of the euro in 1999, (2) that they have worsened in the crisis years, particularly as regards competitiveness across member states and (3) that asymmetries have diminished from 2014 to 2017 but have remained stagnant since then and thus stayed very far from the pre-crisis levels. Finally, they have calculated the same metrics for US states and compare them with those of the eurozone. As shown in the paper, macroeconomic asymmetries within the US did increase in the 2008–2009 crisis years but have returned to pre-crisis levels.

This paper is thus a comparison of how two unions respond to similar shocks. Why the euro area responded so differently from the US is not examined.

1.4   Preserving unions: the eurozone

Roth and Jonung move us on to the politics emphasised by Christopher Mallaby. Several approaches are available to assess the feasibility and the success of a monetary union; for example, the economic criteria countries must fulfil to form a so-called optimal currency area, or the analysis of the degree of macroeconomic convergence or divergence among the economies forming (or willing to form) a monetary area (see the chapter by Castañeda and Schwartz). Jonung and Roth opt for a completely different approach, which consists of the measurement of the popular support for the euro and of trust in the ECB. Ultimately, they claim that it is the public support of the euro that will guarantee its legitimacy and viability in the future. This is so manifestly true that it could be claimed to be tautological, except that Roth and Jonung are the first in many years of writing on the euro to make the point. Using the Eurobarometer dataset produced by the European Commission since 1999, they measure and assess the support for the euro and the extent of trust in the ECB and in national governments before and after the Global Financial Crisis.

As shown in the data, there has always been a net support for the euro within the eurozone member states; this support declined slightly in the crisis years and has returned to pre-crisis levels in the recovery years. A different story applies to the level of trust in the ECB and in national governments. The crisis did have a major impact – there was a loss of trust in both. As might be expected, these losses are even larger in those (periphery) member states most affected by high and rising unemployment since 2008. The authors explain the resilience in the support for the euro even during the crisis years; in their view, the public identify the euro as a sound currency, which has been able to maintain low inflation and thus be suitable as a means of payments and store of value over time. In contrast the public make the ECB and the national governments responsible for the macroeconomic management of the euro crisis, and therefore for the crisis itself and the increase in unemployment rates. This is shown by a regression analysis where the authors identify unemployment as the major determinant in the loss of trust in the ECB and in the national governments; with an increase in unemployment having a more than proportional impact in trust in both the ECB and in national governments. Thus the apparent paradox of the currency being trusted but the institutions which issue and manage it not is removed.

When it comes to the reform of the eurozone, many suggest enhancing a deeper economic integration through a fiscal union among member states as the way forward to tackle another crisis in the future, so that a meaningful "federal" budget can allocate transfers across member states in need and therefore absorb the shock and stabilise the cycle. Tsomocos and Wang acknowledge the economic, social and political difficulties of such a proposal and propose a substitute for fiscal union; namely, the possibility for member states to restructure their debt by, for example, a stock conversion which increased its duration,[12] within a monetary area such as the eurozone. However, for this policy option to be efficient, the conditions for debt restructuring must be set and well known by all parties (creditors and borrowers) ex ante, so that the different member states' debts and banking risks can be properly priced by financial markets.

Tsomocos and Wang use a general equilibrium model to show how, in the absence of debt restructuring, a crisis means that a highly indebted member state under a monetary union has no other option but to bail out failing banks and impose austerity measures (the so-called internal devaluation policies). They have an alternative proposal. To alleviate the effects of a crisis, they suggest allowing member states to restructure their debt but, crucially, according to conditions and criteria specified beforehand with the creditors. If done in this way, financial markets would have had the information needed to charge a market risk premium on each country's debt as a compensation for a default risk. This approach would not require bailouts by the other member states, nor fiscal transfers from a "federal" budget. In addition, the model shows that the economy reaches an equilibrium under debt restructuring, one that leads to more efficiency and an improvement in welfare.

Codogno and van den Noord argue that the only way to share common liabilities in the eurozone is to achieve full fiscal and political union, i.e. unity of liability and control. In the pursuit of that goal, there is a need to smooth the transition, avoid unnecessary strains to macroeconomic and financial stability, and lighten the burden of stabilisation policies on national sovereigns and the European Central Bank while preserving market discipline and avoiding moral hazard. Both fiscal and monetary policy face constraints linked to the high legacy debt in some countries and the zero lower bound, respectively, and thus introducing eurozone "safe assets" and fiscal capacity at the centre would strengthen the transmission of monetary and fiscal policies. The chapter introduces a standard Mundell-Fleming framework adapted to the features of a closed monetary union, with a two-country setting comprising a "core" and a "periphery" country, to evaluate the response of policy and the economy in case of symmetric and asymmetric demand and supply shocks in the current situation and following the introduction of safe bonds and fiscal capacity. Under the specified assumptions, it concludes that a safe asset and fiscal capacity, better if in combination, would remove the doom loop between banks and sovereigns, reduce the loss in output for both economies and improve the stabilisation properties of fiscal policy for both countries, and thus is welfare enhancing.

1.5   *More than a monetary union?*

Tim Congdon's premise is that a multi-government monetary union can maintain monetary and financial stability only under certain conditions. He explains what these conditions are, and examines whether they have been met in the case of the eurozone.

In general terms, in a monetary area there is similarity between the rate of change of the quantity of money and that of nominal output. To maintain price stability, monetary authorities should ensure low and steady monetary growth roughly in line with the growth of real terms national income. In the eurozone, given the trend growth of real output and the price stability target as defined by the ECB, a reasonable working assumption is that price stability is maintained with an increase in nominal output of about 2.5% per year. However, the financial liberalization which accompanied the introduction of the euro allowed a slightly faster growth of the money supply. Since in Europe bank deposits are the main component of the relevant stock of money (Congdon favours a broad measure, such as M3) and the prescribed bank capital ratio is around 10% of bank liabilities, a growth of their assets at 4/5% of the stock of money, on a yearly basis, would be consistent with a broad money expansion up to around 3.5/4.5%, and there-fore consistent with monetary stability as defined by the ECB. But, in fact, credit growth has been characterized by great volatility (faster in the first decade of the eurozone) with variations in the inflation rate, and marked cyclical fluctuations in output and employment.

The legal framework established by the Maastricht Treaty includes a "no bail-out" clause, which puts responsibility to repay each nation's public debt with national governments; an "excessive deficit procedure", imposing fines on govern-ments if their deficit/GDP ratio exceeds certain limits; and prohibition of overdraft financing of governments by the ECB, while market purchase of (mostly govern-ment) securities by the ECB is nevertheless allowed for monetary policy purposes. If these securities are not held only temporarily, for technical reasons, but for longer periods, and if these purchases are not made on the basis of a legally deter-mined proportionality, the distribution of resources and output among member states can be affected. This is a contentious issue. Which national governments' securities have to be bought, at what price and in what amounts, depends on the different fiscal policies and levels of public debt of individual member states.

In addition, in the absence of treaty guidance, bank financing by the ECB can be controversial both with regard to the national banking system involved, and to the possibility of an extension of credit at below-market rates in certain cases, with consequent different treatment of different borrowers. As a result, inter-state resource transfers may occur, even though the EMU's aim was promoting a political – not a transfer – union. A bailout might result by stealth, indeed almost inadvertently.

What do the data show? Dividing the period of the existence of the euro into two decades, the first was marked by a surge of bank credit to the private sec-tor while central bank financing was negligible; the second decade, following the financial crisis, shows a very modest growth of bank credit, related to the authorities' clampdown on banks' risky assets, while the central bank involve-ment greatly increased to prevent deflation, and the acceleration of money growth was mainly due to the ECB involvement, through its exposure to governments ("quantitative easing"), and its privileged, low-cost and quasi-permanent financ-ing to commercial banks.

The result has been a de facto transfer union, through an enormous exposure of the ECB to governments and banks, Spanish and Italian in particular, with a parallel increase in the TARGET2 debit/credit positions. This explains Germany's TARGET2 credit position, and could not have occurred without the growth of the ECB's domestic assets. To prevent a transfer union, an agreement should have specified that the central bank would not hold large claims on any government, and that the task of emergency lending should be carried out at a national level.

Roland Vaubel explores the recent proposals made by the European Commission to reform the eurozone: among others, the "Investment Stabilisation Function", the "Structural Reform Support Programme", the "Convergence Facility" for ERM II countries, the "European Deposit Insurance Scheme", the transformation of the European Stability Mechanism into a European Monetary Fund, and the appointment of a "Finance Minister" of the eurozone as proposed by the French President Emmanuel Macron. He analyses these proposals in detail and highlights the risks they bring about and, in some instances, their incompatibility with the EU treaties and the principle of subsidiarity. Vaubel provides here, by focusing on the medium to the long-term effects of the reforms and the new institutions proposed by the European Commission, an excellent example of workings of the "law of the unintended consequences". By doing so, he illustrates some undesirable effects of such measures. Further, in the analysis of each of them, he shows the political tension within the EU member states and how different their views and preferences are as regards the reform of the euro's architecture.

Vaubel does not only provide a critique of the "roadmap" offered by the European Commission to reform the eurozone. He also offers an alternative option, one that does not require further centralisation of macroeconomic power in the Commission or any other EU institution, but a reform which, he suggests, is much more compatible with "sound market principles". These include the following: *"(1) Government bonds should no longer be privileged in the risk management of banks. (2) The eurozone needs an orderly insolvency procedure for governments. (3) The eurozone needs an orderly exit procedure"* (Vaubel's italics).

Along with the completion of the banking union and the termination of the ECB's purchase of government bonds, Vaubel suggests a further step. This would be rather more controversial: the regular settlement of TARGET2 balances and the reform of the ECB governing bodies, so each national central bank's voting rights are linked to its contribution to the capital of the ECB.

2   Concluding observations

The papers in this volume all take somewhat different perspectives on how the architecture of the euro area should be changed, so as to alleviate political and financial strains and perhaps facilitate faster economic growth in some members.

The conference raises the question of why, notwithstanding severe political and financial strains and the lack of major institutional reforms, the eurozone has not collapsed. Some papers put in evidence many angles from which its governance can be criticised. The papers on the "political" aspect help to explain the present situation. A good few countries benefitted from the lower, and more stable, inflation the euro brought them. Hence the voters like the euro, although they are somewhat unhappy with the institutions behind it. This does not seem to be a stable situation, for the "endowment effect" of low inflation is fading in memories, and of course some countries, Germany for one, did not experience such an effect. Pressure for reform will surely increase.

The papers in this volume certainly do not provide a complete and easily attained set of reforms. But they are all of benefit in the endeavour to improve the working of the euro area, as they provide a range of approaches, varying from modest changes to major reform. Which will ultimately be chosen is of course not clear. But the range of proposals is such that those for alleviation would not prevent the subsequent adoption of what major reforms are ultimately chosen.

Notes

1 M. Friedman's article in *Wall Street Journal*, 22 September 1992.
2 The single market is mentioned in art 3(d), the monetary union and the convergence are mentioned in the Preamble and the single and stable currency (not explicitly the euro, which did not exist at the time) is also mentioned in the Preamble.
3 Mallaby's remarks raise the fascinating question of why Britain, as full a participant as any in the European wars, did not feel any real pressure for political union so as to prevent another such war, but it is a question far beyond the scope of this book.
4 See P. Schwartz (2004) *The Euro as Politics*. London: IEA.
5 See P. Kenen (1969) "The optimum currency area: An eclectic view". In R.A. Mundell and A.K. Swoboda (Eds.), *Monetary Problems of the International Economy*. Chicago: University of Chicago Press.
6 McCallum quotes J.S. Mill as writing as if this were inevitable with the passage of time. And it is a perspective that held up to the 1930s, and indeed to the Bretton Woods Agreement, which was consciously seen by many as a way of getting the benefits of gold without its disadvantages.
7 In a comment on McCallum's paper, Wood (2003) suggests that the climate was also propitious for development of the optimum currency area concept in the 1870s. But this increases still further the puzzle McCallum notes.
8 See M. Brunnenmeier, H. James, and J.P. Landau (2016) *The Euro and the Battle of Ideas*. Princeton, NJ: Princeton University Press, pp. 2–3.
9 What happens in the US is discussed in Hartland's pioneering paper (1949) and in work on the inter-district settlement account of the Federal Reserve (see Wolman, 2013).
10 There is thus the assumption that not only can we learn from the past in general, but that we can learn in the case of the euro, a currency without a precedent.
11 The authors use the new historical database of central banks' statistics, collected by the Banque de France.
12 See Capie, Mills, and Wood (1986) for examination and appraisal of such an operation.

References

Brunnenmeier, M., James, H. and J. P. Landau (2016): *The Euro and the Battle of Ideas*. Princeton, NJ: Princeton University Press.
Capie, F. Mills, T. and G. Wood (1986): "What Happened in 1931?". In Capie and Wood (Eds.), *Financial Crises and the World Banking System*. London: Palgrave Macmillan.

Capie, F. and G. Wood (2002): "Can EMU Survive Unchanged?" In A. A. El-Agraa (Eds.), *The EU and Britain: Implications of Moving into EMU*, pp. 93–117. London and New York: Prentice Hall.

Friedman, M. (1953): "The Case for Flexible Exchange Rates". In *Essays in Positive Economics*, pp. 157–203. Chicago: University of Chicago Press.

Hartland, P. C. (1949): "Interregional Payments Compared with International Payments". In *Quarterly Journal of Economics* 63 (August), pp. 392–407.

Kenen, P. (1969): "The Optimum Currency Area: An Eclectic View". In Mundell and Swoboda (Eds.), *Monetary Problems of the International Economy*. Chicago: University of Chicago Press.

Lutz, F. A. (1954) "The Case for Flexible Exchange Rates". In *Banca Nazionale del Lavaro Review* 7, pp. 175–185.

McCallum, B. (2003): "Theoretical Issues Pertaining to Monetary Unions". In Capie and Wood (Eds.), *Monetary Unions. Theory, History, Public Choice*. Routledge. Chapter 2.

Mallaby, C. (2017): *Living the Cold War. Memoirs of a British Diplomat*. Amberley Publishing.

Mundell, R. (1973): "The economics of common currencies". In H. Johnson and A. Swodoba (Eds.), *The Economics of Common Currencies*. Routledge. Chapter 7, pp. 114–132.

Mundell, R. A. (1961) "A Theory of Optimum Currency Areas". In *American Economic Review* 51, pp. 657–665.

Schwartz, P. (2004): *The Euro as Politics*. London: IEA.

Sohmen, E. (1957): "Demand Elasticities and the Foreign-Exchange Market". In *Journal of Political Economy* 65, pp. 431–436.

Wolman, A. (2013): "Federal Reserve Interdistrict Settlement". In *Federal Reserve of Richmond Economic Quarterly*, 99(2), pp. 117–141.

Wood, G. (2003): "Comments on Theoretical Issues Pertaining to Monetary Unions". In F. Capie and G. Wood (Eds.), *Monetary Unions: Theory, History, Public Choice*. London: Routledge.

Yeager, L. B. (1959): "Exchange Rates Within a Common Market". In *Social Research* 25, pp. 415–438.

Part 1

Lessons from previous currency and monetary unions

2 The flexibility of the classical gold standard (1870s–1914)

Any lessons for the eurozone?

Guillaume Bazot, Eric Monnet and Matthias Morys

1 Introduction

A large number of papers have looked at the history of the gold standard for inspiration for the European Monetary Union (EMU), initially for guidance on the EMU's architecture, and later to address the eurozone's pertinent problems.[1] A distinctive feature of this literature is to acknowledge the stability of the pre-WWI gold standard and turn it into a possible model for Europe, with a somewhat narrow focus on the constraints imposed by this system on member countries.[2] Such constraints are typically presented in the framework of the macroeconomic trilemma, also referred to as the impossible trinity of international finance (Obstfeld & Rogoff 1995; Obstfeld & Taylor 2004). In this approach, the euro area and the gold standard are compared with each other precisely because they are both systems of fixed exchange rates with full capital mobility, resulting in the complete absence of an autonomous monetary policy. The policy implication from this framework is that better financial risk sharing and fiscal policy should play the role that independent monetary policy or floating exchange rates are no longer able to play. To be fair, some of the work mentions that the gold standard exhibited some short-term flexibility and that adjustment was far from automatic. Yet these side remarks are conveniently left aside when it comes to the policy conclusions.

In this contribution, we take the opposite perspective and emphasize instead how the stability of the gold standard may be partly explained by the fact that it was *not* a rigid framework. Based on our recent quantitative study on central bank balance sheets under the gold standard (Bazot et al. 2019), we argue that central banks had several ways to cope with the short-term constraints imposed by fixed exchange rates. The "active policies" (Bloomfield 1959, p. 47) pursued by central banks served as a "buffer between the internal and external economy" (Polanyi 1944, p. 295), yet did not prove incompatible with the high (and rising) level of financial integration of the 1870–1914 period. Moreover, central bank cooperation (through swaps and emergency loans) played an important role during the gold standard to avoid spillovers from financial crises (Eichengreen 1992; Bordo & Schwartz 1999).

Turning to potential lessons for today, we then highlight that some mechanisms – which are often underestimated in their efficacy or discussed only at the margin – already exist in today's euro area to absorb asymmetric shocks between countries, confronting similar macroeconomic problems in a new institutional setting (i.e. a unified European Central Bank (ECB) today as opposed to a multitude of national central banks under the gold standard). In particular, we discuss the ECB's standing facility, macroprudential policy, Emerging Liquidity Assistance (ELA) and, in the last resort, capital controls as such instruments. As the reaction to the recent crisis has shown, the ECB is committed to ensure the convergence of credit conditions (bank lending rates and market interest rates) across countries – that is, to fight against financial fragmentation. As Benoit Coeuré, member of the ECB board, writes, "In response to this [fragmentation], we have put in place a range of measures, particularly the longer-term refinancing operations (LTRO and TLTRO), and announced our readiness to conduct outright monetary transactions (OMT). Such measures were specifically designed to counter the impairment to monetary transmission caused by this fragmentation" (Coeuré 2017). Elsewhere he writes, "Monetary policy cannot eliminate such persistent differences, but it can accommodate them. We have proven that a carefully calibrated package of non-standard policy measures . . . can successfully overcome even significant causes of heterogeneity, such as the impairment of the bank lending channel across large parts of the single currency area in the wake of the euro area's sovereign debt crisis" (Coeuré 2019).

This commitment implies that (short-term) asymmetric financial shocks can be absorbed by liquidity injections (by long-term refinancing operations [LTRO] or, in emergency, ELA) in response to increasing demand of domestic banks at their national central bank (within the eurosystem). If a specific country experiences an idiosyncratic shock that drives its interest rate up, the domestic banks will turn to the standing facility of the ECB (marginal lending facility or LTRO) to obtain funding. The provision of liquidity by the ECB will push domestic interest rates down and ease convergence towards the euro area average and the ECB policy rate.[3] As revealed by the Greek case, capital controls can also be used as a last resort if eurosystem liquidity injections are insufficient to maintain confidence in the banking sector and to keep domestic interest rates at a reasonable level. As in the gold standard, capital controls have a similar objective to the provision of liquidity, since they avoid an overly wide divergence between target and actual interest rates. In the current context, they are also a means of transferring risk off the eurosystem's balance sheet (because they are substitute to further emergency liquidity injections). In this sense, they break the singleness of the euro (i.e. one euro in one country is no longer fully convertible), as they broke convertibility between gold and domestic currency during the gold standard. Consequently, today as in the past, balance sheet policies and capital controls are tools of a very different political nature, although they may share the same objective. The OMT program was designed to help governments facing too high yields on securities which could not be reduced by the usual purchase of securities by the central bank.[4] To be eligible to the OMT, a state needs to have received financial support from the eurozone's bailout funds (ESM) under strict conditions. Therefore, even if the ECB maintains a single objective and single interest rate for the euro area, all these policies have the effect of reducing the consequences of asymmetric shocks on domestic financial conditions.

The main difference between the gold standard and the eurosystem is that the latter is an organised and managed monetary area. In this managed system, TARGET II is responsible for the settlement of cross-border payments in euro. Consequently, the (im)balances between countries are reflected in the (im)balances of TARGET II, i.e. the claims and liabilities of the national central banks (NCBs) of the euro area vis-à-vis the ECB resulting from cross-border payment flows executed via TARGET2. During the gold standard, a country that increased central bank lending to the economy (faced with a negative economic or financial shock) reduced its foreign exchange reserves relative to the other gold standard countries. In the euro area, this is equivalent to increasing TARGET II's liabilities to other eurosystem members. This comparison reminds us that TARGET II is an integral part of the decentralised implementation of the single European monetary policy (Jobst et al. 2012; Eichengreen et al. 2015), and that TARGET II's claims are similar to holding foreign exchange reserves under a fixed exchange rate regime. The history of the gold standard shows that central bank balance sheet policies are far less heterodox than commonly argued for. Their logic was in fact integral part of the functioning of the classical gold standard. Although there are important differences between the euro area and the gold standard, both systems are able to respond to the asymmetry in credit demand, within the borders of the fixed exchange rate area. It operates through the central bank's balance sheet and can be done without moving interest rates in a way that would be against the constraints of the fixed exchange rate (or the unity of the policy rate in the case of the euro area). This logic does not only apply to credit to the national economy. Today's argument according to which financial aid to a country in times of crisis is necessary to avoid spillovers to other countries of the monetary union has its precedents in the gold standard emergency loans between major central banks (Eichengreen 1992, Bazot et al. 2016). To be sure, as in the gold standard, such mechanisms are insufficient to offset divergent productivity trends or to sustain prolonged episodes of fiscal imbalances (at the time, countries left the gold standard when facing large expenditures due to wars or sovereign debt defaults, see Bordo & Kydland 1995).[5] Yet crucially, the classical gold standard shows that they can work in the context of high financial market integration where capital controls can only be allowed *in extremis*. The 1870–1914 experience shows that financial market integration, fixed exchange rates and economic stability are not incompatible with a key role of central banks in taming the potentially adverse short-term effects of financial flows. A limited autonomy of monetary policy did not mean that central banks were inactive in smoothing an asymmetric short-term cycle. This is also true for the ECB today. As already acknowledged by Polanyi (1944) and Bloomfield (1959), the functioning of the classical gold standard during the first era of globalization actually required a great deal of management by central banks.

In the remainder of this paper, we first present our new database (section 2). In section 3, we describe how central banks could cope with domestic and international shocks during the gold standard era. We then present our current estimates on how central banks reacted to a discount rate shock emanating from the Bank of England, the "conductor of the international orchestra" at the time, and how these results should be interpreted (section 4). These two sections summarize the main results of Bazot et al. (2019). We finally add concluding remarks linking the gold standard experience to the current policy of the ECB (section 5).

2   Our new database from the archives of the Banque de France

Our contribution is based on an ongoing research project highlighting the role of central banks as "shock absorbers" during the gold standard (Bazot et al. 2019). This new study shows that the actual functioning of the gold standard offered a significant amount of flexibility and autonomy to central banks. It worked through two mechanisms. First, the central bank balance sheet was used systematically to offset domestic and international shocks; i.e. the domestic money supply was kept constant, rather than hastening the adjustment process of the price-specie flow mechanism (also known as the "Rules of the Game"). Such sterilization policies were facilitated by the fact that many central banks used foreign exchange interventions rather than sales or purchases of gold to adjust. Second, we document that restrictions on the convertibility of bank notes into gold were widespread at the time. In practice, this constituted a form of capital control in that the domestic currency was no longer fully convertible into the key international currencies of the time and pound sterling in particular (Bloomfield 1959).[6] This allowed many countries to benefit from wider bands of exchange rate fluctuations than the ones implied by the gold points.[7]

A great deal of this has been known for some time, or at least plausibly speculated upon since the seminal study of Arthur Bloomfield on "Monetary Policy under the Classical Gold Standard" (1959). There certainly has been considerable evidence on the level of individual country studies.[8] Yet our study is the first to offer a detailed analysis of the reaction of central banks to international shocks at a monthly frequency and to cover all central banks of the gold standard, including those on the periphery. We have assembled a monthly database of the balance sheets of 21 central banks from 1890 to 1913, together with discount rate and exchange rate series at a similar frequency.[9] Our dataset is based on an exceptional source that has never been exploited before: the French central bank (Banque de France) began systematically collecting the weekly or monthly balance sheets of all the world's central banks in 1891. We thus have the chance to rely on the knowledge of the economists of the time who collected, classified and built homogenous and comparable categories for each central bank's assets and liabilities of the panel.

3   How can central banks offset domestic and international shocks?

Bloomfield (1959) famously argued that there was some evidence that central banks even under the classical gold standard before World War I did not play the "rules of the game". He documented that what Nurkse (1944), in another seminal study, had identified as an aberration of the interwar gold standard from the supposed gold standard orthodoxy, had in fact been a regular feature of the classical gold standard itself.

What kind of orthodoxy did these "rules of the game" command? According to the textbook model of adjustment, a country faced with a current account deficit (i.e. depreciation of the exchange rate relative to the center parity, associated with a drain of gold reserves) has to decrease its price level compared to other countries (see O'Rourke & Taylor 2013 for a current restatement), which was to be achieved by means of decreasing the money supply. According to the "rules of the game", central banks were, on their part, supposed to hasten such adjustment by increasing interest rates and exacerbating the impact on the money supply by reducing its domestic component as well. Yet contrary to theoretical expectations, Bloomfield noticed that in practice domestic and foreign portfolios of central banks were often negatively correlated. He inferred from this that central banks were offsetting the loss of foreign reserves by expanding their credit to the domestic economy, i.e. they pursued sterilization/neutralization policies when they were supposed to do precisely the opposite.

Bloomfield was interested in the case when gold reserves were pulled out of a given country because of financial arbitrage (i.e. differential between interest rates). Yet the negative correlation between the domestic and international portfolios documented in his work might not necessarily constitute a "violation of the rules of the game" in response to an international shock, but reflect a – perfectly understandable and legitimate – central bank response to a domestic shock. This important distinction – of which Bloomfield (1959, p. 62) was fully aware, though was subsequently overlooked in the literature on the matter – is important conceptually and empirically. As explained in detail in Bazot et al. (2019), the quantitative analysis of Bloomfield actually lacked a proper method of identification: the simple correlation between domestic and international portfolio is unable to point out whether the central bank is responding to a domestic or an international shock. It is important to distinguish two different mechanisms.

First, a central bank absorbs a domestic shock, real or financial. During this period, economies were subject to strong seasonal credit shocks, mainly due to the large share of agriculture in domestic economic activity. Domestic portfolios of central banks were indeed very seasonal. We have calculated that, on average, seasonal credit accounted for around 25% of the domestic portfolios of central banks during the seasonal peaks. Central banks played a key role to absorb the seasonal demand for credit.[10] Likewise, there might be a domestic shock emanating from a domestic banking crisis, to which the central bank responded by increasing its domestic loans. Yet such domestic shocks would typically also have an effect on the balance of payments (and hence on the international assets of the central bank). In these circumstances, we will often observe a negative correlation between the international and domestic portfolios of the central bank: a poor harvest and/or a domestic banking crisis creates financial outflows and a balance of payments deficit while increasing the demand for domestic borrowing at the central bank discount window.

Second, the central bank reacts to an international shock. The quintessential "international shock" is when the Bank of England increased its discount rate, thereby creating an interest rate spread with London and hence an arbitrage opportunity. Because of the related decline in capital account, the exchange rate depreciated compared to the sterling, and central banks used their international assets to maintain the parity. According to the "rules of the game", central banks were supposed to hasten such adjustment by exacerbating the impact on the money supply by reducing its domestic component as well. In this stylized model behavior to an international shock, we should then observe a positive correlation between the international and domestic portfolios of the central bank.

4   Neutralization of international shocks

Given this lack of a clear identification in earlier work, we propose an alternative estimation and expand on earlier work by Bazot et al. (2016) for the purpose of a cross-country study involving all countries with (proto-)central banks in the classical gold standard period. In Bazot et al. (2019), we estimate how central banks reacted to an increase in the discount rate of the Bank of England, the conductor of the international financial system at the time. This is a straightforward way to identify an international shock, thereby avoiding the issues which had plagued the earlier literature (cf. the previous discussion). Our sample – excluding England for the purpose of estimation – covers all the central banks of the period – that is, 20 central banks (18 countries, since Italy had 3 banks of note issue). Only 2 countries in our sample (Spain, Portugal) did not belong to the gold standard at all during our estimation periods (1891–1913). Several countries adhered to the gold standard only for a sub-period (Austria-Hungary, Italy, Russia, Bulgaria, Serbia, Japan, Greece, Romania, Spain).

In all gold standard countries, we find that an increase in the English interest rate is followed by a depreciation of the domestic exchange rate. Markets were sufficiently integrated, confirming that a change in the English rate constituted an "international shock". Yet we also document that not a single central bank followed the so-called rules of the games: no central bank decreased its domestic portfolio after an increase in the Bank of England rate. Likewise, no central bank increased its discount rate by the same amount as the Bank of England. Crucially, countries with highly integrated capital markets – Germany, France, Belgium, the Netherlands and Austria-Hungary, often referred to as "core countries" – exhibited higher pass-through (24% on average) than peripheral countries such as Romania, Russia, Italy, Serbia and the Scandinavian countries (17% on average), whose capital markets tended to be less connected with the rest of the world.

Earlier research focused on the impact of an English shock on the exchange rate and interest rate, yet we estimate simultaneously the impact on the central bank balance sheet. Central banks in *core countries* experienced a decrease in their international portfolio (gold + foreign exchange), yet their domestic portfolio *increases*. While this is clear evidence of systematic sterilization policies, – and hence the exact opposite of following the "rules of the game" – our quantification also reveals that the increase of the domestic portfolio was larger than the decrease of the international portfolio. For core countries, for example, the reaction of the domestic portfolio is, in percentage terms, more than three times larger than the reaction of the international portfolio, namely 5.5% versus 1.9% after one month (a factor consistent with the result of Bazot et al. 2016 on France).

By contrast, central banks in *peripheral countries* experienced a much smaller decrease in their international portfolio (in fact, the negative point estimate is not statistically significant), but their exchange rate varied by a larger magnitude than in the case of core countries (0.14% versus 0.08%). This finding is consistent with research suggesting that peripheral countries implemented restrictions on gold convertibility (i.e. capital controls in today's parlance), thus widening their exchange-rate band (Morys 2013).

Peripheral countries were able to shelter from the global cycle by potentially imposing capital controls. This deviation from a central pillar of the gold standard made their adherence less credible (Mitchener & Weidenmier 2015), – or, vice versa, low credibility forced them to impose restrictions on gold convertibility – but it did allow them to combine quasi fixed exchange rates (albeit with larger bands) with a certain level of monetary policy autonomy.

Incidentally, a comparison of all responses core versus periphery helps explain why peripheral gold standard countries limited convertibility. Core countries raise their discount rate fast and sizably, bringing in foreign funds quickly given high levels of financial integration between Europe's main financial centres. Adjustment was further helped by private agents who deemed the core countries' adherence to gold credible and bought domestic currency when it was "cheap", i.e. depreciated within the gold points (Bordo & MacDonald 2005). By contrast, lower levels of financial integration and reduced credibility meant that the discount rate was a less sharp weapon for peripheral countries. The transmission mechanism of monetary policy (i.e. a change in the discount rate) was also less likely to be effective, because of the lower development and higher fragmentation of the domestic banking system. This, in turn, created a reliance on – partial or complete – inconvertibility to make the gold standard work in this set of countries. Practice differed between countries (see Bloomfield 1959; Ford 1989, for a review of gold devices), but immediate and unlimited convertibility remained a characteristic of the core countries until the end of the classical gold standard period (Martín-Aceña et al. 2012; Morys 2013, 2014, 2017).

Last but not least and fully in line with the predictions of the trilemma (Obstfeld & Taylor 2004), countries that are not in the gold standard simply float their exchange rates in response to an international shock. Only the exchange-rate response is statistically significant, but this particular variable reacts more strongly by a wide margin than in gold standard countries. It falls 0.45% in month 1 – that is, approximately five times as much as in core countries and three as much as in peripheral countries on gold, and the exchange rate remains at depreciated levels thereafter. In floating countries, the burden of adjustment is borne entirely by the exchange rate, so that the central bank exhibits no statistically significant reaction either in its discount rate or on its balance sheet.

An important caveat applies (Bazot et al. 2019): while documenting systematic sterilization policies on behalf of core country central banks, it is important to note that such actions should not necessarily be seen as *deliberate policy* (an observation already made by Bloomfield himself, cf. Bloomfield 1959, p. 47). Indeed, as far as we know, central banks were not involved in asset purchases intended to keep the money supply constant (or even expanded in our estimations) in a deliberate way. Yet this important caveat still leaves space for sterilization as *active policy*: central banks were fully aware that they were not raising interest rates while they were facing a decline in their international reserves and other central banks were increasing their rates. In order to appreciate this fine-yet-crucial distinction, let us summarize how a negative correlation between the national and international portfolios emerges (explained in more detail in Bazot et al. 2016). In a world of perfect capital mobility, any increase in the international rate pushes the domestic money market rate up due to arbitrage. At the same time, domestic economic agents raise their demand for foreign assets (gold or foreign exchange) from the central bank to obtain a higher return abroad. The central bank's international assets are declining and the money market rate approaches the level of the central bank discount rate. When it becomes cheaper to borrow from the central bank rather than from the market (at least for a fraction of the banking system), the demand for borrowing increases at the central bank. Consequently, the central bank's domestic assets increase. Thus, the negative correlation between the central bank's international and domestic assets is explained by the increasing demand for borrowing at the central bank's discount window when the central bank refuses to increase its rate in line with the international rate (that is, to act in accordance with the rules of the game). Put differently, while the injection of domestic credit into the economy is not "deliberate", the central bank is fully aware of the mechanism outlined and "condones" the increase of the domestic portfolio in contravention to the "rules of the game".

Such role could be reinforced by central bank cooperation. One of the most well-known examples is the loan from the Bank of France to the Bank of England in 1890 during the Barings crisis (Bazot et al. 2016; White 2016). In this case, maintaining a stable discount rate did not imply to expand domestic credit but foreign credit. As explained clearly by the governor of the France central bank: "We avoided the threat of a monetary crisis in England, which would have affected the French market and thereby obliged the Banque de France to increase its discount rate" (quoted in Ramon 1932, p. 400). Hence, as already pointed out by Eichengreen (1992), central banks in the gold standard were willing to act on international markets and play a cooperative game in order to avoid the spillover of foreign crises on their domestic credit conditions.

5   Comparison with the eurozone

Does the eurozone have similar mechanisms? In fact, the common policy of the ECB also plays a role to absorb asymmetric shocks since operations are decentralized to national central banks and the eurosystem is committed to meet the

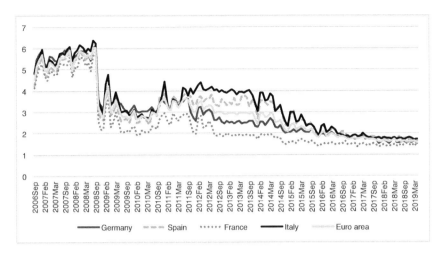

Figure 2.1 Composite indicator of the short-term cost of borrowing (percentages per annum)

Source: ECB Statistical Data Warehouse.

(asymmetric) demand for credit in all countries in order to reduce the fragmentation of financial systems. This is done to achieve a convergence of credit conditions (Figure 2.1).[11] The outcome of this balance sheet policy to stabilize interest rates in the euro area is especially visible in the very asymmetric distribution of loans for the LTRO across countries (Figure 2.2).[12] If standard operations are not enough, the ECB can implement ELA. As a last resort, capital controls offer a temporary solution, as in Greece today. They are a de facto temporary suspension of convertibility.

As in the gold standard, an "active" policy is defined as a policy where the central bank accepts to provide credit to a banking system which experienced a negative shock (which can be country specific), rather than to let market interest rates increase in this country. Today, macroprudential tools can also be used if – on the contrary – credit conditions in a specific country are too loose. As in the gold standard, these tools might be enough to stabilize interest rates in the short term, but they may not solve chronic current account imbalances.

In the euro area today, liquidity injections by national central banks to stabilise local money market conditions give rise to TARGET II liabilities (Jobst et al. 2012; Eichengreen et al. 2015; Eisenschmidt et al. 2017). Current account imbalances between countries are reflected in the imbalances of TARGET II. As in the gold standard or other fixed exchange rate regimes, claims on and liabilities to other countries not only reflect central bank policies but also more broadly reflect a country's net international investment position. During the gold standard period, European countries held foreign exchange reserves (mainly liabilities of England, France and Germany; see Lindert 1969) in addition to gold. Today, eurosystem's

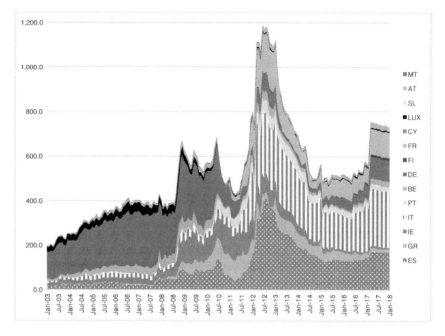

Figure 2.2 Country use of main and long-term refinancing operations at the European Central Bank (millions EUR)

Source: Bruegel database of eurosystem lending operations developed in Pisani-Ferry and Wolff (2012)", updated Dec. 2017. http://bruegel.org/publications/datasets/eurosystem-liquidity/.

central banks hold balances vis-à-vis the ECB. Some people today may regret that gold is no longer available to settle balances of payments between countries in a rather anonymous way. But, apart from gold nostalgia, there is little reason to consider the TARGET II system as an abnormal creature.

6   Conclusion

The flexibility of the classical gold standard should not be overestimated. As Eichengreen (1992) recalls, the sterilization observed by Bloomfield was a response to short-term shocks; persistent imbalances were not sustainable. Similar issues arise today in the euro-area, and the rules of the European monetary union impose further constraints on budget deficits (although not on current account imbalances). Moreover, gold standard central banks used their autonomy to maintain stable interest rates rather than to run countercyclical monetary policies. Yet, our new results show that sterilization of international shocks was so systematic under the gold standard that it cannot be interpreted as anything but the norm. Such flexibility was probably a key factor of the stability of the classical gold standard. As already suggested by Polanyi (1944, p. 295), central banks acted "as a buffer between the internal and the external economy" and "the absence of such a mechanism would have made it impossible for any advanced country to stay on gold without devastating effects as to its welfare, whether in terms of production, income, or employment". In such an historical perspective, the recent policies implemented by the eurosystem to respond to asymmetric shocks and harmonize credit conditions across the European monetary union do no longer seem "unconventional".

Notes

1 See among others, Foreman-Peck (1991), Panic (1993), Friedman (1997), Flandreau et al. (1998) for the first wave, and Ógren & Oksendal (2011), Eichengreen & Temin (2010), Dellas & Tavlas (2013), O'Rourke & Taylor (2013), Morys (2014) for the second wave after the global financial and European debt crises.
2 For sure, differences between the gold standard and the European monetary union are also highlighted, prominently the facts that the gold standard did not have a unique central bank and that no formal agreements linked countries. See in particular O'Rourke & Taylor (2013).
3 The quantitative easing program works differently, with targets of purchases for each country. The announcements of this program had, however, different effects across countries and also led to a convergence of interest rates (De Santis 2016).
4 There are still debates on whether the ECB could have provided a stronger backstop to sovereign debt (Corsetti et al. 2019).
5 On how a persistent pattern of fiscal dominance kept a country out of the gold standard for good, see Martínez-Ruiz & Nogues-Marco (2018) on the Spanish experience.
6 In a case of exchange rate depreciation, it meant that it was then more expensive to convert the domestic currency in another international currency (typically sterling). Bloomfield (1959) also mentioned some direct controls on foreign exchange, for instance in the case of Russia.
7 The gold point corresponds to the exchange rate value above (respectively below) which it becomes profitable to make arbitrage through the transportation of gold from one country to one another.
8 Lindert (1969) was the first to follow Bloomfield by studying the role of foreign exchange interventions from 1900 to 1913. His work was also comparative and, as Bloomfield, he relied on annual data. Since then, scholars have confirmed Bloomfield's results showing a negative correlation between the international and domestic assets of some individuals central banks: Drummond (1976) for Russia, McGouldrick (1984) for Germany, Dutton (1984) and Pippenger (1984) for England, Bazot et al. (2016) for France, Reis (2007) for Portugal before 1887, Jonung (1984) and Ögren (2012) for Sweden and Oksendal (2012) for Norway. They have also provided a detailed description of foreign exchange intervention in some countries: (Reis (2007) and Esteves et al. (2009) for Portugal, Jobst (2009) for Austria-Hungaria, Ugolini (2012) for Belgium and Oksendal (2012) for Norway.
9 Flandreau et al. (1998) rightly point out that the gold standard really started to become "international" in the 1890s although the common views still dates its origin around 1880 when all core countries were on gold.
10 By contrast, in the US, which did not have a central bank, seasonality of agricultural credit was damaging for the financial and real economy (Mankiw & Miron 1986; Hanes & Rhode 2013).
11 See these two speeches by Benoit Coeuré (2017, 2019).
12 The offsetting effect on domestic credit/money is reinforced in the case of TLTRO, or if the fund of LTRO is used by promotional banks to invest directly in domestic economy; see Monnet et al. (2014).

References

Bazot, G., Bordo, M. D., & Monnet, E. (2016). International shocks and the balance sheet of the Bank of France under the classical gold standard. *Explorations in Economic History*, 62, 87–107.

Bazot, G., Monnet, E., & Morys, M. (2019). Taming the Global Financial Cycle: Central banks and the sterilization of capital flows under the Classical Gold Standard (1891–1913). CEPR Discussion Papers N°13895.

Bloomfield, A. I. (1959). *Monetary Policy under the International Gold Standard: 1880–1915*. New York: Federal Reserve Bank of New York.

Bordo, M. D., & Kydland, F. E. (1995). The gold standard as a rule: An essay in exploration. *Explorations in Economic History*, 32(4), 423–464.

Bordo, M. D., & Schwartz, A. J. (1999). Under what circumstances, past and present, have international rescues of countries in financial distress been successful? *Journal of International Money and Finance*, 18(4), 683–708.

Bordo, M. D., & MacDonald, R. (2005). Interest rate interactions in the classical gold standard, 1880–1914: Was there any monetary independence? *Journal of Monetary Economics*, 52(2), 307–327.

Coeuré, B. (2017). Convergence matters for monetary policy. Speech at the Competitiveness Research Network (CompNet) conference on "Innovation, firm size, productivity and imbalances in the age of de-globalization" in Brussels, 30 June 2017.

Coeuré, B. (2019). Heterogeneity and the ECB's monetary policy. Speech at the Banque de France Symposium & 34th SUERF Colloquium on the occasion of the 20th anniversary of the euro on "The Euro Area: Staying the Course through Uncertainties", Paris, 29 March 2019.

Corsetti, G., Eichengreen, B., Hale, G., & Tallman, E. (2019). The Euro Crisis in the mirror of the EMS: How tying Odysseus to the mast avoided the sirens but led him to Charybdis. *Federal Reserve Bank of San Francisco*, February.

Dellas, H., & Tavlas, G. S. (2013). The gold standard, the euro, and the origins of the Greek sovereign debt crisis. *Cato Journal*, 33, 491–512.

De Santis, R. A. (2016). Impact of the asset purchase programme on euro area government bond yields using market news. Working paper (No. 1939). European Central Bank.

Drummond, I. M. (1976). The Russian gold standard, 1897–1914. *The Journal of Economic History*, 36(3), 663–688.

Dutton, J. (1984). The Bank of England and the rules of the game under the international gold standard: New evidence. In *A Retrospective on the Classical Gold Standard, 1821–1931* (pp. 173–202). Chicago: University of Chicago Press.

Eichengreen, B. (1992). *Golden Fetters*. Oxford: Oxford University Press.

Eichengreen, B., Mehl, A., Chitu, L., & Richardson, G. (2015). Mutual assistance between Federal Reserve Banks: 1913–1960 as Prolegomena to the TARGET2 debate. *The Journal of Economic History*, 75(3), 621–659.

Eichengreen, B., & Temin, P. (2010). Fetters of gold and paper. *Oxford Review of Economic Policy*, 26(3), 370–384.

Eisenschmidt, J., Kedan, D., Schmitz, M., Adalid, R., & Papsdorf, P. (2017). The Eurosystem's asset purchase programme and TARGET balances. *ECB Occasional Paper*, 196.

Esteves, R. P., Reis, J., & Ferramosca, F. (2009). Market integration in the golden periphery: The Lisbon/London exchange, 1854–1891. *Explorations in Economic History*, 46(3), 324–345.

Flandreau, M., Cacheux, J. L., & Zumer, F. (1998). Stability without a pact? Lessons from the European gold standard, 1880–1914. *Economic Policy*, 13(26), 116–162.

Ford, A. (1989). International financial policy and the gold standard, 1870–1914. In P. Mathias and S. Pollard (Eds.), *The Cambridge Economic History of Europe*, volume 8 (pp. 197–249). Cambridge: Cambridge University Press.

Foreman-Peck, J. (1991). The International Gold Standard as a European Monetary Lesson. In J. Driffil and M. Beber (Eds.), *A Currency for Europe*. London: Lothian Foundation Press.

Friedman, M. (1997). The euro: Monetary unity to political disunity. *Project Syndicate*, 28.

Hanes, C., & Rhode, P. W. (2013). Harvests and financial crises in gold standard America. *The Journal of Economic History*, 73(1), 201–246.

Jobst, C. (2009). Market leader: The Austro-Hungarian Bank and the making of foreign exchange intervention, 1896–1913. *European Review of Economic History*, 13(3), 287–318.

Jobst, C., Handig, M., & Holzfeind, R. (2012). Understanding TARGET 2: The eurosystem's euro payment system from an economic and balance sheet perspective. *Monetary Policy & the Economy Quarterly*, 1, 81–91.

Jonung, L. (1984). Swedish experience under the classical gold standard, 1873–1914. In *A Retrospective on the Classical Gold Standard, 1821–1931* (pp. 361–404). Chicago: University of Chicago Press.

Lindert, P. H. (1969). *Key Currencies and Gold, 1900–1913* (No. 24). International Finance Section, Princeton: Princeton University.

Mankiw, N. G., & Miron, J. A. (1986). The changing behavior of the term structure of interest rates. *The Quarterly Journal of Economics*, 101(2), 211–228.

Martín-Aceña, P., Martínez-Ruiz, E., and Nogues-Marco, P. (2012). Floating against the Tide: Spanish Monetary Policy. In *The Gold Standard Peripheries, 1870–1931* (pp. 145–173). London: Palgrave Macmillan.

Martínez-Ruiz, E., & Nogues-Marco, P. (2018). The political economy of exchange rate stability during the gold standard. Spain, 1874–1914. Working Papers of the Hitotsubashi Institute for Advanced Study; HIAS-E-75. Tokyo.

McGouldrick, P. (1984). Operations of the German Central Bank and the rules of the game, 1879–1913. In *A Retrospective on the Classical Gold Standard, 1821–1931* (pp. 311–360). Chicago: University of Chicago Press.

Mitchener, K. J., & Weidenmier, M. D. (2015). Was the classical gold standard credible on the periphery? Evidence from currency risk. *The Journal of Economic History*, 75(2), 479–511.

Monnet, É., Pagliari, S., & Vallée, S. (2014). Europe between financial repression and regulatory capture (No. 2014/08). Bruegel Working Paper.

Morys, M. (2013). Discount rate policy under the Classical Gold Standard: Core versus periphery (1870s–1914). *Explorations in Economic History*, 50(2), 205–226.

Morys, M. (2014). Gold standard lessons for the eurozone. *JCMS: Journal of Common Market Studies*, 52(4), 728–741.

Morys, M. (2017). A Century of Monetary Reform in South-East Europe: From Political Autonomy to the Gold Standard, 1815–1910. *Financial History Review*, 24(1), 3–21.

Nurkse, R. (1944). *International currency experience: Lessons of the interwar period*. Geneva: League of Nations.

Obstfeld, M., & Rogoff, K. (1995). The mirage of fixed exchange rates. *Journal of Economic Perspectives*, 9(4), 73–96.

Obstfeld, M., & Taylor, A. M. (2004). *Global Capital Markets: Integration, Crisis, and Growth*. Cambridge: Cambridge University Press.

Ögren, A. (2012). Central banking and monetary policy in Sweden during the long nineteenth century. In *The Gold Standard Peripheries* (pp. 17–36). London: Palgrave Macmillan.

Ógren, A., & Øksendal, L. F. (2011). The Euro and the gold standard: What are the lessons? In *The Gold Standard Peripheries* (pp. 231–44). London: Palgrave Macmillan.

Øksendal, L. F. (2012). Freedom for Manoeuvre: The Norwegian gold standard experience, 1874–1914. In *The Gold Standard Peripheries* (pp. 37–57). London: Palgrave Macmillan.

O'Rourke, K. H., & Taylor, A. M. (2013). Cross of euros. *Journal of Economic Perspectives*, 27(3), 167–192.

Panic, M. (1993). *European Monetary Union: Lessons from the Classical Gold Standard*. London: Springer.

Pippenger, J. (1984). Bank of England operations, 1893–1913. In *A Retrospective on the Classical Gold Standard, 1821–1931* (pp. 203–232). Chicago: University of Chicago Press.

Pisani-Ferry, J., & Wolff, G. (2012). Propping up Europe? *Bruegel Policy Contribution 2012|07*, April.

Polanyi, K. (1944). *The Great Transformation*. Boston: Beacon Press.

Ramon, Gabriel. Histoire de la Banque de France d'après les sources originales. Paris, Grasset, 1932.

Reis, J. (2007). An 'art', not a 'science'? Central bank management in Portugal under the gold standard, 1863–87. *The Economic History Review*, 60(4), 712–741.

Ugolini, S. (2012). Foreign exchange reserve management in the nineteenth century: The National Bank of Belgium in the 1850s. In *The Gold Standard Peripheries* (pp. 107–129). London: Palgrave Macmillan.

White, E. N. (2016). How to prevent a banking panic: The barings crisis of 1890 revisited. Mimeo.

3 A measurement of asymmetry in the running of the classical gold standard

Juan E. Castañeda, Alessandro Roselli and Simeng He

1 Introduction: how symmetry should work

Any system of fixed exchange rates should imply the adoption of macroeconomic policies – both monetary and fiscal policies – aimed at avoiding fundamental disequilibria inside the system, through symmetry of behaviour of both surplus and deficit countries – that is, expansionary domestic macroeconomic policies in surplus countries and tight policies in deficit countries. It is, however, very difficult to translate this pattern of behaviour into positive, binding provisions. A good example in this regard is the Bretton Woods system, based on fixed exchange rates, which was born out of the idea of Keynes that adjustments between creditor and debtor nations should be symmetric. The Articles of Agreement of the International Monetary Fund (IMF) introduced the concept of a "fundamental disequilibrium" as the trigger of changes in the parity rates if symmetric policies could not be attained, without distinction between surplus and deficit countries. However, the United States, at the outset of the system the overwhelmingly dominant economy and the most powerful creditor nation, – the "hegemonic" country – did not accept a system that would force it to adjust its policies or to revalue its currency. The system lacked an institutionally sanctioned symmetry. The dollar being the world's reserve currency – the only currency directly convertible into gold – the US creditor position meant a shortage of dollars for deficit countries and worked mainly as a mechanism of adjustment for these countries, which had either to adopt deflationary policies or, in case of a fundamental disequilibrium, to adjust their parities. Similarly, when the US moved later on to a position of trade deficit and external liabilities exceeded the value of its gold holdings, the United States preferred to avoid any adjustment, rather suspending the convertibility of dollars into gold, in 1971. This marked the end of the Bretton Woods system, and the start of floating currencies, while the gold anchor was abandoned. The asymmetry of the system brought in the end to its demise.

All the more so symmetry is required when the system is not made of currencies of different countries, but of a single currency adopted by all the countries participating in the system – that is, when we have a monetary union (Capie and Wood, 2003), as the eurozone. However, in the eurozone an issue of symmetrical monetary policies cannot arise, just because there is a single monetary policy even when, de facto, countries remain, structurally and cyclically, in a different macroeconomic position. To rebalance disequilibria, and to avoid deflation in the deficit (or "peripheral") countries, the only available macroeconomic instrument is fiscal policy, which would mean expansionary policies by the surplus countries, and the opposite by deficit countries. Aggregate demand management through fiscal policies is, however, severely constrained in the eurozone by the behaviour of the hegemonic country – Germany – and more generally by the fiscal consolidation embedded in the balanced budget principle, introduced in some countries by a constitutional amendment. Moreover, the "escape lane" sanctioned by the IMF Articles of Agreement – exchange rate parity adjustments – is precluded by the very existence of a single currency, while crucially no exit procedure from the monetary area is even envisaged in the legislation (some attempts were made in this direction at the height of the Greek crisis, as a temporary return to the drachma, but they didn't come to fruition).

These experiences seem to point out that, if a specific country emerges at the centre of the system as the hegemonic country, and if it sticks to an asymmetric behaviour, the whole system becomes dysfunctional. For "peripheral" countries that are in a situation of deficit, the only possible resort appears to lay in internal devaluations of prices and wages, and/or in supply-side measures, aimed at giving them the competitiveness that cannot be recovered through currency devaluations. As observed in the recent eurozone crisis, these measures may well be needed, but they do not seem to have been enough to achieve the intended macroeconomic stabilisation within the eurozone.

In this paper, we consider the experience of an international monetary system – the gold standard – which is generally seen as a major historical case of (quasi) fixed exchange rates, and wonder whether the gold standard countries complied with the symmetry requirement, as just described. Specifically, we look at the relevant features of the gold standard and how symmetry works within the system (section 2); the gold convertibility ratio, which is the pivot of the whole system (section 3); central banks' attitudes to symmetry (section 4); and the obstacles to symmetry in the gold standard (section 5). We then develop an empirical analysis to measure symmetry in five European countries (section 6), and finally draw conclusions, including whether the gold standard collapsed because of asymmetries (section 7).

2   The gold standard and symmetry

The gold standard has often been praised for its potential, market-induced, non-discretionary symmetry, which would automatically rebalance positions of credit and debit between countries adhering to the system. In a simplified model of the gold standard (gold *specie* standard), the money supply consists entirely of gold, which is also accepted in the settlement of debt between countries, and the underlying theoretical assumption is that prices adjust passively to changes in the money supply, barring changes in the real product and in the velocity of money (i.e. the quantity theory of money). If, for some reason, in a certain country a payment deficit and an outflow of gold occur, the money supply is by definition reduced and the price level falls. As a consequence, the economy becomes more competitive, exports increase and foreign accounts are finally rebalanced, while exchange rates remain unchanged: an affirmation of "internal" over "external" devaluations.[1] The opposite of course happens if a country is in surplus. The gold standard functions symmetrically in this basic model without any government intervention.

The use of gold as the only domestic currency, if ever it existed, was then followed by government induced changes, which is by the use of gold substitutes as currency: paper currency, and the demand deposits created through the banking system. If, differently from the model discussed, in the real world the money supply is made – rather than of gold only (which may instead assume a very limited role, for reason of convenience if not for other motives) – of these substitutes, there is not a market induced, automatic mechanism that reduces the amount of money in case of an external deficit and an outflow of gold (and vice versa in case of surplus): there is not an embedded symmetry. Governments have to "create" a threshold to contain the supply of money in relation to the available gold in reserve – that is, they have to define a legally binding ratio between the gold reserve and the money supply, the "conversion ratio".

Therefore, any gold standard country has two targets: (1) a legal, binding target: the gold convertibility of its currency at a fixed rate, assured by maintaining a certain, legally defined, ratio between the gold reserve and the money supply (whose components are in turn legally defined, including certain money aggregates); and (2) a non-statutory "rule of the game": to make changes in the monetary aggregates coherent with the evolution of the country's foreign balance, in order to reach that symmetry which, in the theoretical model, is by definition assured.

The historical evolution of the gold standard shows the relevance of the interaction of these two targets and their relative importance in abiding by symmetry, or in preferring certain degrees of asymmetry. Three factors favoured symmetry: (1) a solid anchor was provided by gold, as the common standard to which every adhering currency was legally bound; (2) socio-political conditions allowed macroeconomic domestic policies, particularly flexibility in wages and prices adjustments, that would have been very difficult to achieve in subsequent times; and (3) parity changes (changes in the gold content of the national currency) and even temporary inconvertibility might occur, though under exceptional circumstances. Point 1 – currency convertibility into gold – was the real pivot of the whole system and, being a legal requirement, represented the most compelling constraint of policy behaviour; point 2 was particularly notable in the period before WW1, but conditions radically changed during the war and in its aftermath; point 3 permitted some flexibility in entering and exiting the standard, a particularly relevant alternative during and after the war. As a matter of fact, the erosion – sometimes gradual, other times abrupt – of conditions under points 2 and 3 led to increasing difficulties in preserving the anchor, the currency link to gold (point 1), and finally to the collapse of the system in the 1930s.

If we consider the three components of money creation by the central bank – the foreign channel (changes in the gold and foreign exchange reserve induced by the foreign balance), the banking and market channel (discount and advances to the banking sector, open market operations), and the Treasury channel (advances to the Treasury and purchase of government securities on the primary market) – in a gold standard regime the first component is the most critical, while the other two (Treasury and "banking/market") are, or can be, under a more direct control of the central bank. The balance of payments has a potential impact on the country's reserves that lies at the centre of the monetary system: in principle, a foreign surplus generates an inflow of gold, and an increase in the gold/foreign exchange reserve as a consequence. Changes in the gold reserve are, therefore, the main variable that the monetary authorities have to follow closely in order to maintain the domestic and foreign convertibility of the national currency. The other two, being more directly under central bank's control, can be adjusted in order to offset or enhance the effects of the first channel.

As we shall see in our quantitative analysis in section 6, under the gold standard the amount of money that the central bank creates is a dependent (endogenous) rather than an independent variable, and it is not fully subject to government or central bank determination.

The domestic and international targets were linked. The link between these two objectives was given by the role of gold as backing of both the national currency and the country's exchange rate against other gold currencies. A loss of gold reserves due to a balance of payments deficit might hinder the domestic convertibility and therefore cause restrictive monetary and credit policies. But an increase in the gold reserve due to a foreign surplus might not cause an expansion in the monetary aggregates. We shall examine, in section 5, the reasons for which this course of action might be followed. Here it is sufficient to mention two reasons of concern for the central bank: (1) an expansionary monetary policy could potentially endanger the legal requirement of gold convertibility of its currency and (2) this policy might create inflationary pressures and risk price stability. In both cases asymmetry would result. Worthwhile to note that the conversion ratio was a binding legal constraint; while symmetry – to which a scholar of today pays attention as a balancing factor in an international monetary system and defines it as one of the "rules of the game" of the gold standard – was perhaps not always in the minds of policymakers, in the absence of any macroeconomic framework to evaluate the effects of their initiatives on the international arena and in the prevalence of domestic interests over international cooperation.

As our analysis will show, the observance of this rule – any influence of external factors on domestic monetary aggregates – might find a formidable obstacle in the compliance with binding provision regarding convertibility and in the prevalence of the national interest. These were perhaps the main, embedded sources of asymmetry.

In questioning the degree of symmetry or asymmetry of the gold standard, previous studies have been focused on changes in interest rates (the official "discount rate") to proxy changes in monetary policy; we use for the same purpose changes in the monetary base. The reasons for this are twofold. On the one side, monetary conditions could be affected by the central bank not only by changes in the discount rate and open market operations (money creation through the "banking/market" channel), but also through Treasury financing (depending on the relevance of the Treasury channel in money creation). On the other side, there is the practical motive that changes in the monetary base were more frequent than those in discount rates, and thus allow us to identify better and more accurately changes in policy.

Our paper is far from exploring a new ground, as demonstrated by the long list of references at the close of every book dealing with this topic.[2] Our task – to trace the reaction of monetary policy to the evolution of the country's foreign accounts and international reserve, i.e. a monetary policy complying with symmetry – deals, however, with an issue that is receiving renewed interest: the analysis and measurement of the supposed symmetry in the behaviour of countries either on a fixed exchange rate system or on a single currency, as a way to maintain the system stable, and in the end to insure its survival, in particular in periods of international stress.

We deal with the period between the second half of the 19th century (specific starting years vary according to the availability of data for different countries), as the beginning of the "universal" or classical gold standard era, and the start of the WWI, which marked the first crisis of the system and perhaps the beginning of its collapse. During that period, conditions existed for a relatively smooth functioning of the system and – therefore – for the potential implementation of symmetric policies. As mentioned, we focus on five central banks representing the most important European economies in terms of real GDP (UK, Germany, France, Italy and Spain).[3]

We consider these five countries as gold standard members. In fact, the situation was more complex. The institutional framework of these countries changed over time, so that various situations of convertibility, de jure, de facto and inconvertibility occurred. The French franc gold content was defined in 1803, at 290.322 milligrams of fine gold. For the lira the Italian government adopted in 1862, after the creation of the Kingdom of Italy, the same parity. From 1865 these currencies belonged to the Latin Monetary Union (LMU). For a while, the two countries were on a bimetallic standard (gold and silver). They were in and out gold convertibility depending on different circumstances. Italy was in the years preceding the WWI on a de facto convertibility. Spain's peseta was introduced as the national currency in 1868, with the same metallic content as the French franc and the Italian lira. It also passed through phases of inconvertibility, and was for a while on a bimetallic standard. It did not however formally belong to the LMU, and finally suspended convertibility in gold in 1883, though restricted by law the amount of notes issued by the central bank. Germany joined the gold standard in 1871–1873, having the Reichsmark a gold content of 358.422919 milligrams of fine gold. The United Kingdom was on a gold standard basis since 1821, with a gold content for the pound of 7.322882 grams of fine gold (123.2745 troy grains of gold of 22 carats). These countries had to suspend convertibility at the outbreak of WWI in 1914.

3 Conversion ratio and "apprehension ratio"

We will measure whether, and to what extent, the monetary policies of those five countries were coherent with symmetry as defined previously; since these policies were constrained by the binding provision of a certain currency conversion ratio, it is necessary to consider how this ratio can be used for an international comparison.

As mentioned earlier, in the basic model of gold standard (gold *specie* standard) each ounce of gold that leaves the country to pay for a trade deficit means, at the same time, a reduction of the central bank's reserve and of the money supply in an equal amount. The ratio reserve/money supply is thus always "one". But, if the money stock is made, mainly, of paper currency (circulation) and bank deposits, a ratio lower than "one" is the norm. In order to reach and maintain the objective of convertibility, it is necessary that the ratio is kept at a certain, prudential level. To use Bagehot's terminology, that ratio should not fall below an "apprehension minimum" (Bagehot, 1931, p. 303).

Two issues arise, for the purpose of calculation: the assets and liabilities to be included in the ratio and the appropriate level of the ratio. They varied according to different legislations and we consider the two issues separately.

Regarding the international assets to be included in the ratio, suffice to say here that in some countries gold only was considered, but in other countries that came to adopt the gold *exchange* standard regime, foreign currencies held by the central bank were also included in the international reserve.

In reference to liabilities, the concept of money supply (the various monetary aggregates) as a broad measure of money – important as it is to detect inflationary pressures and for assessing the monetary policy stance – was never adopted to calculate the legal conversion ratio.[4] According to some legislations, circulation only was included, but more often, also the bank reserves – that is, the balances held by the banking system at the central bank. In this case, the denominator of the ratio coincided with the "monetary base", or "central bank money": a much narrower definition of the money supply in the country. Moreover, in some countries circulation was composed not only of central bank's banknotes but also of notes and coins issued by the Treasury. Finally, few countries had, at least for a while, a plurality of banks of issue (Italy had three, until 1926), and in other countries (the UK, for instance) banknotes issued by commercial banks were also in circulation.

Regarding the level of the conversion ratio, as determined by law, it might also vary according to different countries and legislations, and change over time, also according to specific assets and liabilities to be covered.[5] An exemplification of calculations of this ratio in different legislations is given here:[6] In France, a maximum of note circulation was prescribed, irrespective of the amount of the reserves. In the UK, the amount of notes should not exceed the amount of the gold reserve by more than a stated amount, the "fixed fiduciary issue" (UK Bank Act 1844). While, for instance, in the US, the gold reserve should not fall below a fixed percentage of the note issue, the percentage lying "between 30 and 40 percent"; this percentage system sometimes applies to bank reserves also.[7]

The ratio was of an "arbitrary and variable character" (Keynes, 1932, p. 166). Hawtrey noted, "A gold reserve is held with a view to contingencies, particularly to . . . an adverse balance of payments. . . . It is impossible to calculate beforehand the magnitude of these contingencies, and the conclusions arrived at on the subject have everywhere been empirical. They have been picked up from experience with little assistance from the theory. . . . Accordingly gold reserve laws are commonly enacted requiring the gold held to be not less than, say, 30 per cent or 40 per cent, or 1/3 of the note issue" (Hawtrey, 1931, p. 50).

Not considering specific legislations, Hayek empirically assumed that "to start with a gold reserve amounting to only a third of the total monetary circulation [he means here "all sight liabilities of the central banks plus the circulation of government paper money"] . . . would probably provide a margin amply sufficient" (Hayek, 1935, p. 87). As noted, Bagehot preferred to speak of an "apprehension minimum", below which the authorities would consider their currency's convertibility in danger. However, he observed that "there is no 'royal road' to the amount of the 'apprehension minimum'. . . . The apprehension minimum is not always the same" (Bagehot, 1931, pp. 304–305). So, he did not give any specific percentage or absolute level, only observing that London, as an international financial centre, had an enormous amount of short-term foreign liabilities, at the mercy of foreign holders, with a very small amount of assets (gold in reserve).[8] Bagehot perhaps ironically wrote of whatever percentage that may "assuage their [the central banks'] fears".

Considering the different legislations, our approach to the calculation of the appropriate ratio for an international comparison could have been twofold:

1   Either to rely on a "legal approach", that is to rely on the specific legislations of any country here considered, both for the aggregates to be included in the calculation, and for the appropriate ratio to be chosen. This approach has two major difficulties: we should look very carefully at those legislations, that are often quite complex and changing over time and thus difficult to interpret and be used for international comparisons (as noted, often the ratios were different according to different types of liabilities, and coverage might sometimes be made of different instruments – that is, not only of metal or foreign currencies). In addition, from an economic perspective, legal provisions might be "inadequate" because, for instance, circulation not issued by the central bank, important as it might be from a monetary point of view, might not be included in the legal ratio, which could well lead to a misleading picture on the true inflationary pressures in the economy.
2   Or to use an "economic approach", by choosing (1) a common definition of assets and liabilities that may encompass the various components of the money supply and reserves, in order to have a more economically significant measure of the monetary policy stance; and (2) a single ratio of the chosen assets and liabilities, notwithstanding the diverse ratios/limits used in the various countries considered in our analysis. If our aim is to compare monetary policies of different countries and assess the stance of their policies in relation to these two objectives, it is relevant to take a common yardstick.

It is evident that if the statutory conversion ratio was different, a country might be compelled to adopt a certain policy that another country, with a different statutory ratio, might well avoid. This brings us to adopt in this paper the "economic approach",[9] comforted in this by previous studies on similar subjects (see Bloom-field, 1959; Nurkse, 1944). By using a common definition of "monetary base"[10] and "reserve", and a common ratio, the inter-country comparison is made simpler and coherent. Regarding the choice of the monetary aggregates, by "assets" we shall mean the components of the international reserve (gold and foreign exchange); by "liabilities" we shall mean the monetary base, that is, notes in circulation and the reserves held by banks at the central bank ("bank balances"). We shall not include, however, in the monetary base metallic coins; this is in the assumption that they – mostly used for retail transactions – were not directly convertible into reserve assets (gold, foreign currency). Therefore we have adopted here a narrow definition of the monetary base, made of the total amount of notes in circulation plus banks' reserves at the central bank.

About the level of the conversion ratio, even being well aware that any choice is ultimately to some extent arbitrary, rather than simply discretionary, on the basis of the actual experience of how monetary policy was conducted at the time, and of the comments and estimates given by the economists mentioned previously, a certain percentage might be tentatively adopted. We shall call it "apprehension ratio" (AR), using Bagehot's terminology. Broadly following Hawtrey and Hayek, we might assume that a ratio of 35% could be considered as the "apprehension level", below which any actual coverage ratio would be seen as insufficient.

Following the economic approach, we have therefore included in the ratio the following components:

$$Coverage\ Ratio\,(CR,\%) = \frac{Metalic\ Reserves + Foreign\ Exchange\ Reserves}{Circulation\,(notes) + Banks\ Reserves}$$

Therefore, the "apprehension ratio" (AR), in our approach, takes the place of the different "conversion ratios", defined by law in any observed country; while – to add another acronym – by "coverage ratio" (CR) we mean the actual ratio that can be historically observed, year by year, in those countries.

4   Central banks' attitudes to symmetry

We intend to measure symmetry in section 6 by observing how and to what extent a change in the international reserve of the central bank is accompanied by a change in the same direction of the monetary base. We need to clarify this point.

Let's suppose that the central bank has an international reserve of (say) 35 million and a monetary base of 100 million. The coverage ratio is 35%, compliant with what we have called "apprehension ratio" (AR), as the yardstick on which to measure symmetry. If the reserve falls by 5 million (for instance, because of a trade deficit), and if the monetary base (notes circulation, plus bank balances) declines by the same amount, the required 35% AR would not be reached.[11] In order to maintain the required ratio of 35%, a bigger fall in the monetary base, from 100 to 85.7 million, would be needed (35:100 = 30:85.7). The deflationary effect of a fall in the reserve is powerful indeed. This necessary, huge fall in the monetary base cannot be reached other than by also decreasing the central bank's domestic assets: advances to the banking system and/or Treasury securities held by the central bank.

In a system made of just two countries, what should the second country do following an increase of its reserve from 35 to 40 million (due, for instance, to a trade surplus with the first)? The monetary base should rise – one might argue in a similar way – from 100 to 114.3 million, in order to maintain the 35% ratio. If the increase in the monetary base were just equal to the increase in assets, i.e. from 100 to 105 million, the coverage ratio would exceed the apprehension level of 35%.[12] The central bank's domestic assets should also increase by the same percentage in order to avoid "excess reserves", i.e. a coverage ratio higher than the AR. The central bank has thus an available margin to expand the monetary base further.

Symmetry can therefore be interpreted in two ways: (1) in a passive sense, the central bank complies with symmetry (the rule of the game) simply by permitting an *absolute* correspondence between a change in its international assets – that is, in the gold/foreign exchange reserve, and a change in its liabilities – even though the coverage ratio falls below the AR (in case of a foreign deficit) or increases above that level (in case of surplus); and (2) in an active sense, whereby a deliberate action of the central bank aims to stick to the AR. This means a *proportional* contraction (increase) of domestic assets.

5   Obstacles to symmetry

All the obstacles to symmetry can be related to one overwhelming factor: the asymmetrical consequences of the ratio required by law (the AR, in this paper). While a deficit country incurring a shortage of gold/foreign exchange had to deflate in order to bring the coverage ratio back to the required level (the AR), a surplus country with an available margin was "under no similar compulsion to take measures of the opposite kind" (Bloomfield, 1959, p. 23). (Interestingly enough, we find this same issue in the dysfunctionality of the Bretton Woods system, at least until the US was in a position of creditor, and of the eurozone). Regarding the gold standard, this meant that a foreign surplus – and a consequent increase in the international reserve – did not oblige the central bank to expand its policy. The central bank might follow this course of action for different reasons: a precautionary motivation, an inflationary concern, national prestige, bank's profitability. In this regard, a short explanation is due. The binding target of the conversion ratio might induce the central bank not to expand its monetary policy, because this action might potentially endanger that ratio. The central bank might prefer, in other words, to have a cushion to defend convertibility, and maintain a higher coverage rate, in case of a future gold outflow in different circumstances. This behaviour tended to maintain in the system excess reserves.[13]

Another obstacle to symmetry goes under the generic name of national interest. Both created what has been termed as the restrictive, deflationary bias of the gold standard, the result of an "ideology" (Eichengreen and Temin, 2010, p. 4) rather than the application of the rules of the game. Related to this argument of "prestige", the surplus country has a vested interest in maintaining the asymmetry. First, there is sort of a "moral issue": the surplus country sees its surplus as "an indication of the virtuous qualities of its policy, to which all other countries should aspire" (Goodhart and Tsomocos, 2014, p. 4). Second, any attempt to cooperate internationally, symmetrically, in order to soften any deflationary pressure elsewhere, would mean to try to rebalance its position, towards reducing, or eliminating, its surplus through expansionary, inflationary, measures, and its very (perceived) political and economic hegemony as a consequence.

In the pre-WWI period, there was, both in legislation and in the prevailing public opinion, a strong emphasis on the necessity to curb any monetary over-expansion, for a better defence of a country's price stability and economic competitiveness. Underlying this view was the belief that money should be solidly anchored to a scarce commodity (gold). Powerful policy instruments were in force to potentially deflate the money supply, as regulatory ceilings to paper circulation and burdensome, progressive taxation if it exceeded certain levels. All this reinforced the "restrictive bias" of the gold standard in those years.

An additional obstacle to symmetry was the fact that, particularly in the pre-WWI period, central banks' policy was largely influenced by considerations related to their own profitability as quasi-private concerns (they were often structured as joint-stock companies, under private ownership), or to their role of assuring orderly conditions in the domestic money market, as *primus inter pares*, rather than as an institution serving a public interest.[14]

Even when central banks behaved symmetrically – for instance, by raising the discount rate or introducing tighter conditions for the availability of central bank funds to the banking system,[15] in case of a trade deficit and a fall in foreign reserves – these measures were taken with the main purpose of changing the composition of the central bank's portfolio, rather than influencing the amount of credit to the economy. On the other side, if the coverage ratio increased thanks to growing foreign reserves, a recourse to lowering the discount rate might occur not so much to favour other countries and rebalance the system (that is, symmetry), but to protect the central bank's profitability by minimising the holding of non-generating-income assets as gold, or for technical reasons related to the smooth working of the money market.

Unrelated to trade balance considerations (flows), another factor of potential asymmetry was related to the country's international investment position (IIP) (stock). A country might experience a significant inflow of foreign capital, in particular when a traumatic event occurs,[16] which may positively alter foreign investors' perspective. While this inflow increases the international reserves, it also generates a foreign debt, which may prove in the end unsustainable. The country's net international investment position might become increasingly negative. In particular, if the maturity distribution of foreign debt is such that it is mostly made of short-term liabilities, the country can be very cautious in adopting a looser monetary stance, being concerned by sudden withdrawals of foreign funds and its inability to repay.

On asymmetry, these considerations lead us to conclude that this rule of the game was not generally observed (as section 6 will show). A similar conclusion was drawn by Bloomfield in his survey on this issue, when he says that monetary policy was not "automatic", but also that – if there was "discretion" – "the quality of management was very poor", responding, we might add, more to criteria of management of a private enterprise than to public policy purposes. We agree with Bloomfield that there was "no awareness of the rules of the game".[17] We shall try to test these points in section 6.

6   Empirical analysis to measure symmetry in five European countries

Our evaluation of the degree of symmetry will not be made on a qualitative basis, which is by taking into account the relevance of the specific possible motivations of asymmetry given in section 5, but on a quantitative analysis, as explained more in more detail in sections 6.1 and 6.2.

We try to address two important questions:

• Whether central banks acted symmetrically according to this rule of the game of the gold standard, and whether a common pattern of behaviour can be detected in a cross-country observation of their policies.
• Whether the observance of the legal conversion ratio was an effective constraint for the central banks to behave asymmetrically, and if so, to what extent.

In order to verify whether central banks acted symmetrically, we measure the degree of correlation between changes in international reserves and in the monetary base. The empirical analysis is carried out by a simulation of the 'monetary reaction function': by which we mean the central bank's reaction, as expressed in changes in the monetary base (MB), to changes in the coverage ratio (CR) and its deviations from the apprehension ratio (CR-AR35%), and in the international reserves (R). Therefore, R, CR and CR-AR35% are the explanatory independent variables, and MB is the dependent variable.

In this way, we can check *ex post* the actual "bias" of monetary policy towards each of these objectives and thus identify and measure the asymmetry bias of the central bank. This check is done in a counterfactual way: what should have been the monetary authorities' policy if they had wanted to be fully coherent with the conversion ratio determined by law (the AR, in this paper)? What should have been their policy had they wanted to keep close track of international reserves, i.e. to observe symmetry? And how close (far) was their actual behaviour to (from) those policies?

We have also analysed changes in the current account (CA) as an independent variable; however, as we show in the following analysis, changes in CA – which are often inconsistent with changes in international reserves – are not a good indicator to explain central banks' policy decisions for two reasons: the current account data are very volatile and do not appear as a reliable source of information for our purposes; the normative variable that central banks had to follow was instead the amount of officially held reserves (gold and foreign currencies). The probable explanation for the often large difference between changes in current account balances and in official reserves is that the monetary authorities preferred to keep these balances within the banking system, that is, to maintain in the private sector part of the foreign investment position of the country, therefore stabilising the monetary base. In addition, reserves and the balance of the current account are somehow correlated: the stock of reserves may well be explained as the running of successive current account surplus in the past. Therefore we have tested for two different specifications in our estimates, one with contemporary reserves as the explanatory variable and another with lagged current account balances.

In order to assess the symmetry or asymmetry of monetary policy we will run in section 6.1 an estimate of the determinants of monetary policy at the time, and then in section 6.2 we analyse how much each country followed symmetry and, when they did not follow it as a policy criterion, which role was played by the apprehension ratio in explaining such a behaviour.

6.1 Estimate of the central bank reaction function

We have estimated a panel with fixed effects from 1894[18] to 1913 to account for the main determinants in the changes in the monetary base in the form of (see Equation 1) changes in either total reserves held at the central bank (R), or the coverage ratio (CR).[19] We have used the Augmented Dickey-Fuller test as well as the Levin-Lin-Chu test to assess the stationarity of the panel, with both the variables in levels and in rates of change. We cannot reject the presence of unit roots when the variables are in levels, while there is no stationarity when using data in rates of change. Therefore we have estimated a panel with fixed effects and the variables in rates of change for the five countries under analysis. The results are summarised in Table 3.1.

Table 3.1 Panel data estimation results (changes in the monetary base as the dependent variable)

Variables	Coefficient (t-statistic)
Constant	0.829 (2,467)***
Total reserves, Central Bank	1.015 (36,892)***
Coverage ratio	−1.081*** (−52.404)
AR(1)	0.311 (3.126)***
R^2	0.958
F-statistic	698,793***
Durbin Watson statistic	2.263
Total observations	95

Note: (***) significant at 2.5% level. An auto-regressive component of order 1 [AR (1)] has been added to the equation to address autocorrelation in the residuals.

$$MB_{(t)} = Constant + Changes\ in\ Reserves_{(t)} + Changes\ in$$
$$the\ Coverage\ Ratio_{(t)} \tag{Eq. 1}$$

The results of these estimates must be interpreted with caution: the value of the coefficients of the reserves and the coverage ratio are significant but seem to point at a close to linear relation between them, which would recommend the specification of a different panel or the assessment of the effects of each variable individually (the latter we do in section 6.2). This is why we have also estimated Equation 2, where we have replaced contemporary reserves for lagged current account balances (two years back). With this specification we address the multicolineality issue observed in Table 3.1.

$$MB_{(t)} = Constant + Changes\ in\ Current\ Account\ Balance_{(t-2)}$$
$$+ Changes\ in\ the\ Coverage\ Ratio_{(t)} \tag{Eq. 2}$$

As shown in Table 3.2, both changes in total reserves held by the central bank and in lagged current account balances are significant variables in the explanation of changes in the monetary base in the countries analysed, and with the expected (positive) sign: an increase in reserves would contribute positively to the expansion of the monetary base. The coverage ratio is also significant but with a negative sign: as discussed in previous sections, central banks operated paying particular attention to an apprehension ratio in order to maintain convertibility. Consequently, an increase in reserves would not imply automatically an increase in the monetary base if it did not raise the coverage ratio to or above the (35%) apprehension ratio. This quite prudent rationale is confirmed by the results offered by our panel estimates; as the sign of the coverage ratio coefficient shows, an increase in the

Table 3.2 Panel data estimation results corrected for multi-collinearity (changes in the monetary base as the dependent variable)

Variables	Coefficient (t-statistic)
Constant	3.852 (5,279)***
Current account balance (t−2)	0.015 (1,824)
Coverage ratio	−0.460*** (−6.576)
AR(1)	−0.155 (−1.395)***
R²	0.468
F-statistic	23,836***
Durbin Watson statistic	1.809
Total observations	85

Note: (***) significant at 2.5% level. An auto-regressive component of order 1 [AR (1)] has been added to the equation to address autocorrelation in the residuals.

coverage ratio was not necessarily followed by an acceleration in the monetary base growth. This result points at an asymmetry in the running of the gold standard.

6.2 Simulation exercise: a normative approach

Even though the results so far confirm that the main driver of changes in the monetary base were changes in reserves and in the difference between the coverage ratio and the apprehension ratio, the previous estimation exercise cannot address the question on how symmetrical or asymmetrical central banks were – that is, how and to what extent they complied with this rule of the game.[20] To do so we must address how central banks should have behaved if changes in the monetary base (notes and banks' reserves) had been fully coherent with (1) changes in their reserves (that is, symmetry in the running of the gold standard, see Equation 3) and (2) changes in their coverage ratio (see Equation 4), and in particular changes in the deviations of their coverage ratio from a 35% Apprehension Ratio (see Equation 5).

1   Reserves-based rule. The gold standard symmetry rule: a policy rule based on changes in the reserves held by the central bank:

$$MB_t = MB_{t-1} \times (1 + \Delta R), \text{ being } \Delta R = R_t - R_{t-1} \qquad \text{(Eq. 3)}$$

2   Coverage ratio-based rule: a policy rule based on changes in the CR irrespective of its level:

$$MB_t = MB_{t-1} \times (1 + \Delta CR), \text{ being } \Delta CR = CR_t - CR_{t-1} \qquad \text{(Eq. 4)}$$

3   Apprehension ratio-based rule: a policy rule based on changes in the deviations of the CR from the AR, 35%:

$$MB_t = MB_{t-1} \times \Delta (CR - 35\%)_t \qquad \text{(Eq. 5)}$$

Concerning our analysis that follows, we use the following sample periods in our five European economies: UK (1870–1913), Germany (1876–1913), France (1860–1913), Italy (1894–1913) and Spain (1874–1913).[21] We have used different reaction functions with several specifications, all of which share a high degree of inertia[22] in the changes made to the amount of money in the economy. Due to the lack of availability of higher frequency data, all the variables used are annual (the sources are detailed in this chapter's Appendix). Finally, the dependent variable is the monetary base narrowly defined, with notes (and not coins) in circulation plus banks' balances at the central bank.

Italy (1894–1913)

1   As shown in Figure 3.1, the trend of the monetary base and the reserves held by the Bank of Italy ran in parallel from 1894 to 1906, which is the expected outcome of a gold standard economy (where – as stressed previously – the

amount of money issued by the central bank is connected to its metallic reserves holdings). From 1907 to 1913, though, the rate of growth of the monetary base is notably higher than that of the reserves, which had a relative stagnation since 1907. The reaction of monetary base changes to changes in the reserves is shown by the correlation coefficient between changes in the monetary base and changes in reserves: it is high and reveals the expected positive value in a gold standard country (0.58, see Table 3.A1). Out of the 20-year period analysed, 70% of the years when reserves increased (decreased) the central bank reacted increasing (decreasing) the monetary base. It is important to note that this does not indicate a one-to-one response of money growth to changes in reserves, but in our view it is a sufficiently strong indication of the underlying determinants of monetary policy at the time.[23] A further analysis of the rate of growth of the monetary base at the time suggests however that the Bank of Italy did not merely follow symmetry – that is, changes in the monetary base following changes in reserves – as a criterion for the running of the gold standard, but also other criteria.

2   We have analysed the correlation between changes in the monetary base and changes in the coverage ratio. Confirming the remarks made previously, the negative sign of this correlation shows that there were periods where reserves grew and the monetary base did not increase accordingly (or even did not increase at all). This result suggests a cautious behaviour followed by the Bank of Italy: overall, for the twenty years considered, the Bank did not expand the monetary base when the increase in reserves was not sufficient to keep the Bank in a safe position to maintain lira convertibility. We have tested this hypothesis by analysing the correlation between changes in the monetary base and those of the coverage ratio in respect to the apprehension ratio: the sign of the correlation with changes in the monetary base is as expected and also quite strong (0.60), as more than 80% of the years when the ratio was above (below) 35% the central bank expanded (contracted) the amount of money in circulation.

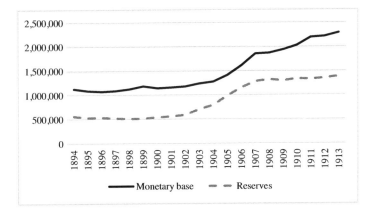

Figure 3.1 Italy: monetary base and reserves, 1894–1913 (in million lira)

The trends and correlations stated previously are confirmed when we address in a counterfactual way which should have been the monetary policy compatible with changes in reserves and in the apprehension ratio. As shown in Figure 3.2, the Bank of Italy's monetary policy decisions from 1894 to 1899 very much followed the prescription of a gold standard symmetry rule, mainly governed by changes in reserves. However, from 1900 to 1908 the monetary base did not follow the same expansionary path in the face of a continuous increase both in reserves and in the coverage ratio. In those years the Bank of Italy seemed to have been more conservative and thus less expansionary than what the application of a symmetry rule would have prescribed.

These discrepancies between the actual monetary base changes and those prescribed by the gold standard symmetry rule can well be interpreted as a *symmetry gap* in the application of the gold standard, where the gap is calculated as the difference between the actual monetary base and the one prescribed by changes in

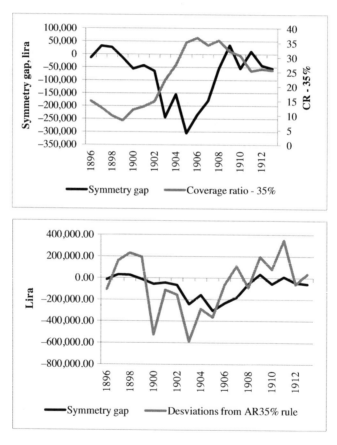

Figure 3.2 Symmetry gap, Italy, 1894–1913: (a) symmetry gap and coverage ratio, (b) symmetry gap and an apprehension ratio rule

reserves (i.e. Equation 3).[24] In the case of Italy, the symmetry gap depicts an over-all negative pattern along the sample, with an average of −131,642 million lire, amounting to −9% under-issue of money on average per year from 1894 to 1913.

When compared to the apprehension ratio rule (see Equation 5), the gap is even greater: from 1899 to 1905, the issue of notes by the Bank of Italy was far below the rate prescribed by the deviations of the coverage ratio from the 35% apprehension ratio (see Figure 3.2b). This was a period when the coverage ratio not only increased but maintained a level well above the 35% ratio, and yet the Bank of Italy would not increase accordingly the monetary base. As shown in Figure 3.2a, only when a comfortable position was reached (1905 onwards), with a coverage ratio well above the 35% apprehension ratio, did the Bank seem to be more willing to increase the amount of notes in circulation, as shown in the fall in the symmetry gap. This suggests a very conservative bias adopted by the Bank in order to preserve an even greater than 35% coverage ratio, which indeed impeded the fulfilment of asymmetry.

In sum, the Bank of Italy did not just mirror every change (either positive or negative) in the reserves in order to change the monetary base but appears to have adopted instead an implicit desired apprehension ratio minimum level deemed compatible with the fulfilment of convertibility, indeed higher than the 35% ratio. Whenever that ratio has not been reached new additions to the stock of reserves were not passed on to the amount of money in the economy but kept at the Bank of Italy as a safety buffer. However, the adoption of such an apprehension ratio seemed to have lost relevance at the end of the sample, in the years running up to WWI.

United Kingdom (1870–1913)

1   The Bank of England was at the epicentre of the world monetary system and followed the prescriptions of the gold standard; thereby changes in reserves were very much followed by changes in the monetary base in the economy: out of the 42 years analysed, more than 81% of the years when reserves increased (decreased) the Bank expanded (contracted) the monetary base accordingly, which is reflected in a quite high correlation ratio between changes in reserves and changes in the monetary base (0.74). Both the monetary base and total reserves held by the Bank of England showed a continuous increasing and very similar pattern throughout the sample (see Figure 3.3).

2   We compare now the actual changes in the monetary base in the UK from 1870 to 1913 to those prescribed by the gold standard reserves' rule (see Equation 3). This analysis suggests that the Bank of England very much followed symmetry: the symmetry gap exhibits very mild fluctuations around the zero line (with a very close to zero average gap, −0.025 million pounds, which amounts to a negligible −0.03% under-issue bias per year on average, see Figure 3.4). More-over, the coverage ratio exceeded the 35% apprehension ratio all throughout the sample and the size of this gap does not seem to have a significant influence in the amount of bank notes issued by the Bank of England. This all suggests a quite symmetrical application of the gold standard.

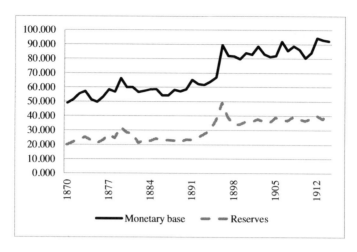

Figure 3.3 UK: monetary base and reserves, 1870–1913 (in million pounds)

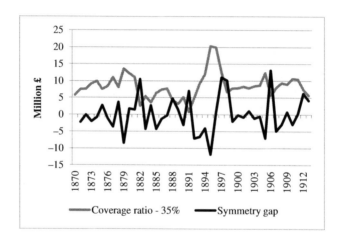

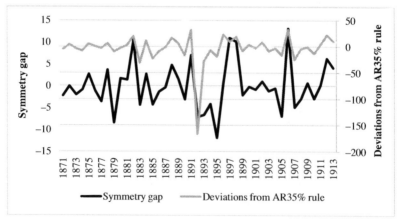

Figure 3.4 UK, gold standard rules as a benchmark: (a) symmetry gap and coverage ratio, (b) symmetry gap and apprehension ratio rule

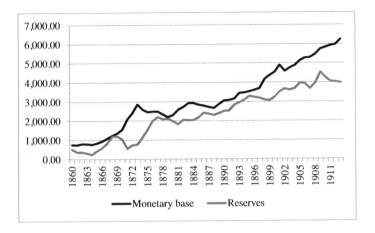

Figure 3.5 France, monetary base and reserves, 1860–1913 (in million French francs)

France (1860–1913)

1   During these years the monetary base grew at a quite stable pace throughout the sample, and at a faster rate than reserves did (see Figure 3.5). The correlations between changes in the monetary base on the one side and in reserves and the coverage ratio are insignificant (−0.05 and −0.38 respectively); as with Italy, what the negative correlation to changes in the coverage ratio indicates is that the Bank of France did not expand the amount of notes when the coverage ratio increased, irrespective of its level. However, 74% of the years in this period the monetary base changed following the sign of the deviation of the coverage ratio from the 35% apprehension ratio: that is, an expansion/contraction in the monetary base when the coverage ratio was above/below 35%. This points at the de facto adoption of other criteria, and not merely the fulfilment of symmetry, such as the achievement of an implicit apprehension ratio, as the criterion to determine the amount of notes issued by the Bank.

2   However, when we compare the actual rate of growth of the monetary base with the running of the reserves and apprehension ratio rules (Equations 3 and 5) we observe important discrepancies (see Figure 3.6b), as well as an overall asymmetric (under-issue) bias in the application of the gold standard (with −33.01 million francs average), accounting for an under-issue of money of −1% on average per year. In order to identify this bias more clearly we can make a distinction between two time periods in the sample:

    a   From 1860 to mid-1870s and with the exception of 1871, the Bank of France's symmetry gap can be explained by the deviations of the coverage ratio from a 35% apprehension ratio. Only when the coverage ratio had been rising well above the apprehension ratio did the Bank of France allow for the monetary base to increase, even above the prescriptions of the symmetry rule (see 1867–1871 in Figure 3.6a).[25] The same rationale applies to the under-issue of money from 1872 to 1877, which was preceded by several years of a fall in the coverage ratio (which even hit the 35% apprehension ratio). This is the time period when the asymmetry bias of the Bank is more acute, with a −8.9% under-issue of notes on average per year, and indicates that it followed a very conservative monetary policy: the monetary base did not grow even when the coverage ratio had reached the 35% ratio, which suggests that the Bank of France may have been adopting (de facto) even a higher apprehension ratio in these years.

b   From 1878 to the start of WW1 the Bank of France seemed to have followed a reserves rule, with the symmetry gap being negligible and fluctuating around zero (see Figure 3.6b).

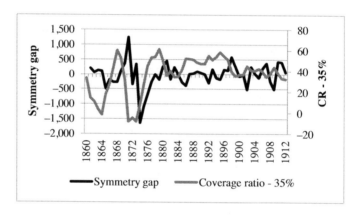

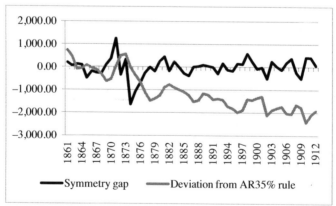

Figure 3.6 Symmetry gap, France, 1861–1912: (a) symmetry gap and coverage ratio, (b) symmetry gap and apprehension rule

Spain (1874–1913)

In 1874 the Bank of Spain was granted the monopoly of notes issue for the whole country and following a monetary contraction in the early 1880s, it suspended convertibility of notes in gold in 1883. Even though not formally on the gold standard since then, the Bank of Spain ran a monetary policy very much linked to the stock of metallic reserves available at the time, which can be interpreted as the running of a gold standard rule "in the shadow".

1   From 1874 to 1881 the monetary base followed a very much stable and low growing pace, in fact slower than that of the reserves held at the Bank (see Figure 3.7), which increased steadily from 1885 on. From 1882 onwards, the monetary base depicts a continuous growing trend, higher than that of the reserves. In more than 60% of the years when reserves increased (decreased) did the monetary base also increase (decrease) as expected; and in 76% of the years when the coverage ratio was above (below) the 35% apprehension ratio did the base also increase (decrease).

2   However, when we compare the rate of growth of the monetary base with the prescriptions of the reserves and the apprehension ratio rules we can observe that, overall, monetary base changes were not always in line with changes in reserves (see Figure 3.8a), resulting in an asymmetry gap: (1) the under-issue of notes from 1866 to 1894, when the Bank seemed to have paid more attention to how close the (falling) coverage ratio was to the apprehension ratio and, in particular, to the need to keep up a considered as a safety ratio around or even higher than 35%; and (2) the over-issue of notes in the mid and late 1890s, which coincides with a very difficult economic and political time – Spain ran successive public deficits to pay for the expenses of the independence wars in Cuba and the Philippines, which in the end imposed a strong pressure on the Bank of Spain to monetise the deficit. After the introduction of a new fiscal and monetary stabilisation plan in 1902 (the so-called 'Villaverde Plan'), the economy resumed more balanced budgets and a more stable monetary policy, which is shown in a significantly smaller symmetry gap.

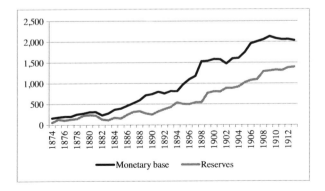

Figure 3.7 Spain: monetary base and reserves, 1874–1913 (in million pesetas)

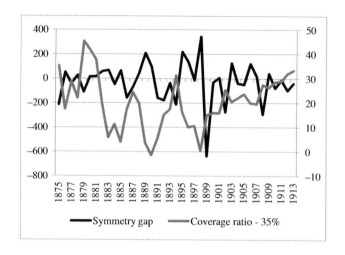

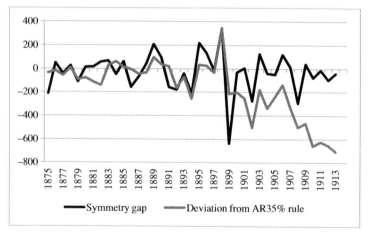

Figure 3.8 Spain, gold standard rules as a benchmark (in million pesetas): (a) symmetry
gap and coverage ratio, (b) symmetry gap and apprehension rule

The Bank of Spain followed consistently a more conservative policy than the one
prescribed by the fulfilment of symmetry, with an overall (average) under-issue
bias of −29 million Pesetas, which amounts to an under-issue of notes of −2.8%
per year on average.

Germany (1876–1913)

1   From approximately 1876 to 1894 the growth of the monetary base fol-
     lowed a very stable path, along with that of reserves. However, as shown
     in Figure 3.9, since the mid-1890s onwards the trend of the rate of growth

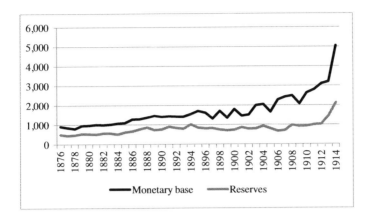

Figure 3.9 Germany: monetary base and reserves, 1875–1913 (in million RM)

of the monetary base was significantly higher than that of reserves, which remained stagnated until 1908. Following James (1997), the main Reichsbank's concerns were the preservation of the gold stock and the ability to respond to financial distress in case needed. So rather than altering the stock of gold, the Bank resorted to its discount rate and to adjustments in its assets portfolio as means to achieve a certain ratio of notes to gold holdings. In practice, this meant the management of the gold standard through the regulation of domestic credit via changes in interest rates. In this sense, the Bank conducted a very "modern" monetary policy through the application of rules rather than personal judgement.

2   The result of this strategy was the overall fulfilment of the symmetry rule until mid-1890s. As shown in Figure 3.10, from 1876 to 1894, the symmetry gap is certainly modest and very similar to that of the Bank of England's (−0.1%). This coincides with a period of an accumulation of reserves by the Reichsbank well above the 35% apprehension ratio. However, the fulfilment of the symmetry rule became much more loose and erratic since 1901, when the coverage ratio fell significantly, even below the 35% apprehension ratio in some years.

Overall, the Reichsbank ran a monetary policy consistent with the symmetry rule, with just an average −19.13 million RM under-issue bias for the whole period, which amounts to a −1.1% under-issue on average per year.

We can summarise our findings in this section as follows:

On the one hand, Italy and Spain exhibit asymmetry, resulting in an under-growth of the monetary base throughout the sample. As regards Italy, the explanation lies in the application of an alternative policy rule, by which the monetary base did not grow following an expansion of reserves until they reached a certain "safety ratio": a desired safety ratio that seems to be higher than the apprehension ratio of 35%. As regards Spain, it was mainly the pressure of the government on

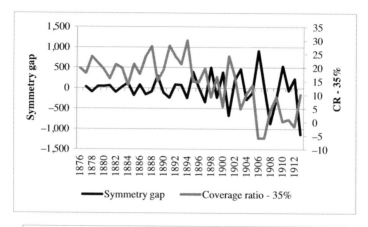

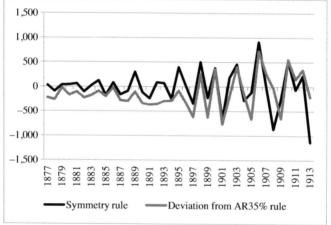

Figure 3.10 Germany, gold standard rules as a benchmark (in million RM): (a) symmetry gap and coverage ratio, (b) symmetry gap and apprehension rule

the central bank that explains the deviations observed from the symmetry rule; once these pressures mitigated in the early 1900s the Bank of Spain followed in greater extent the gold standard rules, even though the country was on an only de facto gold standard. Germany and France did not follow symmetry consistently throughout the sample either, and displayed (though to a lesser extent) a not-negligible under-issue policy bias.

On the other hand, the United Kingdom, the epicentre of the monetary system at the time, followed symmetry in the running of the gold standard. The UK was comfortably within the apprehension ratio, and foreign investors had confidence in the strength of the pound, so that the central bank could promptly adjust its monetary policy to changes in its gold reserve.

The consequences resulting from the running of the gold standard with a deficient degree of symmetry should not be underestimated, as countries like Germany and France refused to let the increase in reserves be reflected in a greater amount of money supply. This created tension in the system, as countries like Italy or Spain would find it more difficult to regain competitiveness, and thus a greater internal devaluation was needed to be able to compete with their trade (surplus) partners.[26]

7   Conclusions and policy implications

We can now try to give an answer to the two questions raised at the beginning of section 6: whether central banks acted symmetrically and whether their policy was affected by the observance of the legal, mandatory conversion ratio. Regarding the first question, our empirical results show that the UK was – on average – the country which followed more closely the symmetry rule of the game; on the opposite side was Italy, which maintained the most pronounced asymmetry, while the other three countries were somewhat in between. The common pattern of behaviour was an under-issue of currency (minimal, in the case of Britain). See Table 3.3.

Regarding our second question, these results point out to an important distinction between the UK and the other four countries. As shown in section 6.2, these four countries seemed to have paid attention to the deviations of the coverage ratio from a (high) "safety ratio" in order to maintain convertibility. What we have observed is that this safety ratio was a sort of benchmark, prudentially adopted, and set well above the apprehension ratio of 35% (needless to remind, we have taken the apprehension ratio as a proxy for the legally required conversion ratio, see section 3), and significantly higher than the figures suggested in the literature. In this vein, only having achieved that safety ratio the interested country would feel comfortable enough to follow the symmetry rule. Or, in other words, our *ex post* analysis suggests that achieving such a safety ratio seemed to have been taken as a pre-condition to be able to abide by symmetry in the running of the god standard. This seems to be particularly relevant for Italy. These countries were fearful that the strict observance of the legal ratio might create difficulties in case

Table 3.3 Summary of results: measurement of asymmetry in the running of the gold standard

Annual percentage deviation from the "reserves rule" (symmetry), $MB_t = MB_{t-1} \times (1 + \Delta R)$	
	(Yearly average, %)
Spain	−2.8%
France	−1%
Italy	−9%
Germany	−1.1%
UK	−0.0003%

Note: A negative/positive sign indicates an under-issue/over-issue of currency as compared to the symmetry rule.

of unfavourable developments in their foreign accounts. Sticking – to a different extent according to the different countries – to this safety ratio ended up by accumulating enormous "idle" reserves: not necessary to cover currency in circulation, and effectively frozen for foreign currency transactions, and by creating powerful deflationary pressures in the system.[27]

Were the asymmetries of the pre-WWI period the origin of the gold standard's final collapse? The straight answer is negative: all the five countries here surveyed had to suspend the standard at the outbreak of the war, if not before such as Spain in 1883; it was the war, with the huge expansion of the money supply, dramatic inflation and social unrest that made later in the 1930s the gold standard unable to survive. In the post-war period, Britain had lost her hegemonic status and symmetry together with it.

And, as pointed out in section 1, the asymmetry of the hegemonic country (the US under the Bretton Woods system) might well explain its collapse.

Should we infer from these experiences that symmetry of the hegemonic country is the precondition for a fixed rate system (or for a currency union with a single currency) to survive? And, referring to the eurozone, should we think that Germany – unquestionably the hegemonic country – is behaving asymmetrically and that the eurozone should collapse as a consequence? Another paper would be needed to answer these questions.

Appendix

Table 3.A1 Correlation with annual changes in the monetary base

	Reserves (annual change, %)	Current Account (annual change, %)	Coverage Ratio (annual change, %)	Apprehension Ratio (deviation from 35%)
Italy	0.58	0.11	−0.06	0.60
UK	0.73	−0.15	0.04	0.28
France	−0.05	0.07	−0.38	−0.08
Spain	0.27	0.40	−0.07	−0.30
Germany	0.20	−0.06	−0.64	−0.45

Source: Own calculations.

Statistical sources

Italy: Monetary Base (MB), Reserves (R), Current Account balance (CA), Coverage Ratio (CR), Apprehension Ratio (AR), 1895–1913. Own calculation of the narrow monetary base as the summation of banks' balances at the Bank of Italy and the notes issued by the Bank of Italy, Bank of Naples and Bank of Sicily (from Caron et al. 1993). Total metallic reserves and foreign exchange reserves of all the banks of issue in Italy (all from Caron et al. 1993); data on the current account balance from B. Mitchell's (2007) "International Historical Statistics. Europe, 1750–2005". Own calculation of the coverage ratio figures.

United Kingdom: Monetary Base (MB), Reserves (R), Current Account balance (CA), Apprehension Ratio (AR), 1871–1913. Own calculation of the narrow monetary base as the summation of banks' balances at the Bank of England, total metallic reserves (both from the Bank of England historical balance sheets' database) and notes in circulation from Mitchell's (2011) "British Historical Statistics"; data on the current account balance from B. Mitchell's (2011) "British Historical Statistics" (coins in circulation have not been included). Own calculation of the coverage ratio figures.

France: Monetary Base (MB), Reserves (R), Current Account balance (CA), Apprehension Ratio (AR), 1860–1913. We have calculated the narrow monetary base figures from B. Mitchell's (2007) "International Historical Statistics. Europe, 1750–2005" and Baubeau (2018). Total metallic reserves from the Bank of France archives; data on the current account balance from B. Mitchell's (2007) "International Historical Statistics. Europe, 1750–2005". Own calculation of the coverage ratio figures.

Spain: Monetary Base (MB), Reserves (R), Current Account balance (CA), Apprehension Ratio (AR), 1874–1913. Total metallic reserves from Martín Aceña and Pons (2005), in Carreras and Tafunell (eds.) *Estadísticas Históricas de España*. Own calculation of the narrow monetary base as the summation of banks' balances at the Bank of Spain (only available from 1900 onwards, from Martín Aceña and Pons, 2005), and total notes in circulation from Anes, 1974). Data on the current account balance has been proxied by the trade balance from Tena's (2005), in Carreras and Tafunell (eds.) *Estadísticas Históricas de España*. Own calculation of the coverage ratio figures.

Germany: Monetary Base (MB), Reserves (R), Current Account balance (CA), Apprehension Ratio (AR), 1876–1913. We have used total metallic reserves from Deutsche Bundesbank (1976): Deutsches Geld- und Bankwesen in Zahlen 1876–1975; data on the current account balance from B. Mitchell's (2007) "International Historical Statistics (1750–2005)". Own calculation of the apprehension ratio figures and of the narrow monetary base.

Acknowledgements

We would like to thank Professors Wood, Goodhart and Capie for their very helpful comments on previous versions of the paper, as well as Dr Jordi Vila and Dr Jose Luis Cendejas for their very valuable technical assistance in section 6.1. We are also grateful to the feedback and comments made by the attendees to the Monetary History Group (October 2018) and the conference on "The Economics of Monetary Unions" (21–22 February 2019, Institute of International Monetary Research and University of Buckingham).

Notes

1 The first author who made clear the proper working of a monetary system based on gold was Hume, David: "On the Balance of Trade", in *Essays and Treaties on Several Subjects*, 1764.
2 Amongst some of the seminal works, Bloomfield (1959), Bordo and Schwartz (Eds.) (1984) and Eichengreen and Flandreau (1985).
3 As per the GDP levels in real terms (million 1990, international Geary-Khamis dollars) in 1914, the world ranking is the following: UK 226,864; Germany 202,207; France 134,230; Italy 95,413; Spain 41,075. See Maddison, Angus: *The World Economy: Historical Statistics*, OECD, 2003.

4 Note that, in line with what has been said so far, the difference between monetary base, created by the central bank, and money stock, which includes bank deposits, is relevant. In Italy, in 1911 for instance, we have:

   – Monetary base 2.6 bln.
   – Money stock (total circulation, plus bank deposits) 9.5 bln.
                    (Source: Banca d'Italia: I bilanci degli istituti di emissione 1894–1990,
                              Laterza, 1993; and website: statistiche storiche).

5 See League of Nations (1930) for a summary of various countries laws on this topic in the post-WWI period.
6 We shall follow Keynes' (1965, pp. 265–269), but it is not the only partition, see also Bloomfield (1959, p. 18).
7 Worthwhile observing that Keynes does not recommend neither this specific percentage, nor a percentage system in general, nor – for what matters – any of the two previously mentioned alternatives. He is, as is well known, in favour of a managed currency, where discretion takes place of any rule, having the central bank policy to be aimed at domestic monetary and financial stability, irrespective of constraints caused by ratios/limits of any kind.
8 Bagehot (1931, p. 322). This was a consequence of the legal provision (the Bank Act of 1844) that linked the amount of gold to banknote only, not considering the bank balances at the central bank.
9 It is however interesting to observe that an attempt made on the basis of the "legal approach" (A), referred to a specific country (Italy), leads to similar conclusions on the monetary policy stance of that country: both the economic and the legal perspective point out to the fact that in the first years of the 20th century, and up to WWI, Italy might have had room for a more expansionary monetary policy thanks to a positive trend in its international reserves, but was reluctant to do that, probably concerned by fears of the lira's convertibility ratio (see Roselli, Alessandro: *Symmetry under the Gold Standard: The Case of Italy 1894–1914*, mimeo, 2016).
10 The adoption of a more "economically significant" ratio would require to use as the denominator the total money supply – M1 or greater aggregate – which would be the best indicator of monetary stability. We have used here the monetary base because it is the best proxy to what different legislations stated as the denominator at the time.
11 $(x:100=30:95; x = 31.6; 31.6<35)$
12 $(x:100=40:105; x = 38.1>35)$
13 It is worthwhile to remember a very different perspective, brought by a critic of the gold standard, John Maynard Keynes. He – as early as in 1923, in front of an enormous inflow of gold in the US – observed approvingly:

   > The Federal Reserve Board began to ignore this ratio [the required coverage ratio] and to accept gold without allowing it to exercise its full influence, merely because an expansion of credit and prices seemed at that point undesirable . . . the gold was not allowed to exercise the multiplied influence which the pre-war system presumed.
   >
   >   (Keynes, 1932, p. 198)

14 This is a very controversial question on the evolution of central banks and their role in modern economies studied in detail in Goodhart (1988) and Congdon (1981).
15 By raising the quality of eligible collateral, for instance.
16 Two cases are exemplary in this regard: after the stabilization of the Reichsmark in 1924, a huge inflow of money occurred in Weimar's Germany (1924–1930), which proved unsustainable when the world crisis erupted and that money flew back. Greece experienced a relevant capital inflow when it joined the euro in 2001 and we are witnessing the consequences now.

17 pp. 26 and 24.
18 This is because 1894 is the first year for which we have all the data available for the five countries considered; 1913 is the final year before the suspension of the gold standard during WWI.
19 We have estimated the model with fixed effects given that it is not a sample of fully homogeneous economies and each country ran the gold standard with its own specificities. In addition, as to the preference for a fixed rather than a random effects panel, the Haussmann test shows no significant differences in the estimated values.
20 This type of simulation, ex post analysis is very much used in monetary policy analysis from the mid-1990s onwards, following the seminal work of John Taylor in 1993 on the analysis of the US Fed policies in the previous decades. Since then, multiple similar analyses have been made by using a policy reaction function as a benchmark to assess ex post the inflationary bias of the central bank (see Taylor, 1993, 1999, 2009).
21 We have not included the US given that the US Federal Reserve did not start to operate as a single central bank for the whole country until 1914. We have added Spain so we can analyse the monetary policy of a formally non-gold-standard country at the time. Further details on the dataset and the sources used can be found in the Appendix. As regards the other countries, we have chosen the starting dates corresponding to the availability of data or a significant monetary event in the country, such as the establishment of the central bank (Italy, Germany) or the monopoly of note issue granted to the central bank (Spain).
22 The analysis of the total and partial correlation of the monetary base series clearly reveal a strong autoregressive structure of order 1.
23 Just to put this analysis in a contemporaneous comparable context, the Bundesbank's monetary targeting policies in the 1970s and 1980s were labelled as a successful rule-based and very much credible monetary strategy, and on average the central bank hit its monetary growth intermediate targets only 50% of the time (see Issing, 2008; Bofinger, 2001). Of course this reinforces the idea that a policy rule is not a mechanistic way to run policy decisions but a consistent strategy to make them and communicate with the public which ultimately enhances credibility over the medium and long term.
24 According to this definition, the deviations of the black line (Figures 3.2) from the zero line reveal asymmetries in the running of the gold standard; either an over issue of liquidity (over-expansionary policy) when there are positive values or too conservative when there are negative values.
25 However France was under a bi-metallic standard before 1873 and thus the interpretation of our estimates in this period must be taken with caution.
26 An alternative would be for the deficit countries to trade more with other countries, not adhered to such fixed exchange rate regime, be it the gold standard or the eurozone.
27 See Nurkse (1944).

References

Anes, G. (1974): 'Una serie de base monetaria [1874–1915]'. In Schwartz, P. and Tortella, G. (eds.) *La Banca Española en la Restauración*. Madrid: Banco de España.

Bagehot, W. (1931): *Lombard Street: A Description of the Money Market*. Homewood, IL: Irwin. (1873).

Baubeau, P. (2018): 'The Bank of France's balance sheets database, 1840–1998: An introduction to 158 years of central banking'. In *Financial History Review*. Vol. 5, Issue 2, August, pp. 203–230.

Bloomfield, A. (1959): *Monetary Policy under the International Gold Standard: 1880–1914*. New York: Federal Reserve Bank of New York.

Bofinger, P. (2001): *Monetary Policy: Goals, Institutions, Strategies, and Instruments*. Oxford: Oxford University Press.

Bordo, M. and Schwartz, A. (Eds.) (1984): *A Retrospective on the Classical Gold Standard, 1821–1931*. NBER. Chicago: University of Chicago Press.

Capie, F. and Wood, G. (Eds.) (2003): *Monetary Unions: Theory, History, Public Choice*. Abingdon, Routledge.

Caron, M. et al. (1993): *I Bilanci degli istituti di emissione in Italia, 1894–1990*. Roma, Bari: Laterza.

Congdon, T. (1981): 'Is the Provision of a Sound Currency a Necessary Function of the State?' In *National Westminster Bank Quarterly Review* (August), pp. 2–21.

Deutsche Bundesbank (1976): *Deutsches Geld – und Bankwesen in Zahlen 1876–1975*. Frankfurt am Main: Knapp.

Eichengreen, B. and Flandreau, M. (1985): *The Gold Standard in Theory and History*. Abingdon: Routledge.

Eichengreen, B. and Temin, P. (2010): 'Fetters of gold and paper'. In *Oxford Review of Economic Policy*, Vol. 26, Issue 3, pp. 370–384, Autumn.

Goodhart, G. (1988): *The Evolution of Central Banks*. Cambridge: The MIT Press.

Goodhart, C. and Tsomocos, D. (2014): 'International Monetary Regimes'. In *Capitalism and Society*. Vol. 9, Issue 2.

Hawtrey, R. G. (1931): *The Gold Standard in Theory and Practice*. London: Longmans, Green and Company.

Hayek, F. A. (1935): *Monetary Nationalism and International Stability*. Fairfield: August Kelly Publishers (1989).

Hume, D. (1984): 'On the Balance of Trade'. In *Essays and Treaties on Several Subjects*. In E. Miller (Ed.), *Part II, Essay V*. Liberty fund, Indianapolis (1764).

Issing, O. (2008): *The Birth of the Euro*. Cambridge: Cambridge University Press.

Keynes, J. M. (1932): 'A Tract on Monetary Reform'. London: Macmillan (1923).

Keynes, J. M. (1965): *Treatise on Money*. Volume 2. London: Macmillan (1930).

League of Nations (1930): *Legislation on Gold*. Geneva: League of Nations.

Maddison, A. (2003): *The World Economy: Historical Statistics*. Paris: OECD.

Martín Aceña, P. and Pons, M. A. (2005): "Sistema Monetario y Financiero". In Carreras, A. and Tafunell, X. (Eds.), *Estadísticas Históricas de España. Siglos XIX y XX*. Bilbao. Fundación BBVA.

Mitchell, B. (2007): *International Historical Statistics. Europe, 1750–2005*. Basingstoke: Palgrave Macmillan.

Mitchell, B. (2011): *British Historical Statistics*. Cambridge. Cambridge University Press. 1988.

Nurkse, R. (1944): *International Currency Experience. Lessons of the Inter-War Period*. Geneva: League of Nations.

Roselli, A. (2016): *Symmetry under the Gold Standard: The Case of Italy 1894–1914*, mimeo.

Taylor, J. B. (1993): 'Discretion versus policy rules in practice'. In *Carnegie-Rochester Conference Series on Public Policy*. Vol. 39, pp. 195–214. North-Holland.

Taylor, J. B. (1999): 'A Historical Analysis of Monetary Policy Rules'. In John B. Taylor (Ed.), *Monetary Policy Rules*. Chapter 7, pp. 319–348. Chicago: University of Chicago Press.

Taylor, J. B. (2009): *Getting Off Track: How Government Actions and Interventions Caused, Prolonged, and Worsened the Financial Crisis*. Stanford: Hoover Institution Press.

Tena, A. (2005): 'Sector Exterior'. In Carreras, A. and Tafunell, X. (Eds.), *Estadísticas Históricas de España. Siglos XIX y XX*. Bilbao. Fundación BBVA.

Part 2

Financing imbalances in a single monetary area

An assessment of TARGET2

4 Payment systems in a multinational currency union – is a reform of TARGET2 necessary?

Uwe Schollmeyer

1 Introduction

Shortly after initial contributions by Sinn (2011) and Deutsche Bundesbank (2011) the so-called TARGET2 (Trans-European Automated Real-time Gross settlement Express Transfer System 2) balances have attracted lots of economists and bankers to contribute to a heated debate. While some papers point out more technical issues such as the mechanics of the TARGET2 balances (Jobst et al., 2012), others have concentrated on recent issues such as the connection to the Eurosystem's asset purchase programmes (Eisenschmidt et al., 2017). Some stress purported risks (Fuest & Sinn, 2018) or rather the absence of such risks (Ulbrich & Lipponer, 2011; Hellwig, 2018). Some authors concentrate on reform proposals for the Eurosystem's architecture including TARGET2, although more from an economist's point of view (Krahnen, 2018; Fiedler et al., 2017) rather than arguing about the technical market infrastructures reform "Vision 2020" as communicated by the ECB (2018b). At a first glance it seems to be hard to add anything new to a years' old debate that appears to be primarily "fought" in Germany.[1] Having reviewed many of the contributions, one could conclude akin to a quote by German comedian Karl Valentin (1882–1948):

> Everything has already been said, but not yet by everyone.

However, the purpose of this chapter is to contribute some aspects in the debate on TARGET2 balances from an integrated central banking perspective. This has so far been missing from the aforementioned debate. The basic question to which all this boils down to is whether alternatives to the current architecture of large-value payment systems and to the setup of the TARGET claims and liabilities between the Eurosystem's central banks could be feasible. To my knowledge, such an approach cannot be found in the literature as of today.

Attributions like "TARGET loans" (Sinn & Wollmershäuser, 2011) or rather emotionally "a madness called TARGET2" (Mayer, 2018) and "Target2 – The eurozone's silent bailout system" (Blake, 2018) cannot be undone. Actually, many papers can mislead the readers in a way that they confuse the actual payment system with the Eurosystem's monetary policy actions before and during the great financial crisis 2008 and the European sovereign debt crisis since. Still it is worth-while to take a step back and have a look at the interwoven issues of payment system architecture, financial stability oversight, monetary theory, accounting and monetary policy implementation within the framework of a currency union. In other words, an integrated perspective of central banking would help. Following Ugolini (2018, p. 2), central banking is to be understood as "a family of public policies aimed at fostering monetary and financial stability, whose provision is nowadays generally (albeit not necessarily) performed by those organizations that we call central banks".

The chapter is organized as follows. After a brief review of related literature, the use of central bank money in payment systems will be addressed in section 3. Economic aspects such as public goods and the microeconomics of financial market infrastructures also fit well into this section as do issues of the settlement of payments and its connection to the often-neglected account keeping. Section 4 introduces the idea of a decentralized system of central banks of issue for a currency area with emphasis on the euro area as a natural example but also looking at a contemporary system (Federal Reserve System of the US) and a historical example (West-German central bank system of the Bank deutscher Länder, 1948–1957). Section 5 will then combine the insights of the two previous sections and shed light on the technicalities of intra-[euro-]system balance sheet positions stemming inter alia from the settlement of payments. With these aspects in mind, section 6 then finally discusses alternative solutions for the setup of large-value payment systems (LVPS) in a multinational currency union. Section 7 concludes.

2   Related literature

Only few authors take a integrated perspective onto central banking; most con-centrate on macroeconomic aspects and/or monetary policy only. Among those taking an integrated perspective, certainly Goodhart (1987, 1988) and Giannini (2004/2011) deserve mentioning in the first places. Very recently, Borio (2019) added insights on the elements of a well-functioning monetary system. The volume edited by Summers (1994) gives valuable insights into the topic of payment systems and central banking from a time when many newly independ-ent countries were to establish their own central banks and financial market infrastructures. The role of central bank money in payment systems is explored by CPSS (2003), whereas Bindseil (2004) adds the aspects of monetary policy implementation from a theoretical perspective and the same author (2018) takes a less Anglo-centric view on the origins of the lender-of-last-resort function of early central banks similarly to Ugolini (2018). More generally, historically oriented studies on central banking such as those by Roberds and Velde (2016) or Jobst and Ugolini (2016) give the reader valuable information on the evo-lution of institutions and the monetary system in general. Schnabel and Shin (2018) extend their findings from the 1620s to aspects of central banking in the digital age.

Textbooks on central banking are still rare. Moenjak (2014) concentrates on monetary and financial stability with only very few regards to the payment system. Herger (2016) focusses in his small booklet for the German market on aspects closely related to monetary and currency policies, occasionally shedding light on some more general aspects. Furthermore, nearly all central banks as well as the International Monetary Fund (IMF), the Bank for International Settlements (BIS) and its committees have published amounts of literature about their respective institutions for different target groups of readers, sometimes even with a didactical approach. One book available from the European Central Bank (Kokkola, 2010) explains the payment system and shows the landscape in the euro area and is thus very relevant for the topic presented in this paper. However, it already gets almost outdated by technical and institutional progress. A new addition to the textbook literature is Berndsen (2018), who informs about money, financial market infrastructures and payments in a metaphorical way by guiding through an imaginative warehouse.

3 The use of central bank money in payment systems

3.1 Payment technologies

Payment systems enable the transfer of money between accounts that can be held by different persons at different financial institutions. It's mainly payment systems, which make sure that a settlement asset has the function of medium of exchange. Only settlement assets that possess all three functions – the others being a unit of account and a store of value – are money. Money comes in different forms. By far the most important form is nowadays money held on accounts at commercial banks, i.e. a claim of a person against a monetary financial institution (McLeay et al., 2014).

Any transfer of this cashless form of money within just one bank would exclusively affect the accounts of two customers of that bank. Depending on the intensity of competition in the market for bank services and consequently on the size of a bank measured in terms of liabilities towards their customers, such an in-house handling of payments may be more or less important in a given economy.

In most countries however, a typical transfer of cashless money would involve at least two different banks. The processing of such a payment leads in the simplest case to a claim of one bank against the other bank, i.e. an increase on the account that the bank of the payment recipient holds at the bank of the sender (Rule, 2015, pp. 5–6). This inter-bank claim comes with credit and liquidity risks that banks are typically not willing to bear if there is a less risky alternative at a given level of cost. Processing the payment through accounts held at a central bank – i.e. the monopolist provider of the monetary base for a given currency – reduces both types of risk to zero (Kokkola, 2010, p. 44). Therefore, payments will normally involve a change of ownership of commercial bank money and a transfer of central bank money (Jordan, 2018).

Transfers that only involve an exchange of claims against a central bank (other than banknotes) are also frequent. The necessary condition for such a transaction is the access to an account at the central bank. There is a variety of access conditions to central bank accounts around the globe. Very generally, commercial banks have access, whereas non-banks (other than the government) would not have access to central bank accounts. The central banks' rules differ across countries mostly with respect to access of non-bank financial institutions to central bank accounts. Examples include payment service providers, clearing houses, securities firms, non-bank credit card issuers, insurance companies, etc. (CPSS, 2003, pp. 26–29). Often this corresponds to the way that financial supervision is exercised.

Most interestingly, the topic of access to central bank money has gained much more attention in the last few years because it is related to two separate debates: On the one hand, the distributed ledger technology (DLT) allows for issuing private currencies as well as a digital form of central bank money which would no longer rely on a central ledger of accounts. The implications for monetary policy and central banking in general are very far reaching (CPMI & MC, 2018) and cannot be elaborated at this place. Interesting from a monetary theory perspective is certainly the link to thoughts of the Austrian School of Economics, especially Menger, von Mises and von Hayek (Sechrest, 1993). On the other hand, a debate around the time of the Swiss referendum on sovereign money highlighted the idea of an access to central bank reserves for all, which would have left commercial banks with a limited business. Similarly, reduction in the usage of cash in Sweden made the Riksbank think about digital alternatives in its E-Krona reports. Again, the implications for the monetary system and central banking would be very far-reaching (Sveriges Riksbank, 2018). Some authors, e.g. Niepelt (2018), find the macroeconomic effects of reserves for all not as far reaching as previously thought. These studies are very interesting in order to take a different perspective on the monetary system. Still, today's LVPSs process the major part of money transfers (measured by the value) and will most probably continue to do so for the near future.

It is quite common that the central bank of a given currency area owns and/or manages the LVPS and sometimes even does the same for retail payment systems. The BIS Statistics Explorer provides the details. The establishment of instant payment solutions for retail payments apparently gets some central banks closer to that part of the payments universe. Since this is a separate topic, I will concentrate on LVPS in what follows. In any case, the net positions of the participants in retail payment systems as well as the cash-legs from the securities and derivatives clearing positions will also settle in an LVPS (see Table 4.1).

The reasons for the involvement of the central bank in LVPS are on one hand a historical nature. The establishment of central banks can in some cases be traced to the necessity of a neutral entity for the settlement of inter-bank transactions (Norman et al., 2011). Even in the other cases, when a central bank was founded by the government or at least using a privilege issued by the sovereign, this government's bank could be the most trustworthy and possibly biggest financial institution around, thus taking naturally the role of a neutral inter-bank payments agent.

Table 4.1 Large-value payment systems in member countries of the Committee for Payments and Market Infrastructures (CPMI)

Name of country/ institution	System	Type	Settlement	Owner	Manager
		LVPS = large-value payment system **RPS** = retail payment system **FX** = foreign exchange settlement system **FPS** = fast payment system	**RTGS** = real-time gross settlement **MN** = multilateral netting **BN** = bilateral netting **G** = other gross settlement **BA** = batch settlement	**CB** = central bank **B** = commercial bank **PA** = payment association **O** = other	**CB** = central bank **B** = commercial bank **PA** = payment association **O** = other
Argentina	MEP – Medio Electrónico de Pagos	LVPS	RTGS	CB	CB
Australia	RITS	LVPS	RTGS	CB	CB
Brazil	STR	LVPS	RTGS	CB	CB
Canada	LVTS	LVPS	MN	PA	PA
China	HVPS	LVPS	RTGS	CB	CB
Hong Kong SAR	HKD CHATS	LVPS+FX	RTGS	CB	B[1]
	USD CHATS	LVPS+FX	RTGS	B	B[1]
	EUR CHATS	LVPS+FX	RTGS	B	B[1]
	RMB CHATS	LVPS+FX	RTGS	B	B[1]
India	RTGS	LVPS	RTGS	CB	CB
	NEFT	LVPS+RPS	MN	CB	CB
Indonesia	BI-RTGS	LVPS	RTGS	CB	CB
Japan	BOJ-Net	LVPS	RTGS	CB	CB
	FXYCS	LVPS	RTGS	B	B
Korea	BOK-Wire+	LVPS	RTGS	CB	CB
Mexico	SPEI	LVPS+RPS+FPS	MN	CB	CB
	SPID	LVPS	MN	CB	CB

(*Continued*)

Table 4.1 (Continued)

Name of country/institution	System	Type	Settlement	Owner	Manager
Russia	BESP System	LVPS	RTGS	CB	CB
	National Settlement Depository (NSD)	LVPS+RPS	RTGS, BA	B	B
	VER	LVPS+RPS	G	CB	CB
	MER	LVPS+RPS	G	CB	CB
	Payments using letters of advice	LVPS+RPS	G	CB	CB
Saudi Arabia	SARIE	LVPS+RPS	RTGS	CB	CB
Singapore	MEPS+(IFT)	LVPS	RTGS	CB	CB
South Africa	SAMOS	LVPS+RPS	RTGS	CB	CB
Sweden	RIX	LVPS	RTGS	CB	CB
Switzerland	Swiss Interbank Clearing (SIC)	LVPS+RPS	RTGS	O[1]	CB
Turkey	EFT	LVPS+RPS	RTGS	CB	CB
United Kingdom	CHAPS Sterling	LVPS	RTGS	CB	CB
United States	CHIPS	LVPS	MN, BN, G	B	B
	Fedwire Funds Service	LVPS	RTGS	CB	CB
	NSS	LVPS	MN	CB	CB
European Union	TARGET2	LVPS	RTGS	CB	CB
	EURO1/STEP1	LVPS	MN	PA	PA

Source: BIS Statistics Explorer, Table PS1: Features of selected payment systems (excerpt).

More recently, banking regulation may also have played a role, especially liquidity regulation for commercial banks. In their role as overseers of the payment and security settlement systems, central banks have since January 2001 formalized their expectations inter alia towards the usage of central bank money in payment systems (CPSS, 2001, Core Principle VI). Since the CPSS-IOSCO (Committee on Payment and Settlement Systems and International Organization of Securities Commissions) Standards have entered into force, Principle 9 regulates the use of central bank money as settlement asset in financial market infrastructures in general (CPSS and IOSCO, 2012).

Additionally, central banks may be the only institutions in a currency area that allow a bank as sender of a payment to address every other bank. This is so because every commercial bank will find access to the central bank useful for funding or just because a minimum reserve requirement makes holding an account at the central bank necessary. The connection of the payment system to the liquidity providing monetary policy instruments is thus very obvious as is the connection to the central banks role as lender of last resort.

3.2   *Competition of large-value payment systems*

No previous considerations rule out, that private providers of an LVPS exist. In such cases a market structure characterized by a duopoly of one private LVPS and the central bank–run LVPS will be the result (Freixas & Holthausen, 2008, p. 445). The explanation for the long-run success of a privately run LVPS side by side with the central bank–run LVPS is in its mutual imperfect substitutability for reasons of risk (i.e. credit risk, liquidity risk, operational risks). The previously mentioned connections of central bank monetary policy operations and values settled in the central bank operated LVPS have also to be borne in mind when comparing settled values. For the euro area the TARGET annual report 2017 (ECB, 2018a, p. 13) shows 7% of the payments as central bank operations. Thus, the overall effect does not seem to be too large.

Not many examples of duopolies in LVPS markets exist. Table 4.2 compresses the information from Table 4.1 to a typology of LVPS ownership and management.

The BIS Statistics Explorer shows some examples of multiple LVPSs in some countries or currency areas. However, in most of these cases the central bank operates different LVPSs for different purposes such as foreign exchange (FX) or retail payments settlement. Only four cases of some kind of competition remain: The euro area, the United States of America, Japan and Russia. The Russian case is quite peculiar, as the (private)[2] National Settlement Depository (NSD) has been built for settling the cash leg of securities transactions. Therefore, the market share in relation to the central bank–operated Banking Electronic Speedy Payment (BESP) is structurally small (Figure 4.1).

Similarly, the Foreign Exchange Yen Clearing System (FXYCS) in Japan is only settling the Yen-legs of FX trades and is thus structurally much smaller than the Bank of Japan Financial Network System (BOJ-Net) Funds Transfer System run by the central bank (Figure 4.2).

Table 4.2 Ownership and management of large-value payment systems in member countries of the Committee for Payments and Market Infrastructures (CPMI)

Countries	LVPS owner	LVPS manager	Remarks
Argentina, Australia, Belgium, Brazil, China, France, Germany, Indonesia, Italy, Korea, Netherlands, Saudi Arabia, Singapore, South Africa, Spain, Sweden, Turkey, United Kingdom	Central Bank	Central Bank	–
India, Mexico	Central Bank	Central Bank	Central Bank operates more than one LVPS for different purposes
Hong Kong SAR	• Central Bank for own currency LVPS • Commercial Bank for foreign currency LVPSs	Commercial Bank	Central Bank is joint owner of the institution which manages the LVPS and owns the foreign currency LVPSs
Russia	• Central Bank • Commercial Bank	• Central Bank • Commercial Bank	Central Bank operates more than one LVPS for different purposes Central Bank is joint owner of the institutions which own and manages the remaining LVPS The semi-private LVPS has a limited purpose
Switzerland	Other (Consortium of Commercial Banks)	Central Bank	–
Canada	Payment Association	Payment Association	–
Euro Area	• Central Bank • Payment Association	• Central Bank • Payment Association	–
Japan, US	• Central Bank • Commercial Bank	• Central Bank • Commercial Bank	Japan: The private LVPS has a limited purpose US: Central Bank operates more than one LVPS for different purposes

Source: Compiled with data from BIS Statistics Explorer, Table PS1: Features of selected payment systems.

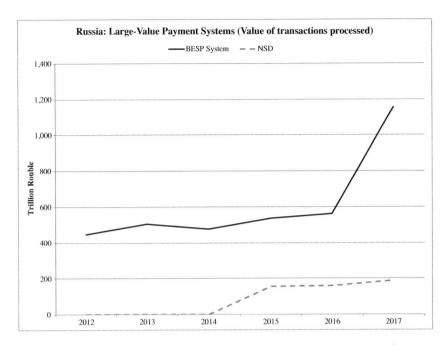

Figure 4.1 Comparison of turnover in Russian large-value payment systems; in black: BESP (operated by the Central Bank of Russia); in grey: NSD (operated by MICEX group)

Source: BIS Statistics Explorer, Table T9: Value of transactions processed by selected payment systems.

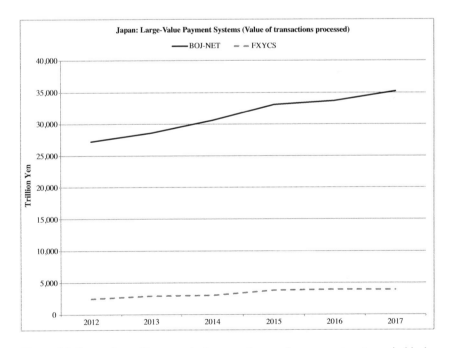

Figure 4.2 Comparison of turnover in Japanese large-value payment systems; in black: BOJ-Net FTS (operated by the Bank of Japan); in grey: FXYCS (operated by the Japanese Bankers Association)

Source: BIS Statistics Explorer, Table T9: Value of transactions processed by selected payment systems.

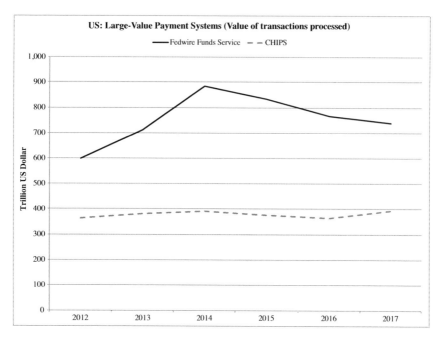

Figure 4.3 Comparison of turnover in US large-value payment systems; in black: Fedwire (operated by the Federal Reserve System); in grey: CHIPS (operated by The Clearing House Payment Company LLC)

Source: BIS Statistics Explorer, Table T9: Value of transactions processed by selected payment systems.

Data about turnover show that in the other two cases (US, euro area) the central bank–operated LVPS settles by far the majority of payments for the reasons discussed previously (Figures 4.3 and 4.4).

One additional case should not be noticed. In Finland, the Pankkien On-line Pikasiirrot ja Sekit-järjestelmä system (POPS) still exists but settles only about 2% of the value in comparison to the Finish legal component of TARGET2 (Bank of Finland, Charts, see references). In terms of market share within the whole euro area (i.e. compared to TARGET2 and EURO1) the settled values are negligible. The Finnish payment system overseers do even not classify POPS as systematically important within Finland.

In the first years after the introduction of the euro, three other national systems that did not become part of the first generation of TARGET operated for a transitional time. The systems focused on the banks in their respective countries. In Germany there was the Elektronische Abrechnung Frankfurt (EAF), which was discontinued after the Bundesbank merged its two systems, Elektronischer Schalter (ELS) and EAF, into a new LVPS called RTGS^{plus} (Real Time Gross Settlement plus) in November 2001, which then was the German TARGET component

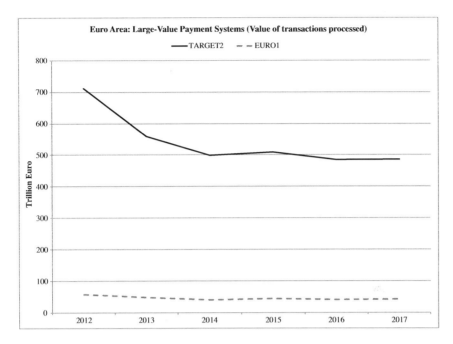

Figure 4.4 Comparison of turnover in euro area large-value payment systems; in black: TARGET2 (operated by the Eurosystem); in grey: EURO1 (operated by EBA Clearing)

Source: BIS Statistics Explorer, Table T9: Value of transactions processed by selected payment systems.

(Deutsche Bundesbank, 2000). In Spain, SPI (Servicio de Pagos Interbancarios) was discontinued in December 2004 with the largest part of the settled volume migrating to TARGET (ECB, 2006, p. 77). The French system Paris Net Settlement (PNS) operated until 2008, after which two-thirds of the traffic went to EURO1 and the remaining third to TARGET2 (Banca d'Italia, 2009, p. 186). The very fact that POPS still survives in Finland is remarkable but in terms of settled volume actually rather unimportant.

3.3 *Microeconomic and governance aspects of large-value payment systems*

A multiplicity of private LVPSs has so far (apart from the transitory period after the euro introduction) not been observed, and it's also improbable that such a structure is to emerge spontaneously. The reason is twofold. On the one hand, financial market infrastructures do typically show a subadditivity of costs. This is because the development and the running of an LVPS incurs a high volume of fixed costs and only few variable costs. Potentially, increasing returns to scale may add to the cost subadditivity. On the other hand, network effects would lead to a positive externality of using the bigger LVPS so that contesting the market for private LVPSs would only pay off once a critical mass of payments can be processed. This in turn would have detrimental effects for the previously existing LVPS so that a multiplicity of LVPSs would only be a transitory phenomenon at the best. However, even contesting these markets has never happened. Only one specific case could be cited as a near miss. Before the establishment of the Continuous Linked Settlement (CLS), a multi-currency payment system that overcomes the settlement risk in foreign exchange markets (i.e. the Herstatt risk), two predecessors as multilateral netting and settlement service called ECHO (Exchange Clearing House Limited) and Multinet had been established. However, the participation among internationally active banks was far from complete. Indeed, the dominant externality was an informational one since committing to one of two standards in the early stages of a market would result in sunk costs. Central banks of the "Group of Ten countries" thus pressed for a solution that would overcome this waiting for a common industry standard (CPSS, 1996). ECHO and Multinet consequently merged into CLS in December 1997.

CLS is also insofar interesting as it is one of only few examples of a privately governed LVPS, which does not face a direct competitor owned or managed by a central bank. However, the CLS settlement positions are also finally transferred by means of payment in central bank money since no money is left overnight on CLS accounts. Therefore, the settlement in CLS is in fact dependent on access to central bank accounts. Two other cases are LVTS in Canada and Swiss Inter-bank Clearing (SIC) in Switzerland. The former is owned and operated by the Canadian Payments Association (CPA), while settlement occurs on settlement accounts at the Bank of Canada. The latter is similar in that SIC Ltd is a subsidiary of SIX Group Ltd, which owns 75% of the shares of SIC Ltd. The other 25% of the shares are held by PostFinance. SIX Group Ltd, in turn, is an unlisted public limited company domiciled in Zurich. Around 140 national and international financial institutions, who are also the main users of the services provided by SIX, own the company. The SIC payment system is operated on behalf of the Swiss National Bank, which also acts as a system manager and settlement agent, providing participants with accounts in central bank money and with liquidity facilities. SIC settles large-value payments including those related to the monetary policy operations of the Swiss National Bank (BIS Red Book, 2011 and BIS Statistics Explorer, Table PS 1).

Hong Kong is also a case in between. The Hong Kong Monetary Authority (HKMA) and the Hong Kong Association of Banks jointly own the Hong Kong Interbank Clearing Limited, the system operator of CHATS in Hong Kong. Settlement of payments denominated in HKD occurs on accounts held at the HKMA. Thus, it can be observed, that the settlement in all three mentioned cases (Canada, Switzerland, Hong Kong) involves the accounts at the respective central banks despite the involvement of private institutions in the governance of the payment system.

4 Governance aspects in decentralized systems of central banks

As has been shown in the previous section, the creation of central bank money and its usage in the inter-bank payment system is closely interlinked. Normally this has no further consequences regarding the balance sheet positions in the central bank of a country because the money creation will just lead to an increase of deposits of commercial banks on the liabilities side and simultaneously to an identical increase on the asset side of the central bank's balance sheet (Rule, 2015). However, if the competence for money creation is divided among many central banks in a system of central banks, things become more complicated.

Not many examples of decentralized systems of central banks exist in the real world. While there are currently four multinational currency unions, only the Eurosystem shows such a decentralized structure. In contrast to the Eurosystem, the central banks of the Eastern Caribbean Currency Union (ECCB), of the West African Economic and Monetary Union (BCEAO) and the Central African Economic and Monetary Community (BEAC) are unitary institutions with branches or agencies in their member states. However, these branches and agencies do not possess competencies beyond operational aspects of central banking, i.e. the accounts management is done centrally. All these three multinational central banks pursue a regime of exchange rate stability (a currency board in the Caribbean and a conventional peg in the African monetary unions, see IMF, 2018) which limits the abilities to create central bank money. A case perhaps could also be made for the central banks of the countries that emerged from the collapsing USSR in the early 1990s and managed the Soviet Rouble separately before introducing national currencies (Orlowski, 1994; Granville, 2016). However, the apparent coordination failures do not make it a good example in the context of a functioning system of central banks. One could even put into question whether this episode could be called a system of central banks at all.

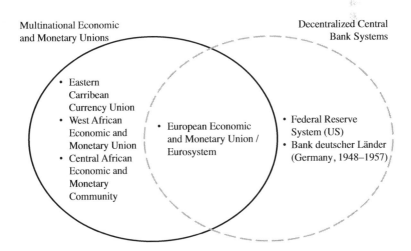

Figure 4.5 Monetary unions and central bank systems

At a national level, the Federal Reserve System of the United States is the only existing case of a decentralized central bank system. A former example would be the predecessor of the Deutsche Bundesbank in Western Germany, i.e. the Bank deutscher Länder with its Landeszentralbanken (State Central Banks) that existed between March 1948 and July 1957. Both cases have in common that the regional central banks were provided with statuary powers (see Section 4 of the Federal Reserve Act and similar provisions for each of the State Central Banks in Western Germany from 1946–1948; see Distel [2003] and the references therein), e.g. maintaining accounts for commercial banks and providing for payment services.

The only example for a decentralized system of central banks in a multinational monetary union is the Eurosystem. Since the structure and the competencies of the different entities in the Eurosystem are very often confused (as in the title of Sinn & Wollmershäuser [2011], to quote a rather prominent example), it is worthwhile to outline the basics again. The Eurosystem's competence for the definition and the implementation of the monetary policy as well as for the promotion of smoothly operating payment systems is defined in article 127 of the Treaty on the Functioning of the European Union (TFEU). These tasks are reiterated in article 3 of the Protocol No.4, which is annexed to the TFEU and is usually known as the European Central Bank (ECB) statute. The independence of the ECB and the national central banks (NCBs) is regulated in articles 130 and 132 TFEU and article 7 of the ECB statute. This means that the other institutions of the EU as well as any institution of its member states must not interfere in, for example, rules concerning the monetary policy, the instruments used, the account structures and issues of the payment system. These tasks are to be implemented by either the ECB or the NCBs (article 9.2 ECB statute) and thus by no one else (Figure 4.6).

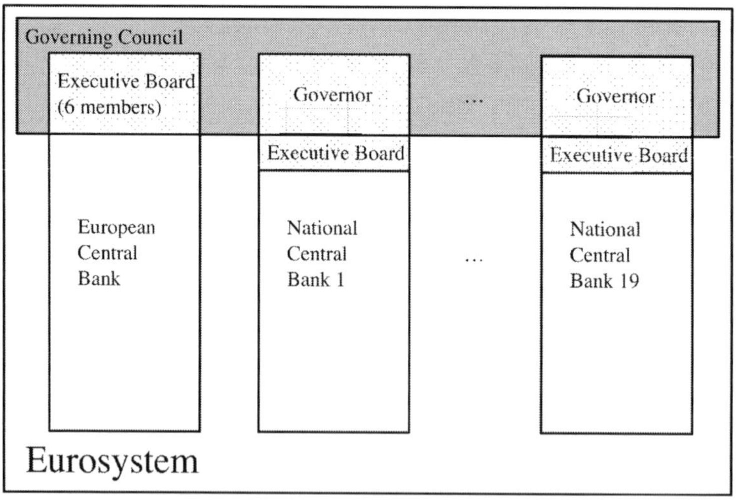

Figure 4.6 Eurosystem governance structures

The ECB together with the NCBs of the EU countries that have adopted the euro are the Eurosystem (article 282 TFEU). It would therefore be wrong to set the ECB equal to the whole Eurosystem. On the opposite, the ECB is just one of (currently) 20 central banks in this system and is as a central bank a Eurosystem member at equal footing to the NCBs. The Eurosystem itself is – in contrast to its members – no legal entity. Therefore, it can only act through its members, and decisions have to be taken centrally at the ECB governing council where the NCB governors are represented and enjoy a majority of votes. The ECB governing council is at the same time also the highest decision-making body for the ECB itself, although the public due to its internal nature rarely notices such decisions. Decisions regarding the monetary policy for the whole euro area receive of course much more attention. The same article 12.1 of the ECB statute that provides for the centralized decision-making does also provide for a decentralized implementation of the operations that form part of the tasks of the Eurosystem.

The rather unobtrusive article 17 of the ECB statute guarantees the ECB and the NCBs the right to open accounts and accept assets as collateral. It is this legal provision that makes a public sector institution to be a bank. Together with the decentralization principle for the implementation of the monetary policy, this article is the key to understanding the legal nature of the intra-Eurosystem claims and liabilities. Among those, the so-called TARGET2 balances have received most of the attention due to their growth since the beginning of the financial market turbulences in summer 2007 and the great financial crisis one year later. The accounting mechanics have been thoroughly explained in many other papers (e.g. Jobst et al., 2012) so that this does not have to be repeated once over here. However, it is interesting to note that a different article 17, which would grant the right to open accounts for banks and accept collateral exclusively to the ECB, would leave the NCBs as empty shells. This would be comparable to what happened in 1957 in Germany when the Bank deutscher Länder and the State Central Banks were merged into the Bundesbank. The regional offices of the Bundesbank kept the name "Landeszentralbank", but their operational independence was replaced primarily by the fact that accounting and account keeping was centralized. If this were ever similarly to happen later to the NCBs, the Eurosystem would in fact be synonymous with the ECB. Of course, today this is not the case and would contradict the very ideas of subsidiarity and federalism that – together with the four basic freedoms – can be regarded as keystones of the architecture European Union.

The liquidity provision to banks in the context of the conventional monetary policy instruments as well as the implementation of the Eurosystem's asset purchase programme (APP) work through crediting the commercial bank's accounts at the NCBs. The role of the ECB is rather limited, as it participates only with a low percentage in the implementation of the APP and does not possess any direct account relationship to the commercial banks. Insofar the ECB is the least of all a bank among the central banks of the Eurosystem and resembles in some ways a coordinating institution such as the Federal Reserve Board is in the Federal Reserve System of the US. However, any cross-country payments via the

Eurosystem's TARGET2 payment system would lead to bilateral intra-Eurosystem claims and liabilities that are consolidated at the end of the business day to a multilateral claim or liability towards the ECB through the accounts that the ECB has opened for each NCB. Other than these accounts, the ECB has opened a few accounts for financial market infrastructures without a clear national anchor such as EURO1 or CLS. However, these payment systems are not eligible counterparties in the monetary policy framework and cannot participate in monetary policy operations. The disaggregated financial statement of the Eurosystem available at the ECB's website reveals this comparatively low level of banking activities of the ECB in comparison to the NCBs: lending to banks is at the ECB always zero whereas money creation through the APP is just shy of 10% of the total Eurosystem volume. In other words, money creation in the euro area happens largely in a decentralized manner at the NCBs.

The same was true in Germany between 1948 and 1957 with the money creation happening primarily at the State Central Banks. Potentially this is also the case in the Federal Reserve System, although in practice the Federal Reserve Bank of New York enjoys a dominant role in the implementation of the US monetary policy, especially concerning liquidity creation.

5   Money creation in a decentralized system of central banks

The primary source of information for anyone who is interested in the amount of central bank money created is the central bank's balance sheet. In case of a decentralized system of central banks, it would be the consolidated financial statement of the whole system, thus not showing any intra-system claims and liabilities. Still, the unconsolidated balance sheets of the system members can be quite revealing as to the detailed working of the monetary policy implementation within the system (Figure 4.7).

Liquidity creation in central bank money happens through the monetary policy operations and/or security purchases on the asset side of the balance sheet. Automatically the bank's current accounts will receive this new liquidity. It may be shifted to the minimum reserve account or the deposit facility, it could be changed into banknotes or it could be used for credit transfers to the government or to foreigners. However, the liquidity would only disappear when the amount of monetary policy operations was to be reduced or the securities were to be sold on a net basis. Increases in the foreign reserves position or other expenses of the central bank would of course also have the same effect.

The intra-Eurosystem positions can neither create nor destroy central bank money. Concerning cash, any change in the claims or liabilities related to the allocation of banknotes would only follow the actual issuing of the physical banknotes (which in itself reduces the amount of reserves that commercial banks hold at their NCB). The intra-Eurosystem position would then just reveal the asymmetries in cash usage in the euro area. The respective positions on TARGET2 similarly show the asymmetries in the flow and the distribution of cashless central bank money

Assets	National Central Bank	Liabilities

Assets	Liabilities
1. Gold and Foreign Reserves	1. Banknotes in circulation
2. Monetary Policy Operations (liquidity-providing), e.g.: • Open Market Operations • Marginal Lending Facility	2. Monetary Policy Operations (liquidity-absorbing), e.g.: • Bank's Current Accounts • Minimum Reserve Accounts • Deposit Facility
3. Securities • Held for monetary policy purposes • Other securities	3. Other Liabilities • Government Deposits • Other (e.g. deposits from foreigners)
4. [Government Debt]	4. Revaluation Accounts
5. Intra-Eurosystem Claims • Participating interest in the ECB • Claims equivalent to the transfer of foreign reserves to the ECB • Net claims related to the allocation of euro banknotes • Other claims net (i.e. TARGET2)	5. Intra-Eurosystem Liabilities • Net liabilities related to the allocation of euro banknotes • Other liabilities net (i.e. TARGET2) 6. Capital and Reserves
6. Other Assets	

Figure 4.7 Stylized version of a Eurosystem NCB's balance sheet

among the commercial banks as account holders at the NCBs. Any central bank money needs to be created before a flow of central bank money can happen. A useful metaphor would show two chefs preparing a sauce: one of them is managing the ingredients whereas the other stirs the pot. Both actions are necessary for preparing a good meal and none is inferior to the other. The same can be said about the monetary policy (i.e. managing the ingredients) and the operation of smoothly operating payment systems (i.e. stirring the pot) by the Eurosystem.

It should be noted that the liquidity provision and the submitting and receipt of payments can also involve branches (or subsidiaries) of foreign banks, i.e. banks established outside the country for which the NCB is responsible. This leads to two important observations. On the one hand, changes in TARGET2 balances do not have a direct relationship to other movements in a country's balance of payments. On the other hand, a reduction of the overall volume of TARGET2 balances would be feasible if the branches of a bank with the head office in a country with TARGET2 liabilities were to take part in monetary policy operations in those countries with TARGET2 claims. When these branches were then to transfer the obtained central bank money to their head offices, the TARGET2 claims and liabilities of the involved NCBs would both decrease, everything else being equal. It follows that the creation of central bank money and the change in TARGET2 claims and liabilities could technically be disentangled.

It is also interesting to note what needs to happen, when the ECB increases its subscribed capital as it happened in December 2010.[3] Technically payments through TARGET2 were submitted by the NCBs and received by the ECB, which either reduced the TARGET2 claims or increased the TARGET2 liabilities of the NCBs. On the other hand, each NCB got an increased position "participating interest in the ECB". This shows clearly that payments among members of a central bank system with decentralized responsibilities for money creation lead to changes in the balance sheet position that keeps track of cashless payments. Within a two-tiered fiat money monetary system, a payment from one central bank to another central bank leads to a situation where the payment itself and the settlement of the payment coincide. The same is also true for payments between the central bank and its account holders, i.e. commercial banks or foreign correspondents.

Therefore, any calls for a settlement of TARGET2 balances are not feasible. The settlement has already happened. Only a payment in any other asset than the central bank money itself would overcome this situation. However, it would be rather absurd if a central bank of issue was to insist on a receiving or sending a payment in anything else than the currency it manages. Only the management of its foreign reserves or the processing of foreign currency payment orders for its customers would lead to obvious exceptions. Other than that, a central bank would face some problems in external communication if trust in its currency by the broader public ever became a serious issue. Alas, there is no need for settlement of intra-system balances in any other asset than its own currency because even for the members of that system the fact that central bank money is less risky than any alternative asset is still true. As long as the currency and the central bank onto which the claim is directed (i.e. in the Eurosystem the ECB) exist, there will be no risk at all.

Even the case of the annual exercise regarding the Interdistrict Settlement Accounts (ISA) and the connected rebalancing of the System Open Market Account (for details see Wolman, 2013) would not prove the opposite since the securities are mainly US Federal Bonds. Thus, the earning are interest payments on US Bonds which (after deductions for operating costs and dividends) will finally be received by the US Treasury department, which is the issuer of the securities. In effect, the securities serve as a means to implement monetary policy whereas the character of an interest-earning asset or even a means of payment between Federal Reserve Banks is clearly subordinated.

Historically, the different positions of the State Central Banks and the Bank deutscher Länder (BdL) in Germany in the post-WWII period were also "settled" through accounts at the BdL. Insofar the Eurosystem works quite similarly.

6   Alternative solutions for large-value payment systems in a multinational currency union

If one was to look for an alternative architecture in order to avoid the building-up of intrasystem claims and liabilities within a system of central banks, one would have to start with some basic decisions. First, the question is whether to have a decentralized approach for the central bank at all. As has been shown, the money creation on central bank accounts is the crucial point. The Eurosystem is unique among the few multinational monetary unions worldwide and can only be compared to one present and one historical case of decentralized central bank systems within one country. This decentralized approach fits well into the broader institutional and historical background of European unification efforts since the 1950s. Giving up well-established central banks like the Bundesbank with its undoubted record of maintaining price stability was (and still is) certainly not a feasible solution for a monetary union. The same is true for many other NCBs in the euro area. When the European economic and monetary union was discussed in the late 1980s and throughout the 1990s, a full dissolution of NCBs was never an alternative. Moreover, as further steps towards a closer political union in the EU are currently not received with overwhelming enthusiasm, one can conclude that the decentralized approach to central banking in the euro area will stay with us for some longer time. This does not rule out other measures as have been taken with the Single Supervisory Mechanism (SSM) in the framework of the banking union a few years ago. In the broader context of the banking union and specifically with a view to liquidity assistance to banks in resolution, views have recently been expressed to centralize the Emergency Liquidity Assistance (ELA) at the ECB (e.g. Draghi, 2018, p. 10). A transfer of the responsibility towards account keeping onto the ECB is still discussed by nobody.

As a contrast to a fiat money system with a central bank at its top, a total privatization of the money creation has never been tested in continental Europe. Historical eras of free banking in some countries such as Scotland or the US have recently gained attention again with new technologies making it potentially possible. However, the provision of the public goods monetary stability and financial stability by entirely private institutions still would have to be tested successfully elsewhere. "In practice, the unconstrained actions of private sector participants have shown themselves incapable of providing these public goods on a sustained and reliable basis" (Haldane & Qvigstad, 2016, p. 628).

Clearinghouses could potentially take over some of the functions that central bank fill out. However, the real test is in crisis times when a lender of last resort could be very necessary. A proposed experiment involving the monetary constitution has proven to be rather unpopular with voters in Switzerland. The same would most probably be true if the citizens of the euro area were asked whether to abolish central banks altogether.

If a semi-private solution for the supply of LVPS services were sought for, the effects on the TARGET2 balances would be rather limited in comparison to the present situation. Indeed, history has shown that a concentration of large-value payments on just two systems has occurred. TARGET2 and EURO1 have taken over the entire volume of previously existing LVPS that worked on a national basis. But even if against all odds a small national LVPS survives to the day, as is the case with the Finnish POPS-system, only payments among banks of one nation are settled so that the TARGET2 balance of the Finnish NCB is not affected at all by the existence of the national LVPS. Were private national LVPS in the eurozone to be spread out at a larger scale over all member countries, the settlement in central bank money would still be necessary so that at the end of the day the TARGET2 positions of the NCBs would not change at all. Even worse in comparison to the present situation would be the effect that national private LVPSs would need an own access to emergency liquidity which would lead to a situation similar to the present discussions about access to central bank money for Central Counterparties (CCPs) after the introduction of the mandatory clearing for over-the-counter derivative financial products.

Any limitation of TARGET2 balances or their future growth (Schlesinger, 2011) would be inappropriate (Ulbrich & Lipponer, 2011) and would have an effect similar to private banks that still retain the right to issue banknotes. While in most countries this is no longer the case, some banks in Scotland and in Northern Ireland issue their own banknotes. As these have to be backed with a deposit at the central bank (i.e. for the United Kingdom the Bank of England) the issuance volume is restricted. Therefore, the bank with the least restrictions leads the course, which in the UK is, naturally, the Bank of England. Within a monetary union and a system of central banks such as the Eurosystem, it would be the national central bank with the highest net inflow of payments that determines whether to swap "large-value payment facilities" with the other NCBs. Insofar, the Eurosystem would de facto go back to a situation with a dominance of one central bank, as was the case during the first European exchange rate mechanism (ERM; 1979–1998). The costs in terms of financial instability were big, as the episode of 1992 (when the UK and Italy dropped from ERM) clearly shows.

7 Conclusion

TARGET2 shows a certain degree of complexity even for payment system experts. The debate around TARGET2 balances has made the topic even more complicated and even confusing for outsiders. Technical aspects of an LVPS play less a role in the debate. Accounting issues and the connection to macroeconomic issues such as the balance of payments take some time to explain. The long-lasting discussion about TARGET2 balances gained some momentum when the numbers increased again after the introduction of the APP of the Eurosystem in 2015 and especially when the Bundesbank was just short of reaching a value of 1 trillion euro TARGET claims against the ECB in 2018. As every argument has been laid on the table multiple times already, I am not inclined to reiterate them again. However, these episodes show that monetary policy and the payment system are very closely interlinked. One cannot have the one without the other.

The current architecture of the accounts structure and the decentralized approach of central banking in the euro area still have their merits. Any of the discussed alternatives show major problems that would potentially be much worse than accumulating TARGET2 balances in the Eurosystem's NCBs. In the end, the basic insight that a claim against a central bank is the least risky asset in our fiat money system still holds true. It even does so for equally ranking central banks within a common central banking system such as the Eurosystem.

Acknowledgement

I would like to thank Christoph Schmidhammer (Bundesbank University of Applied Sciences) for valuable feedback on previous versions of the paper. All errors and omissions are mine. The paper describes the personal opinion of the author and not necessarily the official position of the Deutsche Bundesbank.

Notes

1 Many texts, especially in the press, books and in the blogosphere, are actually written in German only, thus making aspects of the debate largely unavailable to non-German speakers.
2 NSD is part of the MICEX group, which has in fact the Bank of Russia as one of their main shareholders.
3 In order to smooth the transfer of capital to the ECB, the Governing Council decided that the euro area NCBs should pay their additional capital contributions of €3,489,575,000 in three equal annual instalments. On 29 December 2010, the NCBs paid €1.16 billion euro as their first instalment. The remaining two instalments were paid at the end of 2011 and 2012 (ECB, 2011, p. 211, 231).

References

Banca d'Italia (2009): *Annual Report, Abridged Version, 2008–115th Financial Year*, Rome, May 2009.
Bank for International Settlements (BIS) (2011): *Red Book, Payment, Clearing and Settlement Systems in the CPSS Countries*, Volume 1, Basel, September 2011.
Bank for International Settlements (BIS): *BIS Statistics Explorer, Payments and Financial Market Infrastructures*, URL: https://stats.bis.org/statx/toc/CPMI.html
Bank of Finland: *Chart gallery*, URL: www.suomenpankki.fi/en/Statistics/chart-gallery/
Berndsen, R.J. (2018): *Financial Market Infrastructures and Payments*, Tilburg, Ron J. Berndsen.
Bindseil, U. (2004): *Monetary Policy Implementation: Theory, Past and Present*, Oxford, Oxford University Press.
Bindseil, U. (2018): *Pre-1800 Central Bank Operations and the Origins of Central Banking*, URL: https://papers.ssrn.com/sol3/papers.cfm?abstract_id=3177810
Blake, D. (2018): *Target2: The eurozone's Silent Bailout System*, URL: https://briefings forbrexit.com/target2-the-silent-bailout-system-of-the-eurozone-by-david-blake/
Borio, C. (2019): *On Money, Debt, Trust and Central Banking*, BIS Working Papers No 763, Basel, January 2019.
CPMI and MC (2018): *Central Bank Digital Currencies*, Bank for International Settlements, Basel, March 2018.
CPSS (1996): *Settlement Risk in Foreign Exchange Transactions*, Bank for International Settlements, Basel, March 1996.
CPSS (2001): *Core Principles for Systematically Important Payment Systems*, Bank for International Settlements, Basel, January 2001.
CPSS (2003): *The Role of Central Bank Money in Payment Systems*, Bank for International Settlements, Basel, August 2003.
CPSS and IOSCO (2012): *Principles for Financial Market Infrastructures*, Bank for International Settlements, Basel, April 2012.

Deutsche Bundesbank (2000): *RTGS^plus: The Bundesbank's New System for Individual Payments*, Monthly Report June 2000, Frankfurt, pp. 59–71.

Deutsche Bundesbank (2011): *The Dynamics of the Bundesbank's TARGET2 Balance*, Monthly Report March 2011, Frankfurt, pp. 34–35.

Distel, J. (2003): *Die Errichtung des westdeutschen Zentralbanksystems mit der Bank deutscher Länder*, Tübingen, J.C.B. Mohr (Paul Siebeck).

Draghi, M. (2018): *EU Parliament, Committee on Economic and Monetary Affairs, Monetary Dialogue with Mario Draghi, President of the ECB (pursuant to Article 284(3) TFEU), Brussels, 26 February 2018*, URL: www.europarl.europa.eu/cmsdata/140021/ 1147067EN.pdf, p. 10.

Eisenschmidt, J.; Kedan, D.; Schmitz, M.; Adalid, R.; Papsdorf, P. (2017): *The Eurosystem's Asset Purchase Programme and TARGET Balances*, ECB Occasional Paper No. 196, Frankfurt, September 2017.

European Central Bank (2006): *The Evolution of Large-Value Payment Systems in the Euro Area*, Monthly Bulletin, August 2006, pp. 73–81.

European Central Bank (2011): *Annual Report 2010*, Frankfurt.

European Central Bank (2018a): *TARGET Annual Report 2017*, Frankfurt, May 2018.

European Central Bank (2018b): *T2-T2S Consolidation, Business Description Document*, Version 1.0.0, 4 October 2018, URL: www.ecb.europa.eu/paym/pdf/consultations/ Business_Description_Document_v1.0.pdf

Federal Reserve Act (approved Dec. 23rd, 1913, as amended through P.L. 115–174, enacted May 24, 2018).

Fiedler, S.; Kooths, S.; Stolzenburg, U. (Kiel Institute for the World Economy) (2017): *TARGET (Im-)balances at Record Level: Should We Worry?*, In-depth analysis for the ECON Committee of the European Parliament, Monetary Policy Dialogue, Brussels, November 2017.

Freixas, X.; Holthausen, C. (2008): European Integration of Payment Systems, in: Xavier, F., Hartmann, P. and Mayer, C. (eds.): *Handbook of European Markets and Institutions*, Oxford, Oxford University Press, pp. 436–450.

Fuest, C.; Sinn H.-W. (2018): Target Risks without Euro Exits, *CESifo Forum* 4/2018, December, Volume 19, Munich, pp. 36–45.

Giannini, Curzio (2004/2011): *The Age of Central Banks*, Cheltenham: Edward Elgar, 2011 (originally published in Italian, Bologna, 2004).

Goodhart, C.A.E. (1987): Why Do Banks Need a Central Bank?, *Oxford Economic Papers*, Volume 39, pp. 75–89.

Goodhart, C.A.E. (1988): *The Evolution of Central Banks*, Cambridge, MIT Press.

Granville, B. (2016): Lessons from the Collapse of the Ruble Zone and the Transferable Ruble System, *CESifo Forum* 4/2016, December, Munich, pp. 19–26.

Haldane, A.G.; Qvigstad, J.F. (2016): The Evolution of Central Banks: A Practitioner's Perspective, in: Bordo, C. et al. (eds.): *Central Banks at a Crossroads*, Cambridge, Cambridge University Press, pp. 627–671.

Hellwig, M. (2018): Wider die deutsche Target-Hysterie, *Frankfurter Allgemeine Sonntagszeitung*, 29 July, p. 20.

Herger, N. (2016): *Wie funktionieren Zentralbanken?*, Wiesbaden, Springer Gabler.

International Monetary Fund (2018): *Annual Report on Exchange Arrangements and Exchange Restrictions 2017*, Washington, DC, April.

Jobst, C.; Handig M.; Holzfeind R. (2012): Understanding TARGET 2: The Eurosystem's Euro Payment System from an Economic and Balance Sheet Perspective, *Oesterreichische Nationalbank, Monetary Policy & the Economy* Q1/12, Vienna, pp. 81–91.

Jobst, C.; Ugolini S. (2016): The Coevolution of Money Markets and Monetary Policy, in: Bordo et al. (eds.): *Central Banks at a Crossroads*, Cambridge, Cambridge University Press, pp. 145–194.

Jordan, T.J. (2018): *How Money Is Created by the Central Bank and the Banking System*, Speech at the Zürcher Volkswirtschaftliche Gesellschaft, Zürich, 16 January 2018, URL: www.bis.org/review/r180118c.pdf

Kokkola, T. (ed.) (2010): *The Payment System*, Frankfurt, European Central Bank.

Krahnen, J.P. (2018): *Target Imbalances Should Not Be Limited, But rather Call for an Institutional Reform of the eurozone*, SAFE Policy Blog, URL: https://safe-frankfurt.de/policy-blog/details/target-balances-are-no-risk-factor-by-themselves.html

Mayer, T. (2018): Ein Wahnsinn namens TARGET2, *Frankfurter Allgemeine Sonntagszeitung*, 15. July, p. 36.

McLeay, M.; Radia, A.; Thomas R. (2014): Money in the Modern Economy: An Introduction, *Bank of England Quarterly Bulletin*, Volume 54, Number 1, London, pp. 4–13.

Moenjak, T. (2014): *Central Banking*, Singapore, John Wiley & Sons.

Niepelt, D. (2018): *Reserves for All? Central Bank Digital Currency, Deposits, and Their (Non)-Equivalence*, Centre for Economic Policy Research, Discussion Paper 13065, July 2018, URL: cepr.org/active/publications/discussion_papers/dp.php?dpno=13065

Norman, B.; Shaw, R.; Speight, G. (2011): *The History of Interbank Settlement Arrangements: Exploring Central Banks' Role in the Payment System*, Bank of England, Working Paper No. 412, London, June.

Orlowski, L.T. (1994): *The Disintegration of the Ruble Zone: Driving Forces and Proposals for Policy Change*, Aussenwirtschaft, 49. Zürich, Jahrgang, Heft I, pp. 101–129.

Roberds, W.; Velde, F.R. (2016): The Descent of Central Banks, in: Bordo et al. (eds.): *Central Banks at a Crossroads*, Cambridge, Cambridge University Press, pp. 18–61.

Rule, G. (2015): *Understanding the Central Bank Balance Sheet*, London, Centre for Central Banking Studies, Bank of England.

Schlesinger, H. (2011): *Die Zahlungsbilanz sagt es uns*, in: ifo Schnelldienst 64 (16), Munich, pp. 9–11.

Schnabel, I.; Shin, H.S. (2018): *Money and Trust: Lessons from the 1620s for Money in the Digital Age*, BIS Working Papers, no 698, February 2018, Basel.

Sechrest, L.J. (1993): *Free Banking: Theory, History, and a Laissez-Faire Model*, Auburn, The Ludwig von Mises Institute (reprinted 2008).

Sinn, H.-W. (2011): *Neue Abgründe*, Wirtschaftswoche, 21.02.2011, Nr. 8, S. 35.

Sinn, H.-W.; Wollmershäuser, T. (2011): *Target Loans, Current Account Balances and Capital Flows. The ECB's Rescue Facility*, CESifo Working Paper No. 3500, Munich, 24 June.

Summers, B.J. (ed.) (1994): *The Payment System, Design, Management and Supervision*, Washington, DC, International Monetary Fund, December.

Sveriges Riksbank: *E-krona Reports*, www.riksbank.se/en-gb/press-and-published/publications/e-krona-reports/

Sveriges Riksbank (2018): *Sveriges Riksbank Economic Review*, Stockholm, p. 3.

Treaty on the Functioning of the European Union (2016): *Official Journal of the European Union*, C 202, 7 June.

Ugolini, S. (2018): *The Historical Evolution of Central Banking*, in: Battilossi, S.; Cassis, Y.; Yago, K.: *Handbook of the History of Money and Currency*, Springer Nature; URL: https://hal-univ-tlse2.archives-ouvertes.fr/hal-01887004

Ulbrich, J.; Lipponer, A. (2011): Salden im Zahlungsverkehrssystem Target2 – ein Problem?, *ifo Schnelldienst*, Volume 64, Number 16, Munich, pp. 69–72.

Wolman, A.L. (2013): Federal Reserve Interdistrict Settlement, *Economic Quarterly–Federal Reserve Bank of Richmond*, Volume 99, Number 2, pp. 117–141.

5 The credit mechanics of monetary unions

A review of the Eurosystem

Frank Decker

1 Introduction

> But if ESCB [European System of Central Banks] internal balances are not required to be settled . . . [national] central banks will no longer have any control over their assets. . . . The danger is not (only) the creation of a fiscal but (also) of a monetary transfer union.
>
> (Klaus Reeh 1999, 318–319, author's translation)

The Great Financial Crisis (2007) and the European sovereign debt crisis (2012) triggered profound changes in European Central Bank (ECB) monetary policies that have not been able to be reversed. Since March 2016 the rate for daily ECB main refinancing operations has been zero. Fixed rate full allotment has replaced competitive auctions, collateral standards have been lowered and outright asset purchases have become the main policy tool. The scale of these interventions has been substantial and the national central banks (NCBs) of the Eurosystem have become dominant purchasers and holders of government bonds.

No normalisation is in sight, which has put the long-term sustainability of the Eurosystem into question and raised the issue of reform. Recent concerns include the size of the German TARGET2 claims, the health of the Italian banking sector, contemplations of a default on the repayment of Italian government debt held by the Eurosystem and an Italian parallel currency (Mini-Bots). There is also still confusion about the underlying institutional set-up of the Eurosystem 20 years after its formation. The continuing and often heated debate about the significance and proper interpretation of TARGET2 balances, for instance most recently in the German press (Hellwig 2018; Sinn 2018), is a case in point. Moreover, there are views that the loss of monetary sovereignty has gone too far and constitutional rights, parliamentary controls and national interests are being compromised (Kerber 2017; Sinn 2018).

The objective of this chapter is to look at these issues from a new angle by analysing the "credit mechanics" (Lautenbach 1952) of monetary unions and to review the Eurosystem and associated reform proposals on this basis. The term "credit mechanics" refers to the formal (and mechanical) relationships that must hold in a monetary system between bank creditor and debtor accounts. This method provides an important analytical framework and has proved to generate valuable insights on the drivers of money supply changes (Stützel 1958 [1978] and recently Decker and Goodhart 2018), and on international currency and balance of payment problems (Stützel 1973). The TARGET2 debate has brought a renewed interest in inter-bank account relationships.

In the following, I use a legal and economic analysis of a bank credit transfer in a four-party payment mechanism to draw out the credit mechanics of a monetary union, which is then extended to the Eurosystem. The chapter is organised as follows. In section 2, I identify the credit mechanics of domestic and international monetary unions. Section 3 deals with historical examples of international monetary unions. Section 4 develops the credit mechanics of the Eurosystem and explains the proper significance of TARGET2 balances and the key structural issues inherent in the Eurosystem design. Reform options are outlined in section 5. Section 6 adds some concluding remarks.

2   The credit mechanics of monetary unions

The term "monetary union" is often used synonymously with "currency union" and is commonly defined as "groups of countries that share a *single money*" (Rose 2008, 2555, emphasis added). Examples include cases where a smaller country unilaterally adopts the money from a large anchor country or when several countries form a multilateral monetary union as part of a treaty. The latter involves *multiple issuers* based in different legal jurisdictions of independent sovereign member states. In the quoted reference entry, Rose does not elaborate further on what specifically a "single money" is and how it is created in a multilateral setting. This gap is perhaps not surprising given the traditional focus on physical forms of legal tender and the fact that the underlying mechanics of credit-based money creation has only recently been revisited (Decker and Goodhart 2018).

In order to fill this gap and to more systematically analyse how a "single money" is shared and created in a multilateral monetary union, I construct a schematic and simplified example to identify the credit mechanics of a bank credit transfer in a four-party payment mechanism. I assume that two banks X and Y issue notes and/ or create deposits by discounting negotiable instruments, purchasing assets or granting loans. X and Y are located in different geographies. Each bank has 200 units of capital. A is a customer of X and has entered into a secured loan contract with X over 1,000 units to raise working capital. A stays in possession of the asset. B is a customer of Y and previously obtained the same amount of sight deposits via credit.

I assume that A needs to discharge a debt owed to B over 1,000 units, the full amount raised. A will instruct X to transfer funds to B, which will instruct Y to credit B 1,000 units into B's account. After the transaction the deposit balance of A at X has decreased from 1,000 to 0 units, while the deposit balance of B at Y has increased from 1,000 to 2,000 units. A has discharged the debt, but the transaction has also created a new debt (of 1,000 units) that legally X owes to Y (Geva 1986, 11–12) (Table 5.1). Importantly, the so-called funds transfer does not operate as an assignment of A's claim against X to B or a transfer of the same coins or banknotes from A to B. Legally, B does not obtain what was originally owned by A. While A held a claim against X, B receives a claim against Y (Fox 2008, 171–172; Omlor 2014, 133). Hence, B could be better off, if Y is the safer bank.[1]

Table 5.1 Balance sheets of a bank credit transfer with four parties

Customer A – Balance sheet

Assets				Liabilities
Deposit at bank X	~~1,000~~	0	Loan from bank X	1,000
Assets		1,000		

Bank X – Balance sheet

Assets			Liabilities	
Loan to customer A	1,000	Deposit of customer A	~~1,000~~	0
Claims on bank Y	0	Obligation towards bank Y	~~0~~	1,000
Other assets	200	Equity		200
Collateral: assets from customer A				

Customer B – Balance sheet

Assets				Liabilities
Deposit at bank Y	~~1,000~~	2,000	Loan from bank Y	1,000
Assets		1,000		

Bank Y – Balance sheet

Assets			Liabilities	
Loan to customer B	1,000	Deposit of customer B	~~1,000~~	2,000
Claims on bank X	~~0~~ 1,000	Obligation towards bank X		0
Other assets	200	Equity		200
Collateral: assets from customer B				

In a typical domestic inter-bank relationship, Y will accept the claims that it receives on X at par value, which will be settled through a clearing system and paid through the accounts X and Y hold with a central bank. Alternatively, banks that are not clearing banks may settle their mutual obligations through the books of a common correspondent bank. X and Y will have ongoing business relationships and receive payment flows in both directions. X can also raise interest rates to attract deposit inflows and ration lending to stabilise or reverse outflows. In addition, inter-bank loans or settlements can be avoided altogether by strategically positioning bank branches in locations that mirror the flow of funds. If X and Y are branches of the same legal entity then the inter-branch balance is of much lesser significance.

It follows from the credit mechanics of the account interrelationships that inter-bank surpluses must equal inter-bank deficits. This means that the payment flow from A to B has left the consolidated balance sheet of the banking system as a whole unchanged. Inter-bank balances can be sustained as long as surplus banks are willing to advance credit to deficit banks. X can only sustain an outflow of deposits as long as Y is prepared to increase the balance of claims on X, or if X can offer Y acceptable assets to settle its debts. Ultimately, in order to stay solvent, deposit banks must ensure that they have sufficient and suitable assets that are shiftable to those banks that are the recipients of payments. Stützel (1973, 150–151) argued that the shiftability of assets to the recipients of payment outflows is the most important rule of banking. On this basis, Stützel (1958 [1978],

174–175) emphasised that a currency must be backed by assets. Importantly, third parties (i.e. Y or a central bank) and not X will determine whether X's assets are suitable. Y will continuously assess the implied credit risk and request settlement or curtail lending, if required. In the example, with a net outflow of 1,000 units and an equity capital of only 200 units, X would be technically insolvent (negative equity of 800 units), if it had not received a loan from Y. Alternatively, as a last resort, X may refinance the loan to A with the central bank and offer Y central bank liabilities it cannot refuse. Any suspected inability of X to obtain inter-bank or central bank credit, for instance, due to problem loans or low collateral standards, will undoubtedly triggered a bank run. According to Stützel (1973, 151), this solvency risk is the disciplining element that ensures that (domestic) interregional payment imbalances do not trigger the equivalent of an "international balance of payment crisis" with a depreciated currency in a domestic context . Sustained domestic payment imbalances will typically lead to a restructure or winding up of the deficit-counterparty rather than a currency devaluation and non-par-clearing. International monetary unions are constituted in a similar way to domestic unions, but a member country will exit the union, if the par-clearing can no longer be maintained.

The payment and clearing system therefore links the deposit liabilities of all banks including note and deposit liabilities of the central bank (see already Decker 2015, 937). Hence, the associated par-clearing mechanism[2] creates what is perceived by the public as a "single money". As a result of this process, a domestic or international monetary union is constituted and maintained. More specifically, the constituting elements include (1) a common "ideal unit" (Nussbaum 1950, 13; i.e. an abstract money of account such as the names dollar, euro, pound, mark, etc.); (2) standard settlement assets (e.g. gold, specie, legal tender, central bank notes and deposits, securities) to finally discharged obligations (Decker 2015, 933); (3) a "stabilising agreement" (Nussbaum 1950, 508) (e.g. a par-clearing system); and (4) note and/or deposit issuing banks that monetise assets (e.g. by purchase or use as collateral) and in this way provide liquidity and means to discharge obligations (denominated in the common ideal unit) across the entire geographical area of the union.

3 International monetary unions: case examples

In order to illustrate the principles underlying multilateral monetary unions in an international context, I consider some of the most important case examples prior to the Eurosystem. These are the Latin Monetary Union (LMU) of 1865 and the Scandinavian Monetary Union (SMU) of 1873 and 1875. A lesser known but equally important example is the monetary union formed by Australia, New Zealand and the United Kingdom (ANZUKMU) prior to World War I (WWI).

The LMU established a uniform bimetallic standard for coins, which the contracting government treasuries undertook to receive in payments. However, bank notes remained unregulated and court judgements found that each state had in fact retained its separate currencies (Proctor 2012, 88). For instance, Nussbaum (1950, 507) reported that an Italian court held in 1894 that a payment calling for French francs could be lawfully discharged by depreciated lira notes representing the same nominal amount.

The SMU was originally set up as a mint union between Denmark and Sweden in 1873 and later joined by Norway in 1875. The countries adopted the krone ("crown", divided into 100 øre) as the common ideal unit and the gold krone as the main coin. Coins differed only in their national designs. The Scandinavian mint convention did not regulate bank notes, which flowed freely across borders. Note-issuing banks had an obligation to buy and sell coins minted at any of the Royal mints at par value. Notes were denominated in krone/kroner. In 1885, the central banks agreed to grant each other unlimited short-term credit. In 1894, the Sveriges Riksbank and Norges Bank agreed to accept each other's notes as legal tender and convertible into gold at par. Denmark's Nationalbank (Nationalbanken i Kjøben-havn) joined the agreement in 1901. After the political union between Sweden and Norway dissolved in 1905, the Riksbank cancelled the 1885 agreement with the Norges Bank and the Nationalbank. Unlimited credit was replaced by credit lines, and gold had to be shipped when credit limits were reached. There was no common monetary authority, and monetary policies lacked co-ordination. The union performed well until the outbreak of WWI, when the three central banks suspended convertibility into gold and no longer accepted each other's notes at par. In October 1915, the Riksbank ceased to accept Danish notes at par and lowered the rate for Norwegian money . The Scandinavian mint convention was revoked by Sweden in 1926, and the SMU ended (Andersen 2016, 81–93; Wetterberg 2009, 261, 277).

The SMU demonstrates the constituting elements of a monetary union in an international setting. The krone provided the common ideal unit, standardised gold coins served as the ultimate settlement asset and mutual credit lines between national central banks provided the stabilising agreement (Nussbaum 1950, 509) that kept central bank notes from different issuers at par. Importantly, the SMU shows that a successful monetary union does not require a common monetary policy or a supra-NCB.

Similar principles are also found to have operated in the ANZUKMU, which existed for over 100 years.[3] This monetary union was created by the actions of private note-issuing banks. Issued note and deposit liabilities were denominated in a common ideal unit (£ sterling). Banks accepted each other's notes, and inter-bank balances were cleared through legal tender coins (most importantly gold sover-eigns), which provided the final settlement asset. This represented the stabilising agreement. Gold points were not formally recognised. Banks carefully managed inter-bank balances by rationing the volume of bank advances (if required) and shipped gold coins or bullion across locations to replenish reserves. A comprehensive branch network helped to minimise the requirement for inter-bank settlements and ensured that funds could easily be transferred across locations.

The union began to fragment with the outbreak of WWI, when a prohibition was placed on gold exports and notes became irredeemable for practical purposes (Decker and McCracken 2018, 248). By 1931, the private banks buying rate for £100 payable in London had been raised to £130, a clear indication that the monetary union had broken up (Decker and McCracken 2018, 252–253; see also Nussbaum 1950, 133). However, even as late as 1933 the majority of the House of Lords in *Adelaide Electric Supply Company Ltd v. Prudential Assurance Co. Ltd*

(1933) found that the pound remained the common currency of Australia and the United Kingdom. This judgement was only revised in 1950, confirming in law that the monetary union was no longer in place (Nussbaum 1950, 132; Proctor 2012, 91; Fox 2016, 731).

4 The credit mechanics of the EMU

In 1992, the same year that the Maastricht Treaty on European Union was signed, Hans-Joachim Stadermann (1992, 362–364) canvassed different design options for a European Monetary Union (EMU). In his view, a possible option was to retain the system of competing NCBs, but where NCBs would issue notes denominated in the same unit. Notes would identify the issuer and each bank would make an undertaking to redeem its notes in the notes of the other NCBs. This system would have been a fixed rate version of the European Monetary System (EMS) and would not have required the creation of an ECB.

According to Stadermann, note redeemability ensures that the note emission standard is set by the strongest rather than the weakest bank. In such a scheme, an over-issue by one of the NCBs will lead to inter-bank balances in favour of the more conservative NCBs, who can demand redemption of the received notes in their own notes. The over-issuing NCBs with deficit balances are then forced to reduce the volume of their notes. As decisions over monetary policies are retained at a national level, deficit central banks can raise interest rates or constrain lending and, in this way, reverse outflows. As a result, credit standards are equalised across the union. An alternative scheme without the redeemability requirement was also considered by Stadermann (1992, 362) as a possible design choice, but in his view presented a significant concern. Any obligation to accept notes of other NCBs without limit and at a fixed rate implies that the weakest NCB sets the standard. While Stadermann saw the system of competing NCBs as a possible option, his preference was the creation of an independent supra-national ECB.

These considerations suggest that there are three principal design archetypes for a monetary union, including two decentralised types and one centralised type (Table 5.2).

Table 5.2 Design archetypes for a monetary union

#	Type	Stabilising agreement	Standard setter	Monetary policy	Creation of notes and deposit liabilities
1	Strongest standard union	Balances settled periodically	Strongest national central bank	Decentralised	Separate national entities
2	Weakest standard union	Unlimited credit at par, no settlement	Weakest national central bank	Decentralised	Separate national entities
3	Centralised union	N/A	Head office	Centralised	Single entity

Both the SMU and ANZUKMU were type 1 monetary unions. While SMU central banks had at times an arrangement to provide each other unlimited short-term credit (as found in type 2), their liabilities were still subject to redemption in gold coins.

The design eventually chosen and implemented for the Eurosystem is a convoluted hybrid of types 2 and 3, with many characteristics of type 2. The centralised aspects are embodied in the ECB, which was constituted as a separate legal entity. Monetary policy decision making is centralised with the ECB Governing Council (composed of the Executive Board and the governors of the NCBs), which is responsible for the formulation of the monetary policy for the Eurosystem. The ECB Executive Board is responsible for the implementation of the monetary policy decided by the Council, which is achieved (where possible) through the actions of the NCBs (Proctor 2012, 730, 732).

The decentralised aspects follow from the fact that NCBs have been retained as national legal entities. NCBs continue to create the majority of euro bank notes and central bank deposits. Technically, the Eurosystem has therefore retained nationally distinct moneys (notes and central bank deposits),[4] which are denominated in the same ideal unit (€s). NCBs are not branches but follow guidelines and instructions of the ECB. However, this statement must be qualified. The Emergency Liquidity Assistance (ELA) agreement provides NCBs with a large degree of autonomy in providing ELA credits, including the choice of guarantees and collateral, which are not rigidly defined. ELA operations above €2 billion can be prohibited by the ECB Governing Council, but this requires a two-third majority of votes. In addition, NCBs can purchase financial assets including government securities independent of ECB monetary policy operations. This was revealed by the disclosure of the confidential Agreement on Net Financial Assets (ANFA) between the NCBs and the ECB in 2016. The agreement sets a limit for the maximum amount of net financial assets an NCB can hold. Limits can be exceeded in a number of cases, including for the provision of ELA. NCBs also continue to administer the national foreign currency reserves. Losses arising from monetary policy operations are shared by the NCBs in proportion to their shares in the capital of the ECB. Costs and risks arising from ELA are excluded from this risk-sharing arrangement and lie at the national level.

One of the most critical and fundamental design features of the Eurosystem is the choice of stabilising agreement to hold the different NCB note and deposit liabilities at par. It is telling that a description of the agreement chosen for the Eurosystem is buried in the technical procedures of the inter-bank clearing system. However, the underlying principle is stated in no uncertain terms. For instance, the guideline ECB/2001/3 of 26 April 2001 on a Trans-European Automated Real-time Gross Settlement Express Transfer system (TARGET), adopted by the ECB Governing Council, provides in Article 4(b)1 that "each NCB and the ECB shall grant one another an unlimited und uncollateralised credit facility". Hence, despite the no-bailout provisions in the Treaty on European Union and the retention of NCBs, the stabilising agreement chosen by the designers of the Eurosystem is that of unlimited, unsecured inter-bank credit (type 2).[5]

In order to demonstrate the impact of this design decision and to explain the proper significance of TARGET balances, the credit mechanics of the bank credit transfer with four parties discussed in section 2 is extended by including two additional NCBs: CX and CY. It is assumed that CX and CY have equity of €200 each. A, X and CX reside in Eurosystem country 1, whereas B, Y and CY reside in Eurosystem country 2. As a starting point, it is assumed that X and Y have refinanced their loan assets with CX and CY and use these assets as collateral.[6] CX and CY have applied a "haircut" and available central bank funds to X and Y are €800 each. Customer A instructs X to transfer this amount to B.[7]

X processes the payment order from A. Deposit liabilities of A reduce from €1,000 to €200. X's central bank assets reduce to €0 as the sending central bank CX processes the payment order. CX credits the inter-NCB account it holds on its books for CY with €800 (obligations towards CY). CY debits the inter-NCB account it holds on its books for CX (claims on CX) with €800 and posts a credit of €800 in favour of Y's account. Y in turn credits B's deposit account with an additional €800. B's account balance increases to €1,800. See Table 5.3.

Table 5.3 Balance sheets for a payment between two Eurosystem countries

Bank X – Balance sheet					
Assets			**Liabilities**		
Loan to customer A		1,000	Deposit of customer A	1,000	200
Deposits at CX	800	0	Loan from CX		800
Other assets		200	Equity		200
Collateral: assets from customer A					

Bank CX – Balance sheet					
Assets			**Liabilities**		
Loan to bank X		800	Deposit of bank X	800	0
Claims on CY		0	Obligations towards CY	0	800
Other assets		200	Equity		200
Collateral: X's loan to customer A assigned or pledged					

Bank Y – Balance sheet					
Assets			**Liabilities**		
Loan to customer B		1,000	Deposit of customer B	1,000	1,800
Deposits at CY	800	1,600	Loan from CY		800
Other assets		200	Equity		200
Collateral: assets from customer B					

Bank CY – Balance sheet					
Assets			**Liabilities**		
Loan to bank Y		800	Deposit of bank Y	800	1,600
Claims on CX	0	800	Obligations towards CX		0
Other assets		200	Equity		200
Collateral: Y's loan to customer B assigned or pledged					

A has discharged the debt. Similar to the domestic case, A's claim against X has been exchanged with B's claim against Y. At the same time the transaction has created a new inter-bank debt of €800 that CX owes to CY. CY has increased the money supply of country 2 by €800, while CX has reduced the money supply of country 1 by the same amount. If X and Y represented the aggregated balance sheet of all banks in country 1 and 2, respectively, CY would have a positive TARGET balance of €800, while CX would have a negative TARGET balance of –€800.

The TARGET2 system modified the procedures in such a way that the net inter-NCB positions at the end of each day are transferred to the ECB and result in a NCB "obligation or claim towards the ECB" (ECB 2012/27 Article 6[2]). There is no limit on ECB claims. At the conclusion of the bank credit transfer from A to B, CX holds an obligation towards the ECB, while CY holds a claim against the ECB.[8] The outcome is summarised in Table 5.4.

How could this balance be settled? In this example, the only option for CX would be to transfer its loan asset to CY via the ECB, as equity funds are insufficient. However, settlement is not required other than on exit of the Eurosystem.[9] Given the composition of voting rights in the ECB Governing Council, the opportunities of surplus-NCBs to directly influence credit standards and the composition of their assets may be very limited. Therefore, individual NCBs have effectively lost control over the composition of their balance sheets. In a sense, NCB assets are being "mutualised". Klaus Reeh highlighted this structural weakness quite some time ago in 1999 and raised the concern that the Eurosystem could develop into a "monetary transfer union" (Reeh 1999). Public attention was drawn to TARGET2 balances only 12 years later by Sinn (see Sinn and Wollmershäuser 2011).

From the mutualisation of assets follows the mutualisation of individual NCB capital. Given unlimited and unsecured inter-central bank credit, €-denominated money can be created at the NCB with the weakest credit requirements, e.g. via ELA against mere guarantees or debt of a sovereign which is locked out of the market, and then be exchanged into €-denominated money issued by what is regarded as the safest NCB. As of April 2019, TARGET2 claims of the German Bundesbank against the ECB were €919.7 billion or half of its total assets. By contrast, Spain and Italy had obligations of €403.1 billion and €481.5 billion, respectively, also at about half their total assets.[10] In a scenario where claims on the ECB could not

Table 5.4 TARGET2 central bank assets and liabilities after the completion of payment

CX		ECB		CY	
Assets	*Liabilities*	*Assets*	*Liabilities*	*Assets*	*Liabilities*
Loan to 800 bank X	Obligations 800 towards ECB	Claims 800 on CX	Obligations 800 towards CY	Claims 800 on ECB	Deposit 1,600 of bank Y
				Loan to 800 bank Y	

be recovered, which is widely expected in a break-up scenario, surplus-NCBs would require recapitalisation by their respective governments at the expense of the national tax payers. Fresh assets would be required for contractionary operations to reduce the outstanding note and deposit liabilities to pre-crisis levels in order to enable effective monetary policy operations.[11]

This is clearly a highly unusual monetary union design unlike any of the historical precedents. Individual surplus-NCBs have practically lost any disciplining mechanism over deficit-NCBs, but carry additional risks on their balance sheets over which they have no control. Arguably, this represents a more significant loss of monetary sovereignty than was ever communicated to the public at the beginning of this European project and is not well aligned with the current level of fiscal and political integration. It is a significant shortcoming that the credit mechanics of the EMU was not more broadly understood and debated prior to the union's creation.[12]

5   Monetary reform proposals for the Eurosystem

How should the Eurosystem be reformed?[13] The proposal to settle TARGET2 balances is already contained in Reeh (1999), Sinn and Wollmershäuser (2011) and has most recently been supported by Homburg (2019). Assets could periodically be transferred from deficit- to surplus-NCBs, in analogy to the Federal Reserve Interdistrict Settlement process. Reeh (1999) has argued that designated high-quality assets could be mandated for inter-NCB settlements. In his view, this would improve the alignment and integration of the Eurosystem and the quality of the currency. Homburg would even accept risky assets as part of a loss mitigation strategy for a Eurosystem break-up scenario. However, given the strong position of deficit-NCBs in the ECB Government Council, it appears unlikely that such a reform would have any chance of implementation. Moreover, a truly disciplining impact would only be achieved if surplus NCBs could unilaterally mandate the type of assets required for inter-NCB settlements.

The protracted nature of the current design suggests the need for more wide-ranging reforms. Reform proposals can be broadly classified into those that support state ordering or private ordering. The recent incremental development path has been towards state ordering and a state money system. This is reflected by the large Eurosystem government security holdings and the emergence of the Eurosystem as the de facto lender of last resort (LOLR) to euro area governments.

The call for a state money system is based on the theoretical concept of money as a creature of the state. In this view, money is the result of expenditure decisions by the state and central bank money is to all intents and purposes interchangeable with government debt. The central bank must act as a monetary authority and is guided by general social and economic considerations. Hence, in the state money view, the ongoing outright purchases of euro member government debt conducted over the past years by the Eurosystem appear appropriate. These purchases have contained sovereign bond spreads between German government bonds and securities of peripheral euro area member countries and have protected governments and private institutions, including banks that have held high levels of potentially unserviceable government debt. The state money view argues that if central bank money and government debt are interchangeable, then government debt should not be subject to liquidity and default risks. Bond holders should be protected by the state's unlimited capacity to monetise its debt and its ability to socialise losses by inflation. From this follows that a sustainable reform of the Eurosystem requires the creation of European state money. This would be implemented via a European Treasury, the issue of euro bonds and a European monetary authority that monetises and stabilises the price of government debt across the Eurosystem. Revoking the prohibition of monetary financing in the Treaty (TFEU Art 123[1]) would allow an even deeper implementation of state money principles.

The main argument against state money approaches is that they are in the long run inconsistent with a free society and the rights and liberties associated with private property ownership. Historically, state money systems with extensive monetary financing have been a characteristic of command systems to organise war efforts, totalitarian regimes and regimes with monetary mismanagement and high inflation. Keynesian methods of economic management that combined monetary and fiscal policy emerging from World War II and its aftermath resulted in the misallocation of resources and became discredited in the 1970s Great Inflation. Moreover, a successful implementation of a European state money would undoubtedly require a strong European treasury and the creation of a single European Federal State, both facing well-known political and constitutional complexities even for a sub-set of member countries.

An important but perhaps lesser known reform proposal, with an emphasis on private ordering, is implied in the concept of "property-based money", which was developed by a team of German economists in the 1990s (Heinsohn and Steiger 2013). Similar to Stützel, Heinsohn and Steiger emphasise the underlying asset-backing of money. In their view, money is a derivative or monetisation of property. For instance, money is created when a creditor, such a bank (private or central), issues promissory notes (money) to a debtor as part of granting a secured loan. Creditor-money is backed by assets including the capital of the creditor and the collateral posted by the debtor. Historically, periods with sound money coincided with monetary systems that created money on this basis. Heinsohn and Steiger argue that the concept of fiat or state money fails to recognise the principles of sound money creation.

The implied reform proposal works within the existing central banking framework and formulates a number of rules for the creation of sound central bank money (Heinsohn and Steiger 2013; Stadermann 2010), which can be summarised into five rules:

- *Rule 1: No government financing* – a central note-issuing bank must not monetise state debt or provide direct loans to governments.
- *Rule 2: Sufficient capital* – a central note-issuing bank requires capital and should not take risks out of proportion with its capital.
- *Rule 3: Sound collateral* – money should be created against sound, marketable collateral in transactions between unrelated third parties.

- *Rule 4: Low-risk refinancing operations* – refinancing operations should be conducted through short-term secured credit or repurchase operations. Outright asset purchases should be limited to foreign exchange operations backed by designated capital.
- *Rule 5: Market interest rates* – central banks should follow rather than lead the market on interest rates.

The central bank in this view does not act as a monetary authority. It is foremost a banker's bank, run like a privately held concern and implementing its mandate with a narrow focus on refinancing property at market interest rates. This precludes the central bank from holding large positions of government debt or monetising government debt. The German Bundesbank and Swiss National Bank provided the template for this type of central banking. The current ECB monetary policies with the main refinancing interest rate at 0%, fixed-rate full allotment, reduction of collateral standards and large-scale purchases of government debt clearly violate rules 3–5 and arguably rules 1 and 2.

This narrow model of central banking as a refinancer of property includes the central bank's responsibility as a LOLR, i.e. to advance money against sound collateral in a crisis. However, a central bank cannot directly recapitalise banks nor provide non-banks with the missing loan security required for fresh loans. Only the state can assist or restructure failed institutions and establish lawful ways to restore the citizen's capacity to enter into debt. The model therefore assumes that the state is ready to act as "proprietor of last resort" (Heinsohn and Decker 2010). This reflects a view where direct transfer payments, temporary state ownership or even a redistribution of property are preferred over indirect central bank assisted bailouts. Ultimately, the state's financial capacity is underpinned by its power to raise taxes rather than the presumed access to the printing press.

There are different configurations of how an EMU could be implemented on this basis. A scheme with a single central bank (as the monopoly issuer of €-notes) and the demotion of the current NCBs to mere branch offices could be devised. This would effectively create a type 3 monetary union with a supra-NCB that acts within a narrow mandate as a refinancer of property based on a Bundesbank template. A supra-NCB would discharge LOLR responsibilities on behalf of the system. However, as pointed out by Spethmann and Steiger (2005, 63), an effective European LOLR function requires backing by a strong European treasury "implying some form of strong European tax" . Both, the required central LOLR function on behalf of the system and the central fiscal authority were critical elements missing in the original design of the Eurosystem.

Given the current status of EU political and fiscal integration, an alternative could be to revisit Stadermann's (1992) proposal to create a federation of independent NCBs that issue and mutually accept €-denominated notes. NCBs would retain their autonomy, pursue separate monetary policies and settle inter-NCB balances periodically with high-quality assets at par. In this type 1 model par-clearing will only be maintained for those countries that pursue monetary policies consistent with the other members of the union and that can provide eligible assets to periodically settle inter-NCB balances. Individual countries could exit and re-enter the monetary union dependent on whether they meet these requirements. An enduring monetary union between stability-oriented countries such as Austria, Finland, Germany, Luxemburg, and the Netherlands should clearly be feasible on this basis. Amendments to the EU Treaties would need to be renegotiated and the ECB wound up. The negotiated withdrawal process would need to be led by Germany, which has the largest TARGET2 claims and arguably the strongest NCB.[14]

6   Conclusion

Despite no-bailout Treaty provisions and the retention of NCBs, the Eurosystem is based on unlimited and unsecured inter-central bank credit. This design choice has driven the Eurosystem towards a state money system and will remain an ongoing point of contention between eurozone countries. Reforms are needed (1) to return central banking practices to a narrow mandate and a focus on refinancing property at market interest rates and (2) to create better alignment between the monetary union design and the level of EU political and fiscal integration. The protracted nature of the current design means that incremental change is unlikely to be effective and suggests that more wide-ranging reforms are needed.

Acknowledgements

I would like to thank Gunnar Heinsohn for helpful comments and Justyna Schulz, who triggered my interest in this topic.

Notes

1 This will be relevant in the discussion of TARGET2 balances.
2 Pioneered by English goldsmith bankers who kept accounts with each other and settled with specie at par.
3 The seven colonies of Australasia and the UK prior to Australian Federation in 1901.
4 See Heinsohn and Steiger (2002, 6) and more recently Heinsohn (2012).
5 See Garber (1998) and Reeh (1999).
6 The asset transfer or pledge is accounted for as a secured borrowing, where the transferor continues to carry the loan as an asset and the transferee does not recognise the transferred collateral as an asset.
7 A and B can represent the same person holding multiple accounts.
8 Hellwig's (2018) assertion that TARGET2 balances do not represent inter-bank credit relationships, but are offsetting entries with little significance, is therefore misleading.
9 See letter of ECB President M. Draghi (18 January 2017) to two members of the European Parliament, which states, "If a country were to leave the Eurosystem, its national central bank's claims on or liabilities to the ECB would need to be settled in full".
10 ECB report on TARGET balances, 3 June 2019.
11 Ilzetzki (2014, 129) estimated the Bundesbank exposure in 2013 at €340 billion.
12 Even as late as 2002, there was wide ranging confusion about the true character of the ECB, see Heinsohn and Steiger (2002, 6) for a discussion. Schlesinger (2012, 13) notes that the TARGET2 system 'originally was only supposed to be a clearing system without lending'.

13 This section builds on Decker (2017, 2018). 100% money, commodity money and completing fiat money proposals are discussed in Decker (2017).

14 Kerber (2012) argues that the introduction of a parallel currency is the preferred reform path. He suggests the creation of the "Guldenmark", issued by a single and newly established central bank for the previously named group of stability-oriented countries. However, similar to the Eurosystem, the lack of a supra-national fiscal authority is a potential weakness of this type 3 design. By contrast, a type 1 monetary union with newly established "parallel NCBs" issuing note and deposit liabilities in the same parallel currency unit would be less reliant on supra-national institutions and could provide an alternative design choice for the proponents of this reform approach.

References

Andersen, Steffen Elkiær (2016) *The Origins and Nature of Scandinavian Central Banking*. Palgrave Macmillan (Springer International Publishing AG, Switzerland, ebook).

Decker, Frank (2015) 'Property Ownership and Money: A New Synthesis', *Journal of Economic Issues*, 49(4), 922–946.

Decker, Frank (2018) 'Proposals for Monetary Reform and the Eurosystem', *Bulletin of the Institute for Western Affairs*, Poznan, Special Series "The euro-opportunities and threats" No. 348.

Decker, Frank (2017) 'Central Bank or Monetary Authority? Three Views on Money and Monetary Reform', *Economic Affairs*, 37(3), 343–356.

Decker, Frank and Charles A. Goodhart (2018) 'Credit Mechanics: A Precursor to the Current Money Supply Debate'. *CEPR Discussion Paper*, DP13233.

Decker, Frank and Sheelagh McCracken (2018) 'Central Banking in Australia and New Zealand: Historical Foundations and Modern Legislative Frameworks', in: R. M. Lastra and P. Conti-Brown (eds.), *Research Handbook on Central Banking*. Cheltenham: Edward Elgar Publishing.

Fox, David (2008) *Property Rights in Money*. Oxford: Oxford University Press.

Fox, David (2016) 'Monetary Obligations and the Fragmentation of the Sterling Monetary Union', in: David Fox and Wolfgang Ernst (eds.), *Money in the Western Legal Tradition*. Oxford: Oxford University Press.

Garber, Peter M. (1998) 'Notes on the Role of TARGET in a Stage III Crisis', *NBER Working Paper* 6619.

Geva, Benjamin (1986) 'The Concept of Payment Mechanism', *Osgoode Hall Law Journal*, 24(1), 1–34.

Heinsohn, Gunnar (2012) 'Statt eines echten Euro gibt es 17 Währungen', *Die Welt*, 16 September.

Heinsohn, Gunnar and Frank Decker (2010) 'A Property Economics Explanation of the Global Financial Crisis', in R. W. Kolb (ed.), *Lessons from the Financial Crisis: Causes, Consequences, and Our Economic Future*. Hoboken, NJ: John Wiley & Sons.

Heinsohn, Gunnar and Otto Steiger (2002) 'The Eurosystem and the Art of Central Banking', *ZEI Working Paper* B11.

Heinsohn, Gunnar and Otto Steiger (2013) *Ownership Economics*, translated and edited with comments and additions by Frank Decker. London: Routledge.

Hellwig, Martin (2018) 'Wider die deutsche Target-Hysterie', *Frankfurter Allgemeine Zeitung*, 28 July.

Homburg, Stefan (2019) 'Debatte über die Target-Salden: Replik und Erwiderung', *Wirtschaftsdienst*, 1, 70–75.

Ilzetzki, Ehtan (2014) 'Comment (on Whelan)', in: Karl Whelan, TARGET2 and central bank balance sheets, *Economic Policy*, 29(77), January, 125–130.

Kerber, Markus C. (2012) *Time for a Historical Compromise: Why Europe Needs the Guldenmark and No Longer the Euro as Single Currency*. Berlin: Europolis.

Kerber, Markus C. (2017) *Bürger wehrt Euch! Wie die Europäische Zentralbank unser Geld zerstört*. München: FinanzBuch Verlag.

Lautenbach, Wilhelm (1952) *Zins, Kredit und Produktion*. Edited by Wolfgang Stützel. Tübingen: J. C. B. Mohr (Paul Siebeck).

Nussbaum, Arthur (1950) *Money in the Law: National and International*. Brooklyn, NY: Foundation Press.

Omlor, Sebastian (2014) *Geldprivatrecht*. Tübingen: Mohr Siebeck.

Proctor, Charles (2012) *Mann on the Legal Aspect of Money*. Seventh Edition. Oxford: Oxford University Press.

Reeh, Klaus (1999) 'Zahlungsbilanzausgleich in der Währungsunion: Viele Fragen, aber noch keine Antworten', in: Hans-Joachim Stadermann and Otto Steiger (eds.), *Herausforderung Geldwirtschaft*. Marburg: Metropolis.

Rose, Andrew K. (2008) 'Currency Unions', in: Steven N. Durlauf and Lawrence Blume (eds.), *The New Palgrave Dictionary of Economics*. Second Edition. Basingstoke, Hampshire; New York: Palgrave Macmillan.

Schlesinger, Helmut (2012) 'The Balance of Payments tells us the truth', *CESifo Forum, Special Issue*, January, 11–13.

Sinn, Hans-Werner (2018) 'Irreführende Verharmlosung', *Frankfurter Allgemeine Zeitung*, 5 August.

Sinn, Hans-Werner and Timo Wollmershäuser (2011) 'Target-Kredite, Leistungsbilanzen und Kapitalverkehr: Der Rettungsschirm der EZB', *Ifo Working Paper* No. 105.

Spethmann, Dieter and Otto Steiger (2005) 'The Four Achilles' Heels of the Eurosystem', *International Journal of Political Economy*, 34(2), 46–68.

Stadermann, Hans-Joachim (1992) *Wirtschaftspolitik*. Tübingen: J. C. B. Mohr (Paul Siebeck).

Stadermann, Hans-Joachim (2010) 'Geldangebot der Zentralbank als Marktvorgang', in Detlev Ehrig and Uwe Staroske (eds.), *Eigentum und Recht und Freiheit. Otto Steiger zum Gedenken*. Marburg: Metropolis.

Stützel, Wolfgang (1958 [1978]) *Volkswirtschaftliche Saldenmechanik*. Second Edition. Tübingen: Mohr Siebeck.

Stützel, Wolfgang (1973) *Währung in weltoffener Wirtschaft*. Frankfurt am Main: Fritz Knapp Verlag.

Wetterberg, Gunnar (2009) *Money and Power: From Stockholms Banco 1656 to Sveriges Riksbank Today*. Stockholm: Sveriges Riksbank.

Part 3

When may monetary unions fail?

6 Pros and cons of being a euro country

A behavioral political economy perspective

Donato Masciandaro and Davide Romelli

1 Introduction

The recent global crisis challenged the stability of the European monetary integration process. That process, which is closely linked to the evolution of the European Monetary Union (EMU), has gone through two stages: the Common Market era, which ran from 1958 through 1993, and the Monetary Union era, which started in 1994 and gained new impetus after the global crisis with the publication of the Four Presidents' Report in December 2012. The aim of the EMU has been to stabilize exchange rates, inflation and interest rates in order to boost capital mobility and trade, thereby promoting the growth of member countries. Thus far, the data show nominal convergence of inflation and interest rates, while real convergence of per capita income has not occurred among the original eurozone participants.[1]

The creation of a currency union implies that its member countries can no longer use exchange rates and national monetary policies to deal with real and financial shocks. These limitations need to be compared with the medium- to long-run benefits of a fixed exchange rate and the delegation of monetary policy to an independent, supranational central bank, which is the European Central Bank (ECB) in the EMU's case. In this context, the pros and cons of a currency union need to be evaluated. The relevance of this issue appears even more relevant if we note that since 1946, a total of 123 countries have been involved in a currency union at some point and that 83 countries were involved in one in 2015 (Chen and Novy 2018).

We assume that decisions to join or leave a currency union are adopted on the basis of a political cost–benefit analysis that weighs the expected economic gains and losses through the lens of the electorate and/or certain ideologies. This perspective revisits the classic approach of optimal currency areas (Mundell 1961), but zooms in on the political actors that shape each country's decisions. Traditional theory "ignores the 'political economy' factors that made currency areas coincident with countries in the first place. . . . If the USSR were an optimal currency area before its break-up, it should have presumably remained so afterwards" (Goodhart 1998). The political economy approach, which defines a monetary union as a transfer of sovereignty, seems to be more consistent with a true theory of optimal currency areas (Bolton and Huang 2018).

Thus far, cognitive biases have not been assumed to affect the relevant players. However, what are the effects of behavioural biases that influence the preferences of political actors or citizens? This question refers to behavioural political economics (BPE) (Schnellenbach and Schubert 2015). In optimal currency area (OCA) research, the BPE approach was recently used to analyse a currency union in which expectations were formed through behavioural reinforcement learning (Bertasiute et al. 2018). In this chapter, we examine whether loss aversion among citizens can shape the decisions of national politicians. We find that a status-quo equilibrium is more likely to occur in such cases. This equilibrium can explain the conditions under which eurozone membership can persist.

The chapter is organized as follows. In section 2, we briefly review traditional OCA theory and discuss how the more recent political economy approach enriches that theory. In section 3, we present our BPE framework and use it to analyse the EMU case in which relevant actors (i.e. citizens and politicians) may be affected by behavioural biases, such as loss aversion, when making political decisions. In section 4, we present our conclusions.

2   EMU membership: from economics to political economy

Research on OCA first emerged in the 1960s (see Mundell 1961; McKinnon 1963; Kenen 1969). Over the last three decades, it has become the theoretical basis for evaluating the viability and desirability of the European Economic and Monetary Union (EMU).[2] Today, the OCA approach is used to evaluate whether regional areas – such as the European Union or the United States – can be viewed as OCAs (Bayoumi and Eichengreen 2017). In Europe, this debate started after the launch of the European Monetary System in 1979, when the majority of the countries in the European Community fixed their exchange rates around a central parity known as the European currency unit. The currency union became even more vivid with the introduction of a single European currency – the euro – as an accounting currency on 1 January 1999. The euro came into circulation on 1 January 2002.

The decision to establish the monetary union involved the complete and irreversible separation of countries' monetary powers in terms of both exchange-rate determination and monetary-policy autonomy. When countries join the EMU, they fix their exchange rates and delegate their monetary policies to the ECB, which implements monetary policies at the supranational level. This has economic costs and benefits.

The OCA theory's rationale for the EMU can be summarized as follows. Consider how the citizens of an individual European country *j* may address the decision to join the single currency union. One benefit of fixed exchange rates is that they provided a more predictable basis for trade decisions than floating rates. In other words, monetary transaction costs are likely to be lower. Consequently, monetary transaction gains will be higher the more country *j* trades with other members of the single currency union, which would also favour the mobility and flexibility of the factors of production (i.e. labour and capital). Therefore, the gains from joining the single currency union are positively related not only to the degree of economic integration in the markets for inputs and outputs but also to the efficiency of those markets.[3]

The OCA theory's rationale for delegating monetary policy to an independent central bank is that doing so further insulates monetary and exchange-rate actions from political biases. At the same time, the OCA approach stresses the medium- to long-term advantages of currency union membership, which can be compared to the short-term costs of losing the ability to use national monetary and exchange-rate tools to address short-term macroeconomic imbalances.

On the one hand, EMU membership implies that national policymakers cannot use nominal exchange-rate flexibility to address and fix competitiveness problems. Each country's competitiveness depends on the relative prices of its goods and services (i.e. on its real exchange rate). In general, real exchange rates are assumed to be correlated with total factor productivity (the Balassa-Samuelson Effect).[4] In a currency union, the bilateral nominal exchange rates are fixed. Therefore, any real exchange imbalance implies price and productivity adjustments. On the other hand, in a currency union, national policymakers cannot discretionally manage interest rates and monetary aggregates to address macroeconomic imbalances. In both cases, sovereignty losses emerge owing to the presence of a supranational veto player in the form of the independent central bank. In the debate surrounding the drivers of a country's attitude towards currency area membership, the general conclusion is that the final outcome depends on the preferences of its players – the citizens and the incumbent policymakers.

If we apply the general principles to the EMU case and assume that monetary instability risks are proxied by inflation-rate dynamics, then the monetary stability gains should be higher when country's j inflation is high or volatile, all else equal. Therefore, the EMU-related gains should be positively correlated with the relative degree of inflation-rate instability in country j. This implies that both monetary transaction and monetary stability benefits can motivate a country to join the EMU. At the same time, however, EMU membership might be associated with certain risks, especially risks related to the inability to use exchange-rate and monetary policies to address macroeconomic shocks. In other words, country j may face stabilisation losses or, more generally, sovereignty losses if it becomes a member of the single currency area. All else equal, such losses are likely to increase the more country j needs to address and fix business-cycle problems. Overall, these losses might reduce citizens' interest in joining the currency union. The extent of the stabilisation losses depends on the same drivers that influence monetary gains (i.e. mobility and efficiency in the markets for inputs and outputs). Lower levels of integration and efficiency call for supranational stabilisation policies that differ from the monetary policies. When such policies are missing, the monetary stabilisation losses will be higher.

Furthermore, recent literature on optimal currency areas points out that both gains and losses can be endogenous, rather than exogenous, as they depend on how the currency area is designed and implemented.[5] The shape of the transaction costs; the level of integration in the markets for goods, services and human capital; political biases; and shocks and their absorbers can be dynamically influenced by the currency area's establishment and implementation. Such endogenous transaction costs can be either decreasing or increasing. Consequently, the integration process can deepen or weaken over time, and it can differ across countries.

Almost 20 years after the adoption of the European single currency, it is possible to claim that some of the expected pros of adopting the euro have been realized. For example, monetary stability has reduced inflation and increased trade, leading to growth. While the gains in terms of low and more predictable inflation are self-evident, the positive effects on international trade require deeper inspection. The selection of a certain econometric methodology matters for estimating the effects of currency unions on trade.[6] Consequently, the results are far from clear-cut. However, in general, currency unions have been associated with an increase in trade among member countries of approximately 40%, although the figures vary widely and depend on pre-existing bilateral relationships between member countries, where weak bilateral trade relationships are more sensitive to the establishment of a currency union than strong, well-established relationships. In this regard, the average trade effect in the ECU seems relatively modest, although there is heterogeneity across country pairs.[7]

Overall, the benefits of membership in the EMU have been more evident in the countries in which national policymakers have implemented policies that increase productivity, such as Germany, Austria, Belgium, Finland, Luxembourg and the Netherlands.[8] At the same time, certain national imbalances still need to be addressed, including financial-instability risks, debt and deficit risks, and the divergence in wages and productivity paths that lead to trade imbalances, as in the case of the peripheral eurozone countries (i.e. Greece, Ireland, Italy, Portugal and Spain).[9]

In summary, the analysis of the economic pros and cons of EMU membership does not provide a clear answer on which of the two sides have prevailed thus far. A dynamic framework that can shed light on the evolution of the expected gains and losses – both economic and political – of joining or remaining in a currency union is needed. The historical tales should not be treated as benchmarks but rather as useful food for thought.[10] This observation is strengthened by looking at the degree of financial integration and at the design of banking regulations, which are substantially more prominent today than in the 1990s or early 2000s.[11]

Another area also deserves attention. Thus far, cognitive biases have not been assumed to affect the relevant players. However, what are the effects if behavioural biases influence the preferences of political actors or citizens? This question relates to behavioural political economy. In the next section, we use the BPE methodology to show how the analysis of EMU membership decisions can be further enriched using a key element of the prospect theory approach, i.e. the possibility of loss aversion.

3   EMU membership: a behavioural political economy framework

Consider a population with a continuum of citizens (voters), each of whom is free to express his or her (hereafter "her") choices regarding having the euro as the national currency (*Europhilia*) (Guiso et al. 2015). The variable π represents those policy choices (attitude). We assume that individual choices are a continuous variable, rather than a binary one, and the variable approximates the extent to which each player is in favour of or against euro membership.

3.1 EMU membership and individual preferences

From the previous section, we know that EMU membership implies both expected benefits (i.e. medium-term [MT] monetary stability) and expected costs (i.e. short-term [ST] sovereignty losses). However, each citizen weighs these benefits and costs on the basis of her personal beliefs. The individual heterogeneous preferences are summarized in a parameter, t, which captures the individual's degree of *aversion* to EMU membership (*Emuphobia*). Notably, we assume that Europhilia is an explicit policy variable while Emuphobia is a latent (hidden) variable (preference).

Heterogeneity among citizens can arise from any driver that can affect personal preferences, such as ideology and culture. Using the following utility function,[12] let $V(t_i, \pi)$ be the description of utility of citizen i:

$$V(t_i, \pi) = B(t_i, \pi) - C(t_i, \pi), \tag{1}$$

where $B(t_i, \pi)$ and $C(t_i, \pi)$ are the individual's benefits and costs, respectively, of being citizen of a eurozone country. We assume that, for each individual, the comparative benefits are increasing and concave:

$$\frac{\partial B(t, \pi)}{\partial \pi} > 0 \quad \frac{\partial B^2(t, \pi)}{\partial \pi} < 0. \tag{2}$$

At the same time, we assume that the individual's comparative costs of euro membership are increasing and convex:

$$\frac{\partial C(t, \pi)}{\partial \pi} > 0 \quad \frac{\partial C^2(t, \pi)}{\partial \pi} \geq 0. \tag{3}$$

These assumptions imply that, in principle, each individual can consider the policy option of having the euro as a common European currency. However, as the citizens are heterogeneous with respect to their degree of EMU aversion (Emuphobia), the optimal degree of euro support will differ depending on the extent of that aversion. In other words each citizen subjectively weights the pros and cons of joining such as specific currency union, which depend on a series a factors, including the characteristics of every country, as the standard OCA theory pointed out.

The individuals can be indexed such that more adverse individuals bear higher marginal costs and/or enjoy lower marginal benefits from euro membership:

$$\frac{\partial B_\pi(t_i, \pi)}{\partial t_i} \leq 0; \quad \frac{\partial C_\pi(t_i, \pi)}{\partial t_i} \geq 0. \tag{4}$$

Given assumptions (1) to (4), the equilibrium is interior. In other words, the Europhilia can be infinitely small but not negative. This is a consequence of the previously mentioned assumption that each citizen can consider the possibility of sharing the euro as common European currency:

$$\frac{\partial B(t_i, 0)}{\partial \pi} > \frac{\partial C(t_i, 0)}{\partial \pi}. \qquad (5)$$

For each citizen, the optimal Europhilia policy $\pi_i *$ is such that marginal benefits match marginal costs:

$$\frac{\partial B_\pi(t_i, \pi)}{\partial \pi} = \frac{\partial C_\pi(t_i, \pi)}{\partial \pi} \qquad (6)$$

and that:

$$\frac{\partial \pi *_i}{\partial t_i} < 0. \qquad (7)$$

In other words, the optimal degree of Europhilia is inversely associated with the personal degree of EMU aversion, i.e. $\pi *_i (t_i)$.

People who like the prospect of using the euro as their own currency (i.e. those with lower EMU aversion) will show higher levels of Europhilia. The opposite is true for individuals who dislike the sovereignty losses.

Notably, any shock that modifies the benefits and costs of eurozone membership will change the optimal Europhilia given the individual preferences. For example, any policy or shock that decreases the individual's gains from MT monetary stability or increases the individual costs of ST sovereignty losses will decrease the optimal Europhilia.

Our framework allows us to capture the evolution of the individual euro attitude as a function of structural beliefs (Emuphobia) in an extremely simple way. This attitude can be influenced from time to time by economic and political shocks.

As a concrete example, we can describe the sentiments of a given European population with regards to eurozone membership using the Eurobarometer surveys (European Commission 1974–2018). The Eurobarometer series was launched in 1974 to monitor attitudes towards the Common Market and the European Community's institutions in the member countries.

Of the Eurobarometer questions, we zoom in on questions about attitudes towards the euro (i.e. "support for the single European currency") along the lines of: "One single currency, the euro, will replace the national currencies of the member states of the European Union. Are you for it or against it?" We share the view that such questions assess individuals' attitudes towards a common European currency (Guiso et al. 2015).

For the sake of our exercise, we selected one country – Italy – and recorded the share of respondents who answered "For euro" (80%) in 1993, which was the year the EMU was established (Eurobarometer, October 1993, Figure 3.5, p. 59). The euro was launched in 1999 when it became the official currency of 11 countries, including Italy. The corresponding paper notes and coins were introduced on 1 January 2002. Therefore, we can assume that Italians' sentiments towards the euro (Italian Europhilia) in 1993 corresponded to their attitudes towards future EMU membership.

The level of Italian Europhilia changed over time. The temporal trend shows that between 1993 and March 2018, Italian Europhilia dropped from 85% to 61%. How can this evolution of support for the euro be explained? In our framework, two drivers may be in action: expected MT monetary stability gains and expected ST sovereignty losses. We can proxy the evolution of expected benefits by looking at the Italian inflation rate. At the same time, we can approximate the expected sovereignty losses using the output growth trend.

The descriptive analysis highlights four features. Italian Europhilia is positively correlated with (1) inflation and (2) output growth. In addition, (3) its temporal pattern declines in three steps from between 80% and 70% in 1993 to 2003, to between 69% and 60% in 2004 to 2007, and to less than 60% since 2007 (excluding the March 2018 data). Notably, Italy experienced severe recessions in 1992 to 1993 and 2007 to 2009, as well as declining growth in the years 2000 to 2002 (Bassanetti et al. 2009). Finally, Italian Europhilia is (4) more stable than inflation and output growth if we use the standard deviation as an indicator of stability (Europhilia = 1.12, inflation = 1.31, output growth = 1.89).

The four stylized facts can be consistently explained using a behavioural economics approach in which we specifically apply the loss-aversion assumption. However, for the sake of transparency, we point out that our interpretation is based on only 26 observations.

3.2 Behavioural biases and eurozone membership

Now we adopt a prospect theory approach, which thus far "remains the most important theoretical contribution to behavioral economics" (Thaler 2018). In particular we assume the presence of loss aversion, such that the citizens perceive any outcome as expected gains and losses relative to a reference point, which represents their endowment (Kahneman and Tversky 1979; Barberis 2012, 2018). In addition, the reference point can be based on expectations (Heffets 2018), which is consistent with our framework. Moreover, we assume that the reference point is the "status quo". In other words, the expected benefits and costs of euro zone membership are evaluated relative to the actual situation in the country. Given the status quo, the citizens assess the expected benefits of MT monetary stability and the expected costs associated with ST sovereignty losses.

From this perspective, the evolution of Italian Europhilia can be interpreted as follows. On the one hand, the falling inflation rate triggered a positive but decreasing endowment effect. This phenomenon is consistent with prospect theory, which assumes that individuals display diminishing sensitivity (Thaler 2018). At the same time, a reduction in the level of support only materialized if a sufficiently large drop in output highlights the expected losses due to the lack of sovereignty in the short term. Such a decline is roughly coincident with the three cases of weakness in output growth. Notably, the size of each reduction in support seems to be roughly similar, so whether the reductions in support are segregated rather than integrated may be a subject for discussion (Thaler 2018).

When a lower level of support for the euro becomes the new status quo, the majority of the citizens do not wish to undo it. The status-quo equilibrium is consistent with the role of sunk costs in explaining individual behaviour (Thaler 2018). However, the actual shape of Italian Europhilia is neither irreversible nor foreseeable. It depends on the kinds of shocks that affect the country.

The behavioural political economy approach described previously can be formally developed as follows. Given loss aversion, losses loom larger than gains for every choice and both are evaluated with respect to a given status quo. Let $z > 0$ be the parameter that captures loss aversion and let π^{SQ} be the status-quo Europhilia. Given condition (5), the status quo is not negative, so we can analyse how a given level of euro support can change if a shock occurs. With loss aversion, increasing euro attitude $-\pi > \pi^{SQ}$ – entails more benefits than costs, but higher expected costs in terms of ST sovereignty losses yield psychological losses amounting to:

$$z(C(t_i,\pi) - C(t_i,\pi^{SQ})). \tag{8}$$

In contrast, reducing euro attitude $-\pi < \pi^{SQ}$ – entails fewer benefits than costs, and gives rise to psychological losses due to fewer MT monetary stability gains. These psychological losses amount to:

$$z(B(t_i,\pi^{SQ}) - B(t_i,\pi)). \tag{9}$$

Therefore, the individual goal function with loss aversion, $V(t_i,\pi / \pi^{SQ})$, is given by the basic utility, $V(t_i,\pi)$, minus the psychological losses due to the departure from the status-quo euro support:

$$V(t_i\pi / \pi^{SQ}) = V(t_i,\pi) - z(C(t_i,\pi) - C(t_i,\pi^{SQ})) \; if \; \pi > \pi^{SQ}.$$

$$V(t_i\pi / \pi^{SQ}) = V(t_i,\pi) - z(B(t_i,\pi^{SQ}) - B(t_i,\pi)) \; if \; \pi < \pi^{SQ}.$$

The optimal conditions are as follows:

$$B_\pi(t_i,\pi) = (1+z)C_\pi(t_i,\pi) \; if \; \pi > \pi^{SQ}. \tag{10}$$

$$(1+z)B_\pi(t_i,\pi) = C_\pi(t_i,\pi) \; if \; \pi < \pi^{SQ}. \tag{11}$$

Therefore, each individual will set her preferred Europhilia, π_i, given her level of aversion, t_i, according to the following rule:

$$B_\pi(t_i,\pi) = (1+z)C_\pi(t_i,\pi) \; if \; t_i < t^S$$
$$(1+z)B_\pi(t_i,\pi) = C_\pi(t_i,\pi) \; if \; t_i > t^T \tag{12}$$

$$\pi_i = \pi^s \; if \; t^T < t_i < t^S$$

Notably, t^T and t^S with $t^T < t^S$ represent a lower bound and an upper bound, respectively, of the distribution of aversion that depends on the status-quo euro support. Every population can be divided into three different groups: "euro lovers" (*if* $t_i < t^T$), "euro haters" (*if* $t_i > t^S$) and neutral people (*if* $t^T < t < t^S$).

Each citizen will express well-defined euro policy preferences. With respect to the basic situation, we assume that (1) each individual evaluates any policy option in terms of changes from the status quo and (2) any negative effect of a change with respect to the status quo looms larger than any positive effect of equal magnitude. These assumptions are a simple application of the loss-aversion principle (Kahneman and Tversky 1979; Tversky and Kahneman 1992), and highlight the fact that if there is a loss/gain asymmetry for individuals, inertia is more likely to occur, also in macroeconomic environment (Favaretto and Masciandaro 2016; Yuemei 2018), as we show here.

Given the preferences, each citizen's optimal Europhilia depends on her aversion t_i which has three possibilities: lover, neutral and hater. More precisely, three different equilibria can arise:

$$\pi_i = \pi^{SQ} \ if \ t^T < t_i < t^S,$$

$$\pi_i < \pi^{SQ} \ if \ t_i < t^T \ and \tag{13}$$

$$\pi_i > \pi^{SQ} \ if \ t_i > t^S.$$

The existence of loss aversion influences decisions via a status-quo effect. In other words, the EMU membership outcome will be the euro support π^{SQ} if the individual is neutral.

Furthermore, given that the distance between t^T and t^S is increasing in $z > 0$, the more loss aversion is increasing, the more the individual is likely to be neutral. As such, a status-quo bias in the form of euro support inertia will emerge. More loss aversion among individuals reduces the distance between their positions. As individuals become more loss averse, the number of neutral people increases and the likelihood of a status-quo equilibrium should increase. In other words, with π^* being the equilibrium Europhilia, increasing loss aversion triggers portfolio inertia:

$$\pi^*_i = \pi^{SQ} \ if \ z > 0. \tag{14}$$

The greater the presence of individuals who disproportionally dislike the expected losses, the less there will be a change in euro attitude preferences. All in all, if a series of negative shocks affects euro support, as in the case of Italian Europhilia, the citizen's attitude declines but remains relative stable.

3.3 *Voting on eurozone membership*

Our equilibrium with loss aversion can explain why a eurozone membership is likely to be confirmed. We can assume that our citizens are a population of voters must decide whether and how to leave the eurozone. The overall procedures can be summarized as a unidimensional policy, $p \in R^+$. In addition, we assume that each individual's optimal policy, p, can be proxied using her optimal Europhilia. Therefore, haters vote against euro policies, while the opposite is true for lovers.

The policy outcome will depend on the voting rules. First, what should be the optimal policy if a social planner is in charge? The standard benevolent dictator would maximize the overall sum of individuals' preferences:

$$\int [B(t,p) - C(t,p)] dFt, \tag{14}$$

where the first best euro policy will be defined in order to equalize the average marginal benefits, $\bar{B}_p(p)$, and the average marginal costs, $\bar{C}_p(p)$. That is, the following equation will be solved:

$$\bar{B}_p(p) = \bar{C}_p(p). \tag{15}$$

The social planner's goal is to maximize the effectiveness of eurozone membership. However, the social planner's solution is not necessarily the equilibrium solution if a voting regime is in action.

If, for the sake of simplicity, we assume that the voting regime is governed via majority rule, then the selected euro policy will depend on the choices of the median voter. In other words, it will be equal to p_m. Therefore, an EMU exit will be less likely if the median voter is a euro lover and the opposite is true if in the median voter is a euro hater. The distribution of the preferences among the citizens becomes crucial for defining the actual euro choice.

If we introduce loss aversion, we can assume that the eurozone membership is active in the status-quo situation. In our model, such an assumption implies $p_{ST} = \pi_{ST} = \varepsilon$, where ε is positive. Given the previously mentioned three groups of citizens – lovers, neutrals and haters – if the median voter is neutral, the policy outcome is the status quo and a eurozone exit is less likely.

3.4 Changing the eurozone support: shocks and amnesia effect

Finally, under which conditions is the status-quo equilibrium likely to change? All else equal, we can identify two such situations: the *major shock effect* and the *amnesia effect*.

First, with regard to shocks that affect EMU attitude, only major shocks can trigger a change in euro support. Let us assume that we have a situation of status-quo equilibrium, π_1^s.

Suppose now that a shock, τ, affects the EMU attitudes of citizens such that, for example, aversion increases. Two outcomes can occur. If the shock is relatively minor the median citizen is likely to remain neutral and the euro support will remain the same.

If the shock is relatively strong, the status-quo support, π_1^s, will become too high for the median citizen and the optimal support will decrease.

Second, loss aversion can decrease if citizens have short memories of the costs of monetary instability and/or the inflation target is reached progressively (the diminishing-sensitivity effect). The more there is a loss of memory related to expected gains and losses in having or missing monetary stability, the less the support will be stable.

Again, given that the distance between t^T and t^S is increasing in $z > 0$, the more loss aversion is decreasing and the less likely it is that the median voter will be neutral. A status-quo bias in the form of euro support inertia is less likely to occur and the support for the euro becomes less stable.

All in all, this framework theoretically shows the conditions under which the euro-irreversibility assumption (Draghi 2012) can hold. Notwithstanding the possibility that shocks can weaken euro support, the expected costs in terms of MT monetary stability losses (i.e. the redenomination risk) reduce the likelihood of a definitive step backward.

4   Conclusions

Triggered by the 2007–2008 financial crisis, crucial questions about the macroeconomic costs and benefits of the eurozone have come into focus. In the run-up to the single currency, there was intense debate as to whether the European currency union, which was characterized by an independent, supranational central bank, imperfect and fragmented markets for inputs and outputs, and national, non-monetary policies with incomplete and partial coordination, could progressively reap the net benefits of a currency union via gradual convergence of policies and performance. However, following the establishment of the eurozone, the idea that the economic benefits in various countries were endogenously associated with the EMU's progress dominated, while the possibility of adverse macroeconomic dilemmas remained relatively hidden or country contingent.

The main lesson of the financial crisis is that significant financial shocks intertwined with sensible real and fiscal heterogeneities among member countries can pose a real threat to the sustainability of the eurozone. A country that does not have exchange-rate flexibility or discretionary monetary policies at its disposal may find that the interaction between deep differential growth and financial imbalances, including fiscal imbalances, calls for viable, effective European institutions and policies that can safely and soundly maintain membership in the currency union. In the absence of supranational institutional devices, adverse shocks might magnify the existing real and financial asymmetries, thereby destabilizing the eurozone, especially given that political attitudes toward currency-union membership are dynamic and contingent on economic and political drivers.

The question is this: How can the pros and cons of membership in the single currency union be captured in a simple and systematic way? The aim of this chapter has been to revisit the standard approach of optimal currency areas and to apply a behavioural political economy approach to the euro zone case.

We developed a general framework for discussing the economics and political economy of the European monetary integration process. The bottom line is that the net benefits of a single currency are calculated by national policymakers, who are elected politicians – career-concerned players who try to maximize consensus by pleasing voters and/or lobbyists. In so doing, they influence the country's evaluation of the medium- to long-term benefits of fixing the exchange rate and establishing an independent, supranational central bank, and the costs associated with losing the monetary flexibility needed to smooth out short-term macroeconomic imbalances and/or implement potentially unpopular fiscal and structural policies.

The political willingness to be a more or less active player in the euro process can trigger centripetal or centrifugal forces that can either reinforce or weaken the robustness of the euro's institutional setting. In other words, the direction and speed of the eurozone process depend on two different but intertwined endogeneity phenomena: endogeneity in the evolution of the pros and cons of eurozone membership, and endogeneity in the political weights assigned to the costs and benefits of EMU membership.

We focused our attention on how the politics of eurozone membership are key for understanding what is going on. At the same time, we discussed the effects of behavioural biases influencing the preferences of political actors (i.e. loss aversion). We used the theoretical framework to analyse the support for eurozone membership among Italian citizens and, more generally, to examine the conditions under which the euro-irreversibility assumption is likely to hold.

In general, for each country, the attitude toward the eurozone is an endogenous, dynamic variable that ebbs and flows depending on the political evaluation of the economic costs and benefits of membership in the currency union. In turn, the cycles of national attitudes towards the EMU are likely to accelerate or decelerate its evolution, including the safe and sound functioning of its currency and the credibility of its monetary actor, the ECB. The ways in which individual political decisions in each member country can affect the common path of the economic supranational institution is a particularly interesting issue that deserves further analysis.

Notes

1 Franks et al. (2018).
2 Buiter (1999), Jonung and Drea (2010), Krugman (2012). See also Goodhart (1995) and Bordo and Jonung (1999). Mongelli (2002) describes the evolution of OCA theory as occurring in four phases: pioneering (from the early 1960s to the early 1970s), reconciliation (during the 1970s), reassessment (in the 1980s and early 1990s) and empirical (since the mid-1990s).
3 On mobility and efficiency in EU markets, see Bayoumi and Eichengreen (1996), OECD (1999), Rose and Van Wincoop (2001), Fidrmuc (2001), Bun and Klaassen (2002), Mahlberg and Kronberger (2002), Mongelli (2002), EU Commission (2004), De Grauwe and Mongelli (2005), Dellas and Tavlas (2005), Andres et al. (2008), Buscher and Gabrisch (2009), and Chukwuemeka (2011). On the relationships between labour markets and currency union in the eurozone see Kekre (2019). On the effects of specific ECU membership cases, see Monga (2004), Rabanal (2009) and Baas (2014).
4 On the relationships between real exchange rates and productivity in the eurozone, see Berka et al. (2018).
5 Frankel and Rose (1997, 1998), Glick and Rose (2002).

6 Glick and Rose (2016).
7 Chen and Novy (2018).
8 Dustmann et al. (2014).
9 Thimann (2015).
10 As stated by Kirkegaard and Posen (2018).
11 Aizenman (2016). See also Handler (2013).
12 Alesina and Passarelli (2015), Favaretto and Masciandaro (2016).

References

Aizenman, J., (2016), *Optimal Currency Area: A 20th Century Idea for the 21st Century*, NBER Working Paper Series, n.22097.

Alesina, A. and Passarelli, F., (2015), *Loss Aversion in Politics*, NBER Working Paper Series, n.21077.

Andres, J., Ortega, E. and Valles, J., (2008), Competition and Inflation Differentials in EMU, *Journal of Economic Dynamics and Control*, 19(1), 21–32.

Baas, T., (2014), *Estonia and the European Monetary Union: Are the Benefits from a "Late" Accession?*, RUHR Economic Papers, n. 489.

Barberis, N.C., (2012), *Thirty Years of Prospect Theory in Economics: A Review and Assessment*, NBER Working Paper Series, n. 18621.

Barberis, N.C., (2018), Richard Thales and the Rise of Behavioral Economics, *Scandinavian Journal of Economics*, 120(3), 661–684.

Bassanetti, A., Cecioni, M., Nobili, A. and Zevi, G., (2009), *The Main Recessions in Italy: A Retrospective Comparison*, Bank of Italy, Occasional Papers, n. 46.

Bayoumi, T. and Eichengreen, B., (1996), Ever Closer to Heaven? An Optimum Currency Area Index for European Countries, *European Economic Review*, 41, 761–770.

Bayoumi, T. and Eichengreen, B., (2017), *Aftershocks of Monetary Unification: Hysteresis with a Financial Twist*, IMF Working Paper Series, n.55, March.

Berka, M., Devereux, M.B. and Engel, C., (2018), Real Exchange Rates and Sectoral Productivity in the Eurozone, *American Economic Review*, 108(6), 1543–1581.

Bertasiute, A., Massaro, D. and Weber, M., (2018), *The Behavioural Economics of Currency Unions: Economic Integration and Monetary Policy*, Bank of Lithuania, Working Paper Series, n.49.

Bolton, P. and Huang, H., (2018), Optimal Payment Areas or Optimal Currency Areas?, *American Economic Association, Papers and Proceedings*, 108, 505–508.

Bordo, M.D. and Jonung, L., (1999), *The Future of EMU: What Does the History of Monetary Unions Tell Us?*, NBER Working Paper Series, n.7365.

Buiter, W., (1999), The EMU and the NAMU: What Is the Case for North American Monetary Union?, *Canadian Public Policy*, 25(3), 285–305.

Bun, M. and Klaassen, F., (2002), *Has the Euro Increased Trade?*, Tinbergen Institute Discussion Paper Series, n.108.

Buscher, H.S. and Gabrisch, H., (2009), *Is the European Monetary Union an Endogenous Currency Area? The example of the Labour Markets*, Halle Institute for Economic Research, Discussion Papers, n.7.

Chen, N. and Novy, D., (2018), *Currency Unions, Trade and Heterogeneity*, CEPR Discussion Paper Series, n. 12954.

Chukwuemeka, V., (2011), *Are Optimum Currency Area Theory Criteria Endogenous to Regime Change? The Case of the EMU Before and After 1999*, Department of International Business and Economics, University of Greenwich, mimeo.

De Grauwe, P. and Mongelli, F.P., (2005), *Endogeneity of Optimum Currency Areas: What Brings Countries Sharing a Single Currency Closer Together?*, ECB Working Paper Series, n. 468.

Dellas, H. and Tavlas, G., (2005), Wage Rigidity and Monetary Union, *Economic Journal*, 115, 907–927.

Draghi, M., (2012), *Verbatim of the Remarks Made by Mario Draghi*, Global Investment Conference, London, July 26.

Dustmann, C., Fitzenberger, B., Schoberg, U. and Spitz-Oener, A., (2014), From Sick Man of Europe to Economic Superstar: Germany's Resurgent Economy, *Journal of Economic Perspectives*, 28(1), 167–188.

European Commission, Brussel; Directorate General Communication (1974–2018), *Eurobarometer*, GESIS Data Archive, Cologne. https://www.gesis.org/fileadmin/upload/dienstleistung/daten/umfragedaten/eurobarometer/eb_bibliography/EB_Bibliography.pdf

European Commission, (2004), *EMU after Five Years*, European Economy Special Report, n.1.

Favaretto, F. and Masciandaro, D., (2016), Doves, Hawks and Pigeons: Behavioural Monetary Policy and Interest Rate Inertia, *Journal of Financial Stability*, 27, December, 50–58.

Fidrmuc, J., (2001), *The Endogeneity of Optimum Currency Area Criteria, Intra-industry Trade and EMU Enlargement*, Bank of Finland, Discussion Paper Series, n.8.

Frankel, J.A. and Rose, A.K., (1997), Is EMU More Justifiable ex Post Than ex Ante?, *European Economic Review*, 41(3), 753–760.

Frankel, J.A. and Rose, A.K., (1998), The Endogeneity of the Optimum Currency Area Criteria, *Economic Journal*, 108, 1009–1025.

Franks, J., Barkbu, B., Blavy, R., Oman, W. and Shoelermann, H., (2018), *Economic Convergence in the Euro Area: Coming Together or Drifting Apart?*, IMF Working Paper Series, n.10.

Glick, R. and Rose, A.K., (2002), Does a Currency Union Affect Trade? The Time-Series Evidence, *European Economic Review*, 46, 1125–1151.

Glick, R. and Rose, A.K., (2016), Currency Unions and Trade: A Post-EMU Reassessment, *European Economic Review*, 87, 78–91.

Goodhart, C.A.E., (1995), The Political Economy of Monetary Union, in P. Kenen (ed.), *Understanding Interdependence: The Macroeconomics of the Open Economy*, Princeton, Princeton University Press, 448–505.

Goodhart, C.A.E., (1998), The Two Concepts of Money: Implications for the Analysis of Optimal Currency Areas, *European Journal of Political Economy*, 14(3), 407–432.

Guiso, L., Sapienza, P. and Zingales, L., (2015), *Monnet's Error?*, NBER Working Paper Series, n. 21121.

Handler, H., (2013), *The Eurozone: Piecemeal Approach to an Optimum Currency Area*, Austrian Institute of Economic Research, WIFO Working Papers, n.466.

Heffets, O., (2018), *Are Reference Points Merely Lagged Beliefs Over Probabilities?*, NBER Working Paper Series, n. 24721.

Jonung, L. and Drea, E., (2010), It Can't Happen, it's a Bad Idea, It Won't Last: US Economists on the EMU and the Euro:1989–2002, *Econ Journal Watch*, 7, 4–52.

Kahneman, D., Tversky, A., (1979), Prospect Theory: An Analysis of Decision Under Risk, *Econometrica*, 47, 263–291.

Kekre, R., (2019), *Optimal Currency Area with Labor Market Frictions*, Becker Friedman Institute, Working Paper Series, n. 14.

Kenen, P.B., (1969), The Optimum Currency Area: An Eclectic View, *American Economic Review*, 58, 356–374.

Kirkegaard, J.F. and Posen, A.S., (2018), *Lessons for EU Integration from US History*, Washington, DC: Peterson Institute for International Economics, January.

Krugman, P., (2012), Revenge of the Optimum Currency Area, *NBER Macroeconomic Annual*, 27(1), 439–448.

Mahlberg, B. and Kronberger, R., (2002), *Eastern Enlargement of the European Monetary Union: An OCA Theory View*, mimeo.

McKinnon, R., (1963), Optimum Currency Areas, *American Economic Review*, 53, 717–725.

Monga, C., (2004), *Latvia's Macroeconomic Options in the Medium Term: Fiscal and Monetary Challenges of EU Membership*, World Bank Policy Research Working Papers, n. 3307.

Mongelli, F.P., (2002), *"New" Views on the Optimum Currency Areas Theory: What Is EMU Telling Us?*, ECB Working Paper Series, n.138.

Mundell, R., (1961), A Theory of Optimum Currency Areas, *American Economic Review*, 51, 657–675.

Oecd, (1999), *EMU: Facts, Challenges and Policies*, Paris, France: OECD Publications.

Rabanal, P., (2009), Inflation Differentials between Spain and the EMU: A DSGE Perspective, *Journal of Money, Credit and Banking*, 41(6), 1141–1166.

Rose, A. and Van Wincoop, E., (2001), National Money as a Barrier to Trade: The Real Case for Currency Union, *American Economic Review*, 91, 386–390.

Schnellenbach, J. and Schubert, C., (2015), Behavioral Political Economy: A Survey, *European Journal of Political Economy*, 40, 395–417.

Thaler, R.H., (2018), From Cashews to Nudges: The Evolution of Behavioural Economics, *American Economic Review*, 108(6), 1265–1287.

Thimann, C., (2015), The Microeconomic Dimensions of the Eurozone Crisis and Why European Politics Cannot Solve Them, *Journal of Economic Perspectives*, 29(3), 141–164.

Tversky, A. and Kahneman, D., (1992), Advances in Prospect Theory: Cumulative Representations of Uncertainty, *Journal of Risk and Uncertainty*, 5, 297–323.

Yuemei, J., (2018), *Why Is There So Much Inertia in Inflation and Output? A Behavioral Explanation*, CESifo Working Paper Series, n. 7181.

7 An optimality index of the single currency

Internal asymmetries within the eurozone since 1999

Juan E. Castañeda and Pedro Schwartz

1 Introduction: an index of internal asymmetries

Since the outbreak of the Global Financial Crisis and the subsequent eurozone crisis, the euro member states (MSs) have taken steps towards deepening their economic integration and strengthening supervision and surveillance procedures. As observed in the years running up to the 2007–2008 crisis, trade and fiscal imbalances had been accumulating across the eurozone for some time, thus making it more and more difficult for a single monetary policy to fit every MS. In addition, once the decision was taken not to let any MS abandon or leave the eurozone (in contrast to seceding from the EU), it became clear that the fiscal and economic performance of each MS in a crisis would create spill-over effects right across the eurozone. In an effort to impose common standards, the MSs of the eurozone have agreed on more stringent fiscal rules (the so-called 'Fiscal Compact') and on new macroeconomic criteria (the Macroeconomic Imbalance Procedure, MIP, or so-called 'Six Pack') to avoid the recurrence of asymmetries in this area. With the aim of integrating the economies of the MSs, they have chosen more centralised procedures and rules further constraining the ability of MSs to run their own macroeconomic and fiscal policies.

A number of studies have tried to gauge the degree of economic convergence within the eurozone. In a recent empirical study, Campos et al. (2017) found that the business cycle became more homogeneous across the EU economies, and even more so within the eurozone. In this vein, Glick (2017) found a significant increase in intra-European trade after the introduction of the single currency. Also, the new Macroeconomic Imbalance Procedure adopted in 2011 extends the number of indicators used by the Commission to assess the performance of MSs economies and now includes, among others, current account balances, unit labour costs, real exchange rates and financial indicators, such as private sector debt and house prices. In line with the MIP approach, we have included a wide variety of macroeconomic indicators in our research to assess the performance of the eurozone MSs since 1999, and crucially we have added monetary growth in our calculations.[1] In our view, the lack of any monetary indicators in the Commission's assessment exercise has resulted in an inadequate assessment of the conditions needed for optimality in a monetary zone.

Here we have calculated an overall index to assess the level of economic integration in the eurozone since the introduction of the euro in 1999, as well as partial indices referring to four separate chapters: fiscal performance, cycle synchronicity, competitiveness and monetary dispersion. With these indices we will be able to measure the internal asymmetries within the eurozone, and which partial developments have most contributed to them, thus possibly offering insights about the introduction of reforms in the respective areas. Another contribution of our research is to compare the performance of the eurozone with the more consolidated and, in principle, more symmetrical US dollar zone. To do so, we have used the same methodology to calculate the index of internal asymmetries within the US economy.

The remainder of the paper is structured as follows: section 2 explains how our indices are elaborated, while section 3 shows the results of the indices as applied to the eurozone. Section 4 applies the same indices of dispersion to compare the performance of the eurozone with the US dollar monetary area. Section 5 summarises the findings and briefly draws conclusions on policy issues regarding eurozone performance.

2   The calculation of the indices: the indicators used

We have assessed the performance of the euro on the basis of the volatility or dispersion of the MSs under the four chapters or sub-indices, namely: (1) the business cycle, (2) public finance, (3) competitiveness and (4) monetary. For the business cycle we have included the dispersion of the annual real growth of the GDP and the GDP per capita, as well as the unemployment rate. For public finances, we have used the ratio of the public debt and the deficit to the GDP. With competitiveness, we have used annual inflation (as calculated by the Harmonised Index of Consumer Prices), annual changes in Unit Labour Costs and real exchange rates. We added a monetary sub-index, with the annual rate of growth of broad money (M3) per nation, the ratio of credit to the private sector and the current account balance to the GDP.[2] The measure of dispersion we use is the standard deviation of the indicators given previously, per year. Since the composition of the eurozone has changed from the 11 founders in 1999 (Austria, Belgium, Finland, France, Germany, Italy, Ireland, Luxemburg, the Netherlands, Portugal and Spain) plus Greece in 2001, to 19 today (with Slovenia [2007], Cyprus and Malta [both in 2008], Slovakia [2009], Estonia [2011], Latvia [2014] and Lithuania [2015]), we present the overall index in two forms: firstly, for the 12 countries which have been members of the eurozone throughout the period; and secondly, for the 7 member states which have joined from 2007 onwards. This enables the analysis to discount the effect of the increased number of members on the general dispersion index.

With the business cycle sub-index we want to point out that it would be expected that the introduction of the single currency would foster intra-eurozone trade and economic links across member states, making business cycles more homogeneous (or synchronic[3]). Consequently we should expect a reduction in the dispersion in the rates of growth of the GDP and the rates of unemployment across MSs.

This is essential if the European Central Bank (ECB) is to operate a single monetary policy, as a large cycle divergence within the eurozone would make virtually impossible to design an optimal monetary policy to fit all MSs.

Convergence in public finances across MSs has always been at the core of the efforts of the euro architects since its very design and inception. As evidenced in the eurozone crisis, large fiscal imbalances in individual MSs may end up precipitating a crisis in the whole area, and thus also affecting the credit risk and borrowing costs of both errant and well-behaved MSs. This means that fiscal consolidation, and thus convergence towards fiscal sustainability, should be achieved in the "good years" in order not to suffer a dire fiscal situation in "bad times". However, the pre-Global Financial Crisis deficit and debt to GDP ratios were not low enough to contain the escalation of fiscal imbalances during the crisis time (see Blanchard et al., 2013). So in order to achieve a lower public debt to GDP ratio during the expansionary phase of the cycle in future, the EU MSs approved in 2012 the "Treaty on Stability, Coordination and Governance in the Economic and Monetary Union", which introduced tougher fiscal criteria: a maximum 0.5% to 1% fiscal deficit ratio to GDP and a country-based calendar and criteria for the reduction of the public debt ratio to GDP. If these new regulations prove to be effective, we would expect a lower dispersion in public finance performance after 2013, and thus an improvement in our public finance dispersion sub-index.

Competitiveness across MSs is an essential dimension of the sustainability of the eurozone. Once monetary sovereignty has been delegated to a supranational authority, MSs can only resort to adjustments in costs and prices if they need to regain competitiveness (a so-called internal devaluation). For this to happen, the markets in labour, goods, and services must be flexible. In the absence of such flexibility and in the event of a crisis, markets will be forced to clear by quantity and not by price, that is to say, they will do so through a deeper recession and a higher level of unemployment than otherwise would be the case. This lack of flexibility would also be reflected in excessively high real exchange rates: when the nominal exchange rate is fixed, the only way to depreciate the real exchange rate is by reducing internal costs. This is why one of our sub-indices compares the real exchange rate of the different MSs: a failure to carry out an internal devaluation will make the country uncompetitive, increase its foreign deficit and reduce the national supply of euros.[4]

Crucially, another sub-index included in this study is the rate of growth of broad money supply in the different MSs. In our view, monetary dispersion across the eurozone did not receive enough attention in the years up to the 2007–2008 crisis.[5] As a matter of fact, overall money growth in the eurozone, as well as differences in money growth across MSs, expanded significantly from 2004 to 2007 (see Castañeda and Congdon [2017] for further details). This is relevant for assessing how feasible a single monetary policy controlled by the ECB really is. Therefore, we use in our research two indicators to measure this monetary dispersion. One is the dispersion of the balance sheets of their respective banking sectors. For this we look at the asset side (credit to the private sector) and the liability side

(M3 growth). The second is the dispersion of the current account balance of the different MSs. If a current account is in continuous deficit, the MS will require an inflow of capital from the rest of the world to sustain it.

TARGET2 balances

This latter (monetary) information is especially relevant to some countries in the eurozone. Before 2008, countries such Greece, Spain and Portugal were able to accumulate negative foreign (im)balances, amounting to more than 10% of their respective GDPs without suffering a run on their currencies or the refusal of their foreign suppliers to continue financing them. But why would current account imbalances be a concern at all, provided that the MS with a current account deficit is able to attract foreign capital to pay for it? For a country running its own currency, the market will set the limit to the size of the economy's current account deficit. The difference is that, as a member of the single currency area, these MSs could finance their negative balances continuously and without limit at the ECB through the TARGET2 system.

The TARGET2 pan-European payment system makes it easy (and at the moment, virtually free) for deficit countries to access credit from eurozone surplus countries, provided that they can present adequate collateral (i.e. mainly sovereign debt of each eurozone MS). Unlike in the equivalent US payments system (the "Fedwire"), MSs' TARGET2 balances are not regularly settled (see Westermann, 2018), nor is interest charged to debtors for accumulating such balances. This makes it easier for an economy with a current account deficit to accumulate a debit position over a period of time, with potentially destabilising effects for the euro as a whole when crises come. This is why we have added TARGET2 balances to the calculation of the monetary sub-index as an additional indicator alongside monetary growth, credit to the private sector and current account imbalances.

However, we have needed closely to analyse correlations among the indicators included in our monetary sub-index for the proper interpretation of the empirical results. In particular, the effects of the Quantitative Easing (QE) programme(s)[6] of the ECB on the indicators included in our indices, specifically on broad monetary growth (M3) and on TARGET2 balances, which have been sizeable. First, QE has been effective in stabilising the rate of growth of broad money in the eurozone (see IIMR, 2018) and in diminishing disparities in the rate of growth of money within MSs, which should have the expected effect of an improvement in our monetary dispersion sub-index. Second, regarding the effects of QE on TARGET2 balances, the implementation of the ECB's Asset Purchases Programme (APP) since March 2015 has resulted in an escalation in TARGET2 imbalances which, when included in the monetary sub-index, would show a significant deterioration in the eurozone integration index. As detailed in Cecchetti and Schoenholtz (2018), this is because of the way these APPs are done, with the seller bank typically based in a creditor or core eurozone MS, thus increasing the creditor position of the core central banks at the ECB. This means that a degree of caution is necessary with the interpretation of the TARGET2 balances, particularly since 2015. True, they do reflect imbalances in the financial position of each MS in the eurozone, but the continuous increase in the central banks' balances since March 2015 does not necessarily reflect a deepening of financial fragmentation within the eurozone, but rather the necessary outcome of the ECB's APP. According to our calculations, APP operations may have contributed to approximately half of the increase in TARGET2 balances from 2015 to 2018. This caveat will be taken into account in the interpretation of the results in the following section.

The calculation of the overall index and the sub-indices

In order to avoid distortions in the calculation of the indices when using indicators measured in different units, we have used their standard deviation to measure dispersion. We have collected the information since the inception of the euro in 1999 and adopted it as the base year in our calculations[7] (thus, 1999 = 100). Both the sub-indices and the overall index have been calculated as the (un-weighted) average of the standard deviation of each component of the index as detailed in Table 7.1.[8] Finally, we have noted that the composition of the eurozone has

Table 7.1 Indicators and indices used for the eurozone

	Sub-indices				Overall index
	Business cycle	*Public finance*	*Competitiveness*	*Monetary dispersion*	
Indicators used	Real GDP, annual growth	Deficit (% GDP)	Annual inflation rate (HICP)	Contribution to the eurozone annual M3 growth	Arithmetic average of dispersion in all indicators
	GDP per capita, annual growth	Debt (% GDP)	Unit labour costs, annual growth	Credit to the private sector (% GDP)	
	Unemployment rate		Real exchange rate (a)	Current account balance of each Member State with the rest of the world (% GDP) (b)	
				TARGET2 balances	

Notes: (a) We calculated the real exchange rate as follows: the nominal exchange rate between the euro in one Member State versus the others, times the difference of the price index in a Member State over the price index in the eurozone. (b) These balances do not include intra-eurozone operations.

changed with the addition of seven new economies since 2007. This may well affect the results of our measures of economic integration in the whole area. Therefore, we have needed to assess the level of integration of the MSs for both the whole eurozone (euro-19) and the original euro-12.

3   Eurozone-19 dispersion indices: interpretation of the results

Business cycle sub-index

The cycle has become more convergent across eurozone MSs since 1999. Before the crisis years, the index reflects a trend of improvement in the dispersion of the cycle across MSs, with a peak 48% fall in dispersion in 2006 (see Figure 7.1). This very much confirms the expected effects resulting from the introduction of the new (single) currency, as the economies of the eurozone became indeed more integrated in terms of real output growth, GDP per capita and the rate of unemployment. During the crises years (first the Global Financial Crisis, 2008–2009 and the subsequent eurozone crisis, 2010–2013), the index shows a deterioration in cycle integration, as the crises particularly affected the "peripheral" eurozone MSs' economies as compared to the eurozone "core" MSs. From 2007 the index shows a continuous increase in business cycle dispersion across MSs until 2011, when the maximum level of dispersion stabilised at around 145 (indeed nearly a threefold deterioration in the index in only five years). But since 2011 the index has shown an improvement in business cycle dispersion, with a positive trend that has brought it even lower than pre-crisis levels.

Public finance sub-index

The fiscal criteria established in the Treaty of Maastricht (and the original Stability and Growth Pact) aimed at achieving fiscal sustainability across member states. However, as measured in our index, this did not happen following the inception of the euro. In fact, fiscal dispersion increased by 23% during the expansionary phase of the cycle (1999–2007), which put the eurozone in a very fragile position in the event of a crisis. The eurozone crisis exacerbated the weaknesses in the architecture of the euro, particularly in regard to the rules supposed to keep fiscal balances and debt in check, and the public finance index reached an all-time high in 2010 (228). This meant that dispersion in this chapter more than doubled since the introduction of the euro. In 2010, eurozone MSs approved new fiscal measures to cut deficits and debt (see section 1) that have resulted in more fiscal discipline and convergence in the last eight years, with a gradual reduction in fiscal dispersion since 2011, so that it now stands even lower than in the pre-crisis years (the index fell to 116 in 2018).

We will now summarise the trends observed in the other two sub-indices, which have indeed posed new risks and concerns on the performance of the euro.

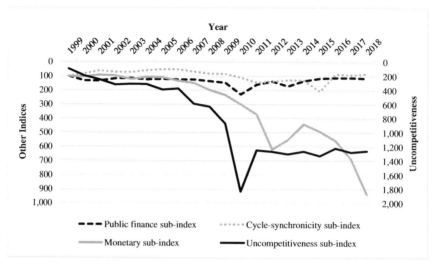

Figure 7.1 Partial indices – euro-19 (1999 = 100)

(Competitiveness index, right-hand scale; all the others on the left-hand scale)

Note: The greater the value of the indices, the greater dispersion.

Competitiveness sub-index

This is one of the main areas in which dispersion has not been addressed effectively since the introduction of the euro. In fact, since the very first year of the adoption of the euro as the single currency, dispersion in competitiveness across member states has increased significantly, and more than trebled in the years running up to the Global Financial Crisis (with the index reaching a value of 377 in 2006). This is mainly explained by the disparities observed in the real exchange rate across MSs. Again, the crisis years triggered even greater dispersion in labour costs and inflation rates across member states, which ended up in a further increase in dispersion in this area, culminating in an all-time record high in 2010 (1,835). It is worth noting that dispersion has diminished since then, which seems to point at the effectiveness of the internal devaluation policies adopted by the MSs in the crisis (see Figure 7.2 with real exchange rates), and the renewed efforts of the EU Commission to improve macroeconomic surveillance in the EU (such as the approval of the MIP discussed in section 1). However, this more favourable trend has stopped since 2016 with the stagnation of competitiveness asymmetries across MSs, still more than 3 times greater than in 2006.

Monetary sub-index

As discussed in section 2, we will be offering the results of this index with and without TARGET2 balances.

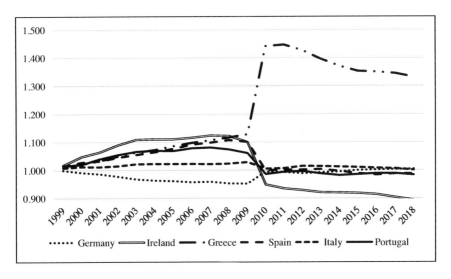

Figure 7.2 Real exchange rates, 1999–2018 (1999 = 100)

Note: Calculated as the nominal exchange rate between the euro in one Member State versus the others (effectively, 1) × (price index in a Member State/price index in the eurozone).

In the first years after the introduction of the euro, monetary dispersion was very much in check. It was only between 2004 and the outbreak of the Global financial Crisis that monetary dispersions started to accumulate in the eurozone. This is clearly shown in the monetary sub-index results, with an accumulated 33% higher dispersion in this chapter from 2004 to 2007 (see Figure 7.3). Indeed, it was during the years running up to the crisis that disparities in our set of monetary indicators increased. The ECB had abandoned its initial monetary strategy, whereby predominant weight was given to the rate of growth of money in the eurozone when making policy decisions, and a "reference value" for annual M3 growth announced. This, in our view, helps to understand why the ECB did not pay enough attention to the excess in (broad) monetary growth in the eurozone as a whole, as well as to disparities in monetary growth across MSs when making monetary policy decisions between 2004 and 2007. With the outbreak of the crisis in 2007 to 2008 (and the subsequent credit crunch) tensions manifested themselves. The sub-index reflects the increase in dispersion across MSs. It reached a record high in 2010 (142). Since then, monetary dispersion has stabilised and even fallen below pre-crisis levels (to 62 in 2018). The fall in dispersion in recent years may well reflect the success of the implementation of the ECB's QE programmes in 2010 and the APP since 2015. As announced by the ECB, APP did cut down the sum of asset purchases from €80 billion (April 2016 to March 2017) to €60 billion (April to December 2017), which was then gradually reduced until ceasing altogether in December 2018.[9]

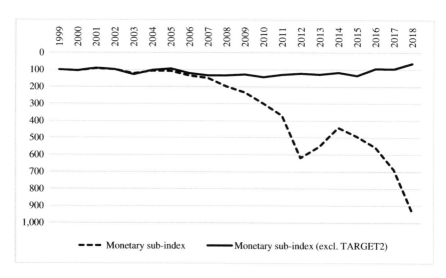

Figure 7.3 Monetary sub-index, euro-19 (1999 = 100)

Note: The higher the value of the indices, the greater the dispersion.

When TARGET2 balances are included in the monetary index of dispersion, asymmetries worsen significantly. The index values are very much similar to those without TARGET2 balances up to 2007 (see Figure 7.3). However, since 2008 the index shows an increase in dispersion, even more notable between 2010 and 2012 with the outbreak of the eurozone crisis. This reflects a redirection of funds from the banking systems of the "peripheral" MSs to those at the "core" of the eurozone (see Cecchetti and Schoenholtz, 2018), which started to result in lower dispersion values once the crisis mitigated in 2013 and 2014. However, as explained in section 2, the implementation of a new QE programme since March 2015 resulted once again in an increase in the debtor position of the "peripheral" MSs' central banks at the ECB, and thus a significant worsening in the TARGET2 balances asymmetries.

Overall index of dispersion: the performance of the euro, 1999–2018

When all the indicators are considered in the calculation of the overall index of dispersion in the eurozone, a common pattern is shown in all the scenarios considered in our research. Either with or without TARGET2 balances or whether applied to the euro 12 or the euro 19, the eurozone has shown an increase in internal asymmetries since the very inception of the euro in 1999, and thus well before the outbreak of the crisis. As detailed in the previous paragraphs, the accumulation of dispersion as regards competitiveness and public finance, as well as the monetary index after 2004, explain this negative trend in the performance of the euro integration index until 2007 (with a 72% increase in overall asymmetries). Even more, as shown in Castañeda and Schwartz (2017), we should not take the dispersion

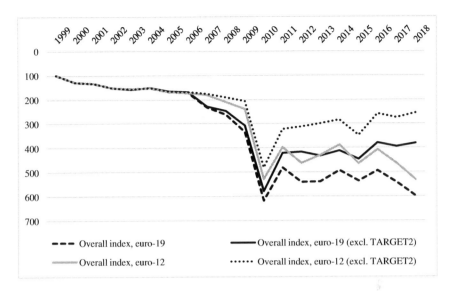

Figure 7.4 Overall index of dispersion, euro-12 and euro-19 (1999 = 100)
Note: The higher the value of the index, the greater the dispersion.

values calculated for 1999 as the desirable or optimum values for the running of the eurozone; in fact, we would expect the introduction of the new currency to foster integration and thus reduce the levels of asymmetries already in place at the time of the introduction of the euro, something that has clearly not happened. The crisis years resulted in a deterioration in the levels of internal asymmetries within the eurozone as measured in our overall index, a trend that has only started to reverse since 2015 (excluding TARGET2 balances), showing a very slow path towards pre-crisis levels of integration. The ECB's APP seems to have been the main driver of greater convergence in the eurozone since 2015, and the resulting increase in TARGET2 imbalances are the consequence of such policy.

As shown in Figure 7.4, the euro-12 have performed better than the enlarged euro-19 area. The addition of new member states since 2007 has not created an increase in the dispersion of the business cycle, public finances or monetary indicators, but has increased competitiveness dispersion. In 2009, with the addition of four new member states in only two years, dispersion in this category in the euro-19 area nearly doubled that of the original euro-12 area.

4   Indices of dispersion for the US dollar monetary area

We have applied the same indices, rationale and method to the USA, in order to offer a comparable picture of the level of internal asymmetries in the US dollar monetary area compared with the eurozone. We have also taken 1999 as the base year. We have considered in our analysis the 50 (mainland) states plus Washington DC and Hawaii. However, there are relevant institutional differences compared with the eurozone that affect the calculation of the indices for the USA (and indeed their interpretation). Though the dollar has been the single currency in the USA for more than a century, neither the regional reserve banks nor the US Federal Reserve, established in 1913, publish monetary growth data per state or per Federal Reserve Bank region. The same applies to the availability of trade (current account) data, which only refer to the whole US economy versus the rest of the world. Even more, there is not a comparable Consumer Price Index calculated at the state level. To overcome these gaps, rather than considering the contribution of each state to the overall rate of growth of money, we have used the ratio of bank deposits held by households as a proxy (using the Federal Deposit Insurance Corporation database as a source). In calculating inflation dispersion, we have resorted to the Consumer Price Index (CPI) per region, as calculated by the Bureau of Labour Statistics.[10] As for state current account balances, we have included the trade balance per state (goods only) as a proxy in the calculation of the indices.[11] See Table 7.2.

Table 7.2 Indicators and indices used for the US dollar

	Sub-indices				Overall index
	Business cycle	*Public finance*	*Competitiveness*	*Monetary dispersion*	
Indicators used	Real GDP annual growth, GDP per capita, annual growth	Deficit (% state GDP), Debt (% state GDP)	Consumer Price Index (CPI), annual growth Labour costs, annual growth	Deposits by households, annual growth Trade balance (% state GDP)	Arithmetic average of dispersion in all indicators
	Unemployment rate		Real exchange rate	Credit to the private sector: • Loans and leases • Real estate loans (both % state GDP) Fedwire balances	

Sources: Bureau of Economic Analysis (Real GDP), Bureau of Labor Statistics (Unemployment rate), US Census Bureau (state deficit, % state nominal GDP and state imports and exports), USgovernmentspending.com (Total debt per state, % state nominal GDP), Bureau of Labor Statistics (for CPI and labour cost) and Federal Deposit Insurance Corporation (for deposits, leases and loans, and real estate loans).

Results for the USA

As shown in the chart in Figure 7.5a, the stability in the indices of dispersion for both the business cycle and public finances in the USA is remarkable. True, dispersion in the business cycle increased approximately 50% in the crisis years (2008–2012), but reversed quite quickly to values which were even lower than those seen pre-crisis and has stayed there ever since. In fact, in 2018 the business cycle dispersion is 33% lower than in 1999. Regarding public finances dispersion across states, the trend has been quite stable since 2010. However, the competitiveness dispersion index did deteriorate in the years running up to the crisis – approximately 80% from 1999 to 2006. Since the crisis, dispersion in competitiveness has deteriorated and shows no signs of a quick return to pre-crisis levels.

The situation looks more worrying regarding the dispersion in monetary indicators (see Figure 7.5b), especially in the years running up to the Global Financial Crisis. Just as in the eurozone, monetary dispersion spiked in 2005 and 2007. Since

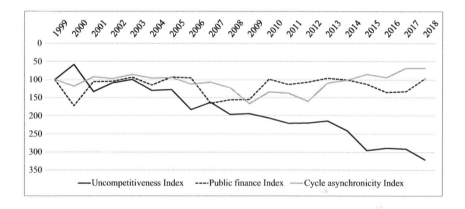

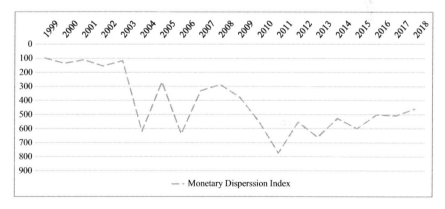

Figure 7.5 US dollar zone dispersion indices, 1999–2018: (a) cycle synchronicity, public finance and monetary dispersion indices, (b) monetary dispersion index

Note: The greater the value of the indices, the greater dispersion.

2011, monetary dispersion has diminished though still far from pre-crisis levels. The US Fed abandoned the publication of its M3 monetary aggregate in 2006,[12] which may well be interpreted as a sign of the diminishing role played by this aggregate in monetary policy decisions. Monetary dispersion displays quite volatile behavior, and the data need to be interpreted with caution. Although we would prefer to have used official money growth data at the state level, as they are not published we used bank deposits by households as a proxy. However as relevant as it may be, monetary dispersion is less worrying in an economy with a more integrated capital and banking markets across the entire country, such as the USA is. This is in sharp contrast with the eurozone, where this level of integration of capital markets has not been reached.

Overall, the US dollar zone index of dispersion shows a better performance than that of the eurozone (see Figure 7.6). The critical difference lies in the years of the Global Financial Crisis: from 2007 to 2010 asymmetries in the eurozone became much deeper than in the US, whereas in both economies asymmetries seem to have stagnated since 2011. However, the size of the asymmetries is significantly greater in the eurozone than in the USA. As observed in both indices, there is not a clear trend towards more integration in either of the two economies in recent years. The overall size of macroeconomic dispersion is much lower and the response of the economy to the crisis seems to have been much more timely and flexible in the USA. Several reasons may explain this result. On the one hand, effective constitutional fiscal rules at the state level

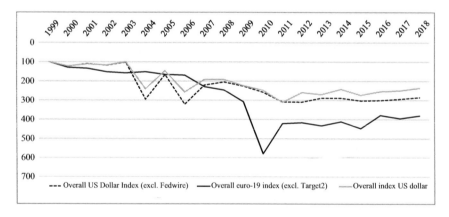

Figure 7.6 US dollar and euro-19 dispersion indices, 1999–2018

Note: We adopt 1999 as the base year for both economies in order to compare their performance since then, therefore focusing on changes in asymmetry. This does not mean that the level of asymmetries in both areas in 1999 was the same. In both cases we have displayed the overall index of dispersion without including the Fedwire and TARGET2 balances for the USA and the eurozone economies, respectively.

have prevented deficits from accumulating to unsustainable levels in the USA. On the other hand, mobility across states and more flexible goods, services and labour markets may have helped to allocate resources across states more efficiently in the event of a crisis, resulting in less business cycle dispersion. As observed in Figure 7.6, Fedwire transfers seem to play an stabisiling role in the USA, in sharp contrast to Target2 in the eurozone. Finally, a sizeable US federal budget[13] provides both discretionary policies as well as automatic fiscal stabilisers that contribute to alleviating income and spending asymmetries across states.

5   Summary and policy conclusions

The euro was launched in 1999 with the expectation that the single currency would lead to greater macroeconomic integration in the eurozone. The general consensus at the time was that, even though not an optimal currency area, the euro would help to mitigate macroeconomic asymmetries among member states. The several indices used to measure the performance of the euro show the following trends. First, with the exception of business cycle synchronicity, asymmetries quickly worsened in all the other areas (fiscal, monetary and, above all, competitiveness). This appears well before the start of the Global Financial Crisis. Second, the policies and new regulations adopted both by member states and the eurozone as a whole, in the aftermath of the Global Financial Crisis and the eurozone crisis, seem to have helped to contain and even mitigate macroeconomic asymmetries. A key contributing factor in mitigating asymmetries since 2015 may have been the adoption of the APP by the ECB. We can see that both monetary (excluding TARGET2 balances) and public finance dispersion have decreased and fallen below pre-crisis levels in recent years. In addition, cycle synchronicity has improved further and it is now better than in 1999. Third, differences in competitiveness still remain quite high and have stagnated since 2011. This seems to indicate that more emphasis should be placed on improving the functioning of trade in goods and services, as well labour markets in the eurozone.

It is important, though, to assess the indices and calculations previously presented within the proper historical context and institutional limitations of the eurozone. The US dollar monetary area is generally used as a benchmark with which to compare the performance of the euro. As detailed in Rockoff (2003), it took nearly a century for the dollar zone to approach optimality. Further research is needed on the influence of institutional and political factors such as the greater labour mobility[14] and the large federal fiscal transfers to the states. Even so, the indices calculated for the eurozone and the US dollar area are informative of the different level and trends in integration currently existing in the world's two major monetary areas, as well as illustrating the greater flexibility in the US economy to absorb a major shock such as the recent 2008–2009 crisis with a single monetary policy.

Appendix

Table 7A.1 Indices of dispersion in the eurozone, 1999–2018

	Competitiveness	Public finance	Cycle-synchronicity	Monetary dispersion	Overall index of dispersion	Overall index of dispersion, excl. TARGET2
1999	100	100	100	100	100	100
2000	195.89	132.14	82.42	105.19	128.91	128.91
2001	247.15	134.73	61.87	92.63	134.10	133.48
2002	320.76	117.35	71.62	97.98	151.93	151.92
2003	313.25	114.21	74.00	122.05	155.88	157.50
2004	315.07	124.74	61.00	107.17	151.99	150.95
2005	392.00	121.37	52.98	108.46	168.71	165.22
2006	377.71	124.39	52.99	134.76	172.46	168.97
2007	590.68	123.76	67.61	148.66	232.68	228.78
2008	633.40	135.88	82.93	198.32	262.63	246.59
2009	873.15	146.07	84.67	232.79	334.17	307.92
2010	1835.48	228.06	109.47	298.52	617.88	578.93
2011	1250.92	159.81	145.02	368.31	481.02	421.31
2012	1270.31	137.80	137.35	617.99	540.86	416.88
2013	1305.70	170.48	127.29	551.88	538.84	432.72
2014	1266.11	134.23	128.70	440.65	492.42	411.36
2015	1328.96	115.72	207.59	492.25	536.13	446.84
2016	1221.67	111.61	86.40	556.24	493.98	378.48
2017	1279.10	111.53	92.20	686.66	542.37	394.67
2018	1257.94	116.49	84.43	936.52	598.84	380.44

Note: The higher the value of the index, the greater the dispersion.

Table 7A.2 Indices of dispersion in the US dollar, 1999–2018

	Competitiveness Index	Public finance Index	Cycle synchronicity Index	Monetary Dispersion Index	Overall US Index	Overall US Index (excl. Fedwire)
1999	100	100	100	100	100	100
2000	58.33	172.50	118.54	136.74	121.53	122.75
2001	133.56	105.64	92.20	112.20	110.90	109.16
2002	108.95	104.81	97.14	155.66	116.64	117.71
2003	99.31	93.17	85.79	118.55	99.20	101.44
2004	130.26	114.74	95.60	620.54	240.28	295.11
2005	127.55	92.58	93.94	270.58	146.16	165.69
2006	183.10	95.18	111.89	637.75	256.98	321.55
2007	162.92	165.42	106.85	331.25	191.61	220.28
2008	196.33	155.94	122.60	288.66	190.88	204.48
2009	193.97	155.14	166.48	377.26	223.21	225.57
2010	206.02	98.53	134.05	551.49	247.52	258.31
2011	220.61	113.12	137.38	773.66	311.19	308.55
2012	219.74	106.70	159.76	553.99	260.05	309.72
2013	214.23	95.75	108.98	661.56	270.13	288.78
2014	241.10	100.38	101.09	527.78	242.59	289.09
2015	295.34	112.33	84.99	600.81	273.37	302.59
2016	288.97	134.75	94.08	501.85	254.91	300.67
2017	291.24	132.31	68.01	509.10	250.17	294.25
2018	320.97	96.91	67.69	460.58	236.54	285.25

Note: The higher the value of the index, the greater the dispersion. Due to the lack of available data at the time of writing, the value for the overall index for 2018 is the average of the cycle and the competitiveness indices only.

Acknowledgements

We want to thank the research assistance provided by Alessandro Venieri, Oyvind Maast, Kirill Rodin and particularly Nong Chen Luis de la Torre in the updating of the index for 2018. We are very grateful for the comments and feedback given by our colleagues at the IIMR euro conference at the University of Buckingham (21–22 February 2019).

Notes

1 A preliminary index has been attempted in Castañeda and Schwartz (2017).
2 We have used Eurostat data for chapters 1, 2 and 3. Regarding 4, we have used the national central banks' datasets for the national contribution to M3 growth, the World Bank's datasets for credit to the private sector and the IMF's for the current account balances.
3 By synchronic we mean that member states share both the timing of the cycle as well as the size or amplitude of their expansionary and contractionary phases along the cycle.
4 This is something particularly relevant for the eurozone and lies at the core of the sound running of a common currency area. This is because, as explained by R. Mundell in his 1961's seminal article, labour mobility across member states does not seem to mitigate the concentration of abnormally high unemployment rates enough in the economies in crisis. In this regard, the calculation and monitoring of the real exchange rate will be key to understanding the accumulation of imbalances across member states, as well as the effectiveness of the measures adopted by member states and the eurozone as a whole to tackle the recent crisis.
5 The ECB had suspended the publication of the "reference value" for the rate of growth on M3 in the eurozone in 2003.
6 Since March 2015 the ECB has re-launched and merged its Quantitative Easing (QE) policies under the new Asset Purchase Programme (APP), which has consisted of the pre-set amount of purchases of private securities, as well as sovereign debt of the member states. This has alleviated borrowing costs on the most debtor economies in the eurozone and thus has helped finance overspending by the private and the public sectors. The size of TARGET2 balances is very much under discussion and indeed a matter of concern in the eurozone.
7 With the exception of those indicators with no information available in 1999, such M3 growth (2000 = 100) and credit to the private sector and TARGET2 balances (both, 2001 = 100).
8 As imperfect as an un-weighted average may be, we do not have the criteria to assign a different weight to each indicator reflecting their (distinctive and asymmetric) impact on the general index of economic integration calculated in our research. This is not unusual in the calculation of economic indices such as the Index of Economic Freedom by the Heritage Foundation. Of course, different weightings might be suggested or recommended in future, depending on the importance given to each of the indicators included in our calculations.
9 With this we suggest that, if credit to the economy does not lead to more positive rates of growth, overall monetary growth in the eurozone and also differences across member states may deteriorate further again in the future.
10 These are the states included in the four (Census) regions: Northeast Region (Connecticut, Maine, Massachusetts, New Hampshire, Rhode Island, Vermont, New Jersey, New York and Pennsylvania), South Region (Delaware, District of Columbia, Florida, Georgia, Maryland, North Carolina, South Carolina, Virginia, West Virginia, Alabama, Kentucky, Mississippi, Tennessee, Arkansas, Louisiana, Oklahoma and Texas), Midwest Region (Illinois, Indiana, Michigan, Ohio, Wisconsin, Iowa, Kansas, Minnesota, Missouri, Nebraska, North Dakota and South Dakota) and West Region (Arizona,

Colorado, Idaho, Montana, Nevada, New Mexico, Utah, Wyoming, Alaska, California, Hawaii, Oregon and Washington).

11 As per the calculation of the real exchange rate per state we have used the same formula as in the eurozone: the nominal exchange rate between the dollar in one state versus the others (1) times the price index in a state over the price index in the US. The sources of the US data are specified on Table 7.2 in the text.

12 As stated in the US Fed press release, November 10 2005: "M3 does not appear to convey any additional information about economic activity that is not already embodied in M2 and has not played a role in the monetary policy process for many years. Consequently, the Board judged that the costs of collecting the underlying data and publishing M3 outweigh the benefits".

13 The US federal budget amounts to around 20% of the US GDP (approximately 50% of total government spending comes from the federal budget, see Bordo et al. 2013), as compared to the eurozone total budget of virtually 1% of the EU GDP.

14 Even though increasing in the last years and thus making the gap smaller, labour mobility in the EU is still lower than in the US: according to the 2016 European Commission report on labour mobility in the EU, 1.78% of the total population changed their country of residence to work abroad, whereas in the USA, following Census data for 2016, 2.26% moved to a different state searching for a job.

References

Blanchard, O., Dell'Ariccia, G. and Mauro, P. (2013): Rethinking Macro Policy II: Getting Granular. IMF Staff Discussion Note. Accessed online. www.imf.org/external/pubs/ft/sdn/2013/sdn1303.pdf

Bordo, M., Jonun, L. and Markiewicz, A. (2013): A Fiscal Union for the Euro: Some Lessons from History. CESifo Economic Studies.

Campos, N., Fidrmuc, J. and Korhonen, L. (2017): Business Cycle Synchronisation in a Currency Union: Taking Stock of the Evidence. Bank of Finland Research Discussion Paper No. 28.

Castañeda, J. and Congdon, T. (2017): "Have Central Banks Forgotten about Money? The Case of the European Central Bank (1999–2014)". In Congdon (ed.). *Money in the Great Recession*. Chapter 4. Cheltenham: Edward Elgar.

Castañeda, J. and Schwartz, P. (2017): "How Functional Is the Eurozone? An Index of European Economic Integration Through the Single Currency". In *Economic Affairs* Vol. 37, No. 3, October, pp. 365–372.

Cecchetti, S. and Schoenholtz, K. (2018): Target-2 Masks Reduced Fragmentation Eurosystem Should Draw Inspiration from Federal Reserve. OMFIF Analysis. Accessed online (12 July 2018). www.omfif.org/analysis/commentary/2018/july/target-2-masks-reduced-fragmentation/

Glick, R. (2017): "Currency Unions and Regional Trade Agreements: EMU and EU Effects on Trade". In *Comparative Economic Studies* Vol. 59, No. 2, pp. 194–209.

Institute of International Monetary Research (IIMR) (2018): July Monetary Update. Accessed online (July 2018). www.mv-pt.org/monthly-monetary-update-archive

Mundell, R.A. (1961). 'A Theory of Optimum Currency Areas'. *American Economic Review*, Vol. 51, No. 4, pp. 657–665.

Rockoff, H. (2003): "How Long Did It Take the United States to Become an Optimal Currency Area?". In F. Capie and G. Wood (eds.). *Monetary Unions: Theory, History, Public Choice*. London: Routledge. Chapter 4, pp. 76–103.

Westermann, F. (2018): Europe's Target-2 Can Learn from US. Euro Area Imbalances Portend Future Crisis. OMFIF Analysis. Accessed online (July 2018). www.omfif.org/analysis/commentary/2018/july/europes-target-2-can-learn-from-us/

Part 4

Preserving unions

The eurozone

8 Public support for the euro and trust in the ECB

The first two decades of the common currency

Felix Roth and Lars Jonung

1 Introduction

The euro, the common European currency adopted in 1999, is now entering its third decade. The euro is unique in at least two ways. First, a large number of independent countries, EU member states, have handed over responsibility for their monetary policy to an independent central bank, the European Central Bank (ECB), while maintaining domestic control over fiscal policy. Second, the euro, to the best of our knowledge, is the only currency for which we have a long and consistent time series showing public support for the currency and public trust in the central bank that supplies the currency. No such opinion poll data exist for the dollar, the pound or any other currency for that matter. This unique data set enables us to conduct innovative studies of the determinants of support for a currency actively in circulation.

The purpose of this chapter is to examine how the European public has viewed the euro throughout its first two decades. We also examine how trust in the ECB and in national governments has evolved among the EU member states within the euro area (EA) and those outside. We stress that we are looking at support for the euro and its governance from the perspective of the public as revealed in public opinion polls, which is not the typical approach adopted by economists. They tend to study the euro by adopting other analytical methods, such as the optimum currency area (OCA) approach developed by Robert Mundell (1961) or the process of divergence and convergence within a monetary union. Our approach should be looked upon as a complementary strategy to these more conventional ways of studying the euro.

Our chapter is structured as follows. Section 2 discusses the role of public support for the sustainability of a common currency within a monetary union. Section 3 summarises previous empirical findings. Section 4 describes the Eurobarometer data used in our study. Section 5 offers a descriptive summary of our measures of popular support and trust. Section 6 presents our macroeconometric findings. Section 7 explains the divergence in support for the euro and trust in the ECB. Section 8 offers an outlook on the future of the euro area. Section 9 concludes.

2   The role of public support for the euro

The literature on monetary unions and monetary unification identifies public support for the common currency as a key determinant of its long-term prospects for survival.

First, the literature on the history of monetary unions suggests that these entities depend on public support for their legitimacy and viability. As long as the common currency enjoys sufficient support, policymakers are able to make adjustments and adequately confront the challenges of political, economic and financial disturbances and crises (Bordo and Jonung, 2000, 2003). According to Bordo and Jonung, the standard OCA criteria are too static to use as a means of evaluating the performance of a monetary union. They stress that ultimately it is the presence of strong political will or glue that holds a monetary union together. An established political bond between European policymakers and their publics/voters guarantees flexible solutions to emerging challenges (Bordo and Jonung, 2003). Strong public support for the common currency may thus act as a shield deflecting the critical rhetoric voiced by populist parties on both the right and the left.

Second, the literature on the political economy of monetary unions based on the OCA approach highlights the concept of commonality of destiny. Echoing the literature on the history of monetary unions, Baldwin and Wyplosz (2019) argue that it is foremost this political OCA criterion that accounts for the survival of the euro. The sense of a shared common destiny helps to find solutions in difficult times. Such a feeling is of key importance for reconciling the conflicting interests of the EA governments, which represent a significant source of the recent crisis in the EA (Frieden and Walter, 2017).

Third, political scientists stress that public support for the euro is crucial for any potential move towards deeper supranational governance (Banducci et al., 2003). In general, public support for the euro is viewed as a necessary condition before European citizens will entertain a further transfer of power from national to European institutions (Kaltenthaler and Anderson, 2001). The political science literature concludes that public support is central for the political legitimacy and thus sustainability of the euro as well (Deroose et al., 2007; Verdun, 2016).

So far, we have discussed the role of public support for the long-term survival of the euro. Public trust in the governing institutions behind the euro, however, is also crucial in this context. For this reason, we also look at two measures of trust: trust in the ECB and trust in the national government.

3   Earlier studies

Empirical studies analysing public support for the euro can roughly be clustered into one of four groups:

1   Studies of public support for a common currency in the years *before* the introduction of the euro, that is from 1990 until 1999, e.g. Kaltenthaler and Anderson (2001) and Banducci et al. (2003).

2 Analyses of public support for the euro in the pre-crisis period from 1999 to 2008, such as Banducci et al. (2009) and Deroose et al. (2007).
3 Contributions dealing with the crisis phase from 2008 to 2013, including Hobolt and Leblond (2014), Hobolt and Wratil (2015) and Roth et al. (2016).
4 Recent papers focusing on the impact of the recovery from the crisis from 2013 onwards, for example Roth et al. (2019).

What can we learn from this body of empirical work? For the sake of brevity, we focus on papers published since the introduction of the euro in 1999.

Looking at descriptive statistics, we find mixed evidence concerning majority support for the euro in the individual countries of the EA. Although Roth et al. (2016) show majority support for the euro since its establishment in 1999 in each individual country, Guiso et al. (2016) and Stiglitz (2016) claim that only a minority of citizens supported the currency in Italy and Germany. A study by Roth et al. (2019) argues that this discrepancy is due to the fact that Guiso et al. (2016) and Stiglitz (2016) use opinion poll data, which do not stem from the Eurobarometer data, which to date provide the sole authoritative data source for measuring public support for the euro across countries and over time.

An examination of the macro-evidence adduced in the literature reveals that the impact exerted by unemployment and inflation on public support for the euro is a controversial question. Whereas Hobolt and Leblond (2014) find no significant relationship between unemployment and net support for the euro, Roth et al. (2016, 2019) establish a weak negative relationship during the crisis, but a stronger impact during the post-crisis recovery.

A similarly controversial finding applies to the effect of inflation on public support. Whereas Banducci et al. (2003) and Hobolt and Leblond (2014) rule out a significant relationship between inflation and net support for the euro in pre-crisis and crisis years, Roth et al. (2016, 2019), who rely on an econometric analysis for 1999–2017, find a strong negative coefficient between an increase in inflation and a decline in net support for the euro before and during the crisis. This effect dissipates during the economic recovery.

Micro-data give support to the findings based on macro-data. Analysing a micro-dataset with 474,712 observations over the time period 1999 to 2017 for an EA19 country sample, Roth et al. (2019) find that perceptions of inflation and unemployment yield negative coefficients, whereas perceptions of the economic situation yield a positive coefficient. The findings concerning socio-economic variables such as gender, education and employment status in the pre-crisis period are similar to the results previously reported by Banducci et al. (2009). They find a stable pattern for education, employment and legal status when comparing the pre-crisis period with the crisis-recovery period. In addition, Roth et al. (2019) detect a halving of the negative female coefficient and report a complete reversal in opinion among the oldest age group (65+) when comparing the pre-crisis with the crisis-recovery period. They conclude that the largest effect on public support for the euro is related to education.

Concerning public support for the euro and trust in the ECB, some first results have been published by Roth (2015), who highlights the contrasting evolution of public support for the euro and trust in the ECB. In addition, Roth et al. (2016) compare the effect of the unemployment crisis on public support for the euro with the effect on trust in the ECB. Here an increase in unemployment is roughly four times more negatively associated with trust in the ECB than in public support for the euro.

To sum up, research on the determinants of support for the euro is evolving. We would expect this to be the case as the new currency is only 20 years old. In addition, the euro area has recently experienced a major crisis and is still in recovery.

4   Eurobarometer data

Our measures of public support for the euro are based upon the biannual Standard Eurobarometer (EB) surveys (European Commission, 2018) from 3–4/1999 (EB51) to 11/2018 (EB90). These surveys ask a representative group of respondents the following question: "What is your opinion on each of the following statements? Please tell me for each statement, whether you are for it or against it. A European economic and monetary union with one single currency, the euro". Respondents can then choose between "For", "Against", "Don't Know", or (since Eurobarometer 90) "Spontaneous Refusal".

Measures for trust in the ECB are based on the following question: "Please tell me if you tend to trust or tend not to trust these European institutions. The European Central Bank". Respondents can then choose between "Tend to trust", "Tend not to trust" or "Don't Know".

Measures for trust in the national government are based on the following question: "I would like to ask you a question about how much trust you have in certain media and institutions. For each of the following media and institutions, please tell me if you tend to trust it or tend not to trust it. The National Government". Respondents can then choose between "Tend to trust", "Tend not to trust" or "Don't Know".

Net public support measures are constructed as the number of "For" responses minus "Against" responses, according to the expression: Net support = (For – Against)/ (For + Against + Don't Know). Net trust measures are constructed as the number of "Tend to trust" responses minus "Tend not to trust" responses, according to the expression: Net trust = (Trust – Tend not to trust)/(Trust + Tend not to trust + Don't Know).

5   Descriptive results

This section describes how support and trust have evolved since the start of the euro as a virtual currency in 1999. We focus first on the whole euro area, then move to individual euro area members and finally to the non-euro area members of the EU. In addition, we account for major differences in the pattern of support for the euro and of trust in the ECB following the crisis that started in 2008.

5.1   *Support and trust in the euro area*

Figure 8.1 plots public support for the euro and trust in the institution that carries out monetary policy in the euro area – the European Central Bank – and trust in

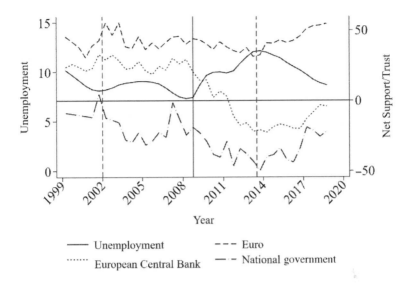

Figure 8.1 Unemployment and net support for the euro and net trust in the ECB and in the national government, average EA19, 1999–2018

Notes: The left-hand y-axis plots unemployment ranging from 7.3% to 12.1%. The right-hand y-axis displays net support/trust in percentage. Since the figure depicts net support/trust, all values above 0 indicate that a majority of the respondents support the euro and trust the ECB. The dashed lines distinguish the physical introduction of the euro in January 2002, the start of the financial crisis in September 2008 and the start of the recovery at the end of 2013. The averages for EA19 are weighted by population.

Source: Standard Eurobarometer data 51–90.

the national governments across the 19 member countries in the euro area as well as the unemployment rate in the euro area. We can draw four central findings from the patterns shown.

First, we see that a large majority supported the euro (>30%) during the first two decades of its existence. Second, whereas a large majority trusted the ECB before the 2008 crisis, only a minority of citizens expressed trust in their national government. Third, while the large majority of support for the euro was only slightly dented by the sharp increase in unemployment during the crisis years of 2008–2013, trust in the ECB and in national governments was strongly negatively affected by the crisis, with the ECB losing the trust of a majority of citizens surveyed and the national governments entering the territory of large mistrust (<−50).

Fourth and finally, the recent recovery in the EA has led to a clear rise in support for the euro from 11/2013 onwards, reaching the average value of 55% in 11/2018, and thus nearly reaching the peak value of 56% from 3–5/2003. The economic recovery also led to a recovery in trust in the national government to a level higher than in the pre-crisis period and a recovery of trust in the ECB. The latter has nearly re-established a majority level of trust, but one not high enough to make up for the decline during the crisis (see Table 8.A1 in this chapter's Appendix).

5.2   *Support and trust among individual euro countries*

Let us now turn to the data for each member state. What do we learn from the disaggregated pattern? Figure 8.2 displays the pattern in each member state of the EA19, split into an EA12 country sample in Figure 8.2a and the EA7 countries in Figure 8.2b, which joined the EA after 2001. (For a figure showing all 19 individual members, including the unemployment rate, see Figure 8.A1 in this chapter's Appendix.)

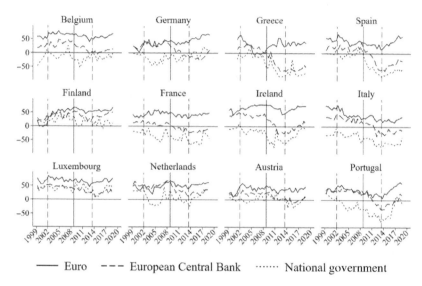

Figure 8.2a Net support for the euro and net trust in the ECB and in the national government, EA12, 1999–2018

Source: Standard Eurobarometer data 51–90.

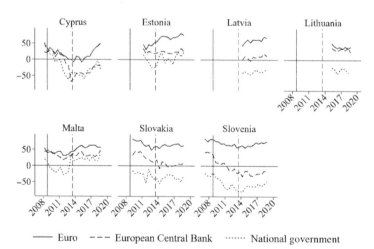

Figure 8.2b Net support for the euro and net trust in the ECB and in the national government, EA7, 1999–2018

Source: Standard Eurobarometer data 51–90.

We identify three striking results. First, with the exception of Greece and Finland in the pre-crisis time and Cyprus in the time of crisis, a majority support for the euro has always existed in each individual EA economy. Second, while there is only a slight decline in support for the euro during the crisis, we detect pronounced losses in trust in the ECB and national governments, in particular in the periphery countries of the EA, i.e. in Spain, Greece, Ireland, Portugal and Cyprus (see also Table 8.A1 in this chapter's Appendix). Third and finally, during the recovery, a pronounced increase of public support for the euro is apparent in almost all countries. A strong recovery in trust in the ECB as well as in the national government is also registered in some periphery countries. The loss in trust has been more than restored in two countries, namely Portugal and Ireland, but this has not happened in Spain and Greece.

5.3 Support and trust outside the euro area

How did public support for the euro and trust in the European Central Bank and the national government evolve outside the euro area? Figure 8.3 reveals four noteworthy patterns.

First, public support for the euro is substantially lower outside the EA than inside, particularly in the UK, Sweden, the Czech Republic and Denmark. Noteworthy is the case of Denmark which de facto has tied its currency to the euro since the start of the common currency. Second, support for the euro declined in a pronounced manner following the euro crisis in all non-euro member states. Third, we detect a recovery in support since November 2013, in particular in the UK. The euro

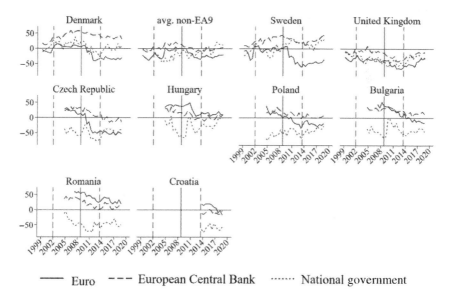

Figure 8.3 Net support for the euro and net trust in the ECB and in the national government, outside the euro area, 1999–2018

Source: Standard Eurobarometer data 51–90.

currently enjoys a fairly high level of support – compared to its time series pattern – although it is still negative. Fourth, in the three older EU member states, Sweden, Denmark and the United Kingdom, trust in the ECB and in the national government is higher than support for the euro. In the new member states, trust in the national government is significantly lower than trust in the ECB and support for the euro.

6   Econometric results

We now turn to some econometric evidence. To analyse the channels that influence public support for the euro and trust in its governance, we adopt a model specification used by Roth et al. (2016, 2019). We estimate support for the euro and trust in the ECB as a function of unemployment, inflation, growth in real GDP per capita and control variables deemed of potential importance in explaining the *within* variation of support. Our baseline model (1) reads:

$$Support/Trust_{it} = \alpha_i + \beta_1 Unemployment_{it} + \chi_1 Inflation_{it} + \delta_1 Growth_{it} + \phi_1 Z_{it} + w_{it}, \quad (1)$$

where $Support/Trust_{it}$ is the net support for the euro and net trust in the ECB for country i during period t. $Unemployment_{it}$, $Inflation_{it}$, $Growth_{it}$ and Z_{it} are respectively unemployment, inflation, growth of GDP per capita and control variables deemed of potential importance lumped together in Z,[1,2] α_i represents a country-specific constant term (fixed effect) and w_{it} is the error term.

We estimate Equation 1 by means of DOLS (dynamic ordinary least squares),[3] a method that permits full control for endogeneity of the regressors. In order to correct for autocorrelation,[4] we apply a FGLS (Feasible General Least Squares) procedure.[5] Both applications lead to the following Equation 2, representing our FE-DFGLS (Fixed Effect Dynamic Feasible General Least Squares) approach – for a detailed explanation of the FE-DFGLS approach, see Roth et al. (2016, 2019):

$$Support_{it}^* = \alpha_i + \beta_1 Unemployment_{it}^* + \chi_1 Inflation_{it}^* + \delta_1 Growth_{it}^* + \phi_1 Z_{it}^*$$
$$+ \sum_{p=-1}^{p=+1} \beta_{2p} \Delta Unemployment_{it-p}^* + \sum_{p=-1}^{p=+1} \chi_{2p} \Delta Inflation_{it-p}^* \quad (2)$$
$$+ \sum_{p=-1}^{p=+1} \delta_{2p} \Delta Growth_{it-p}^* + \sum_{p=-1}^{p=+1} \phi_{2p} \Delta Z_{it-p}^* + u_{it}$$

with α_i being the country fixed effect and Δ indicating that the variables are in first differences. Applying DFGLS, Unemployment, Inflation and Growth turn exogenous and the coefficients β_1, χ_1, δ_1 and ϕ_1 follow a t-distribution. This property permits us to derive statistical inferences on the causal impact of unemployment, inflation and growth. The asterisk (*) indicates that the variables have been transformed and that the error term u_{it} fulfils the requirements of the classical linear regression model.

Table 8.1 shows the econometric results for Equation 2 within our EA19 country sample. Analysing the full period from 3–4/1999 to 11/2018, we detect unemployment to be a significant factor behind public support for the euro, trust in the ECB and trust in the national government (regressions 1, 4 and 7 in Table 8.1).

Table 8.1 Unemployment, inflation, GDP per capita growth and net support for the euro and net trust for the ECB and national government, FE-DFGLS estimation, EA19, 1999–2018

Regression	(1)	(2)	(3)	(4)	(5)	(6)	(7)	(8)	(9)
Dependent variable	euro	euro	euro	ECB	ECB	ECB	NG	NG	NG
Period	FS	BC	CR-RE	FS	BC	CR-RE	FS	BC	CR-RE
Unemployment	-1.3***	-1.7	-2.1***	-4.2***	1.1	-3.4***	-4.6***	-3.1*	-3.7***
	(0.41)	(2.13)	(0.41)	(0.54)	(0.88)	(0.61)	(0.41)	(1.80)	(0.59)
Inflation	-4.9***	-14.9***	-4.8***	0.3	-2.0	-1.4	-0.1	1.2	-0.6
	(1.71)	(5.75)	(1.47)	(1.90)	(3.59)	(1.91)	(2.28)	(7.25)	(2.50)
GDP per capita growth	-0.5	-2.1	0.0	1.2	0.1	0.7	1.2	7.7**	0.2
	(0.78)	(2.33)	(0.71)	(0.84)	(1.58)	(0.89)	(1.10)	(3.49)	(1.24)
Durbin-Watson statistic	2.23	2.49	2.12	2.46	2.14	2.36	2.09	1.96	2.13
Adjusted R-squared	0.81	0.79	0.85	0.90	0.72	0.91	0.84	0.78	0.85
Country fixed effects	Yes	Yes	Yes	Yes	Yes	Yes	Yes	Yes	Yes
Control for endogeneity	Yes	Yes	Yes	Yes	Yes	Yes	Yes	Yes	Yes
El. of first-order autocorr.	Yes	Yes	Yes	Yes	Yes	Yes	Yes	Yes	Yes
Observations	548	218	330	548	218	330	479	149	330
Number of countries	19†	19	19†	19†	19	19†	19†	19	19†

Notes: ECB = European Central Bank. NG =National Government. FS = Full Sample. BC = Before Crisis. CR-RE = Crisis-Recovery. † = econometric results remain robust when analysing an EA15 country sample. ***p < 0.01. **p < 0.05. *p < 0.1.

Source: Standard Eurobarometer Data 51–90.

A 1-percentage-point increase in unemployment is associated with a decline in net support by 1.3 percentage points. The effect is threefold in trust in the ECB and in national governments, with an estimated coefficient of −4.2 and −4.6, respectively.

Analysing the pre-crisis sample (regressions 2, 5 and 8 in Table 8.1), we find unemployment to be insignificantly related to public support for the euro and to trust in the ECB and only slightly significantly related to trust in the national government. However, we find a highly significant and strong effect of inflation on public support for the euro (−14.9). Studying periods of crisis and recovery (regressions 3, 6 and 9 in Table 8.1), it is clear that the negative unemployment coefficient from the full sample is driven by the crisis-recovery period. We detect a highly significant and negative coefficient between unemployment and net support for the euro (−2.1) and net trust in the ECB and the national government (−3.4 and respectively −3.7) during the crisis.

To untangle the effects of the crisis-recovery, Table 8.2 splits the crisis-recovery period into a crisis phase 2008–2013 and a recovery phase 2013–2018. When analysing the crisis period 2008–2013 (regressions 2, 5 and 8 in Table 8.2), we find that whereas the unemployment increase in times of crisis slightly dented public support for the euro (−0.8), it had a six-fold impact on trust in the ECB (−5.3) and a four-fold impact on trust in the national government (−3.5).

In analysing the recovery period (regressions 3, 6 and 9 in Table 8.2), we detect a four times larger coefficient for public support for the euro (−3.6) compared to the crisis period, which indicates a rising effect during the recovery in which a 1-percentage point of decline in unemployment leads to an increase of 3.6 percentage points of public support. The unemployment decline during the recovery more than fully makes up for the decline during the crisis. The same pattern holds for trust in national governments. The compensation effect (−4.1) during recovery is larger than the losses during the crisis (−3.5). Only in our analysis of trust in the ECB did we find a different pattern. The pronounced loss in trust during the crisis due to the sharp rise in unemployment (−5.3) has only partially been restored during the recovery (−2.2).

To sum up the econometric work, the rate of unemployment emerges as a key factor determining support for the euro and trust in the ECB and in national governments.

7 Explaining the divergence in support for the euro and trust in the ECB

Our descriptive and econometric findings highlight an intriguing difference in EA citizens' public support for the euro and their trust in the ECB. Before the crisis, the two sets of time series were stable and strongly correlated at a relatively high level (see Figure 8.1). This pattern changed during the crisis (2008–2013), which brought about a sharp fall in trust in the ECB, while support for the euro declined only slightly. During the recovery (2013–2018), when unemployment started to decline, support for the euro began to rise. Although the same holds for trust in the

Table 8.2 Unemployment, inflation, GDP per capita growth and net support for the euro and net trust for the ECB and national government, FE-DFGLS estimation, EA19, 2008–2018

Regression	(1)	(2)	(3)	(4)	(5)	(6)	(7)	(8)	(9)
Dependent variable	euro	euro	euro	ECB	ECB*	ECB	NG	NG†	NG
Period	CR-RE	CR	RE	CR-RE	CR	RE	CR-RE	CR	RE
Unemployment	-2.1***	-0.8**	-3.6***	-3.4***	-5.3***	-2.2***	-3.7***	-3.5***	-4.1***
	(0.41)	(0.38)	(0.60)	(0.61)	(0.72)	(0.68)	(0.59)	(0.67)	(1.48)
Inflation	-4.8***	-11.2***	-0.6	-1.4	-10.8***	1.5	-0.6	-10.2**	3.6
	(1.47)	(2.58)	(2.06)	(1.91)	(3.85)	(2.33)	(2.50)	(4.74)	(4.99)
GDP per capita growth	0.0	-1.6	0.0	0.7	0.7	0.1	0.2	0.7	-1.0
	(0.71)	(1.07)	(0.97)	(0.89)	(1.44)	(1.11)	(1.24)	(2.00)	(2.28)
Durbin-Watson statistic	2.12	2.14	2.03	2.36	2.11	2.11	2.13	2.27	2.19
Adjusted R-Squared	0.85	0.85	0.90	0.91	0.88	0.94	0.85	0.84	0.87
Country fixed effects	Yes	Yes	Yes	Yes	Yes	Yes	Yes	Yes	Yes
Control for endogeneity	Yes	Yes	Yes	Yes	Yes	Yes	Yes	Yes	Yes
El. of first-order autocorr.	Yes	Yes	Yes	Yes	Yes	Yes	Yes	Yes	Yes
Observations	330	164	166	330	164	166	330	164	166
Number of countries	19†	19	19†	19†	19	19†	19†	19	19†

Notes: † = Inflation coefficient lacks robustness. Excluding the two sets of time periods (EB 70 and 71) in the direct aftermath of the financial crisis renders insignificant coefficients if tested in sensitivity analysis. ECB = European Central Bank. NG = National Government. CR-RE = Crisis-Recovery. CR = Crisis. RE = Recovery. † = econometric results remain robust when analysing an EA15 country sample. ***p < 0.01. **p < 0.05.

Source: Standard Eurobarometer data 69–90.

ECB, the recovery was far more modest. In 2018, the gap between the two series remains much larger than during the pre-crisis period.

How can we explain this difference over time? We suggest that the public makes a distinction between the role of the euro as the currency per se and the role of the ECB as the central bank that supplies the currency and frames monetary policy.

When asked about the euro, the public most likely considers how well the euro performs the standard micro-functions of money, traditionally expressed as that of a medium of exchange, a store of value and a unit of account. The euro has served the public well on all three accounts, particularly as a source of stable purchasing power. Inflation in the euro area has been low and fairly constant since the introduction of the euro, in sharp contrast with the inflationary past of several euro-area members.

This stability is a likely factor behind the support for the euro as a currency even during the crisis years of 2008–2013. Indeed, this line of reasoning is confirmed by our econometric findings, which depict a strong significant negative relationship between inflation and public support for the euro during the crisis period.

When asked about trust in the ECB, the respondents turn their attention from the micro-issues related to the euro as the money they use in daily business and commerce to the macro-problems related to monetary policy, interest rates, unemployment and crisis management. Most likely, they hold the ECB responsible for the state of the macroeconomy, or at least with shared responsibility with other actors such as national governments, as reflected in the decline in trust in the ECB in parallel with the fall in trust in national governments during the euro crisis. During this crisis, the ECB is associated with the flow of negative macroeconomic news, such as the crisis management by countries like Greece, as a member of the troika, and the rise in unemployment due to the austerity programs launched in several euro-countries in response to the crisis.

In addition, the crisis provoked strong criticism of the ECB, which was not present during the first decade of the euro, when its launch was commonly regarded as a success. And again, our interpretation is confirmed by our econometric findings, which depict a six-fold stronger negative impact from unemployment on trust in the ECB compared to public support for the euro during the crisis period.

In short, the ECB is judged as a policymaker, whereas the euro, as a currency, is regarded as falling outside the immediate policy sphere. When its policies are viewed as being insufficient, as reflected in failing outcomes and rising unemployment, public trust in the ECB declines. When the economy of the euro area starts to improve, trust in the ECB is eventually restored.

Still, the euro-crisis has left a scar on the trust invested in the ECB. The level of trust has not recovered to the level it obtained before the crisis. The gap between support for the euro and trust in the ECB suggests that it will take a long time for trust in the ECB to reach pre-crisis levels.

8 Why is popular support of the euro so important? Two recent cases

We have argued that popular support of the common currency is crucial for its sustainability. Here we illustrate this argument by discussing two recent cases.

First, we suggest that the case of Italy in 2018 demonstrates how public support for the euro is crucial for the long-term survival of the common currency, in particular if there is a loss of trust in the ECB and in the national government. After more than a decade of economic distress, higher than EA-average unemployment and lower than EA-average trust in the national government, a coalition government of major populist parties was formed in May 2018. The new coalition government intended to nominate a finance minister known to be critical of the euro. Such a nomination would have damaged cooperation among EU policymakers. The Italian president ultimately prevented the nomination.

The most likely explanation for his action is found in the fact that a majority of Italian citizens has supported the euro for over three decades, since the first plans of monetary unification were floated in 1990. Similarly, a referendum on the euro, initially considered by the populist government, was not held due to the popularity of the common currency.

In short, attempts by the Italian populist coalition government to dismantle EA cooperation was effectively countered by the popularity of the euro, serving in this way as a shield against populism. Most likely, this effect will persist in the near to medium future as well. In our opinion, a similar story has played out in France. The populist party of Marie Le Pen has dropped or at least moderated its criticism of the euro.

Second, the decision by the ECB to become the lender of last resort in the government bond market of the EA in 2012 was facilitated by the popularity of the euro. It took the ECB four years after the start of the crisis in 2008 to assume this role, but the announcement by the president of the ECB in July 2012 to "do whatever it takes" swiftly resolved the sovereign debt crisis in the EA. The quantitative easing (QE) programme implemented from 2015 to 2018 also contributed to the EA's recovery from the euro crisis. Given the loss of majority trust in the ECB during the crisis, we speculate that the large public support for the euro granted the ECB political legitimacy to secure its independence against growing criticism of its actions.

9 Conclusions

In our analysis of Eurobarometer data for the first two decades of the euro's existence, from 1999 to 2018, we find that a majority of respondents has supported the euro in each member country of the euro area. Although the crisis in the EA led to a slight decline in public support, the recovery since 2013 has triggered an upturn in support. As the euro turns 20, the currency enjoys historically high levels of support among the citizens of the EA. We detect a similar, although less pronounced, rise in trust in the ECB.

Looking ahead, we argue that the present esteem with which the euro is held by a persistent majority of citizens makes it equipped to weather the challenges it will surely face in its third decade. Our results suggest that keeping unemployment and inflation at bay, particularly the former, will be important for sustaining public support for the common currency and public trust in the ECB. Ultimately, euro-area citizens assess the euro and the ECB on the basis of their economies' performance. This makes policymakers in the member states responsible for designing measures that succeed in enhancing growth and employment, and thereby fostering support for the common currency and trust in the ECB.

Acknowledgements

We gratefully acknowledge constructive comments received from participants at the conference "The Economics of Monetary Unions: Past Experience and the Eurozone" at the University Buckingham, and from Fredrik N.G. Andersson, David Laidler, Felicitas Nowak-Lehmann, Thomas Straubhaar and Joakim Westerlund.

Notes

1 The components of Z could potentially be macroeconomic or socio-political control variables. However, given the cointegrating relationship between support for the euro and our macroeconomic variables (see Tables 8.A3 and 8.A4 in this chapter's Appendix), we can be confident that these Z variables do not cause bias in the coefficients of unemployment, inflation and growth.
2 Data on inflation (the change in the harmonized index of consumer prices), seasonally adjusted unemployment rates, as well as seasonally and calendar adjusted data on GDP per capita are taken from Eurostat. A summary of the data utilized can be found in Table 8.A2. The matching methodology between our macroeconomic variables and public support for the euro and trust in the ECB follows the approach of Roth et al. (2016, 2019).
3 A prerequisite for using DOLS is that the variables entering the model are non-stationary and that all the series are in a long-run relationship (cointegrated). In our case, all series are integrated of order 1, i.e. they are I(1) (and thus non-stationary); non-stationarity of inflation and growth of GDP per capita is due to non-stationarity (non-constancy) of the variance of these series and they are cointegrated. The panel unit root tests and Kao's residual cointegration test are displayed in Tables 8.A3 and 8.A4 in this chapter's Appendix.
4 We found first-order autocorrelation to be present.
5 FGLS (in the ready-to-use EViews commands) is not compatible with time-fixed effects. It picks up shocks and omitted variables in the period of study. In addition, it has been found that running the regression with time-fixed effects (without applying FGLS) does not tackle the problem of autocorrelation of the error term.

References

Baldwin, R.E. and Wyplosz, C. (2019). *The Economics of European Integration* (London: McGraw-Hill).
Banducci, S.A., Karp, J.A. and Loedel, P.H. (2003). 'The Euro, Economic Interests and Multi-Level Governance: Examining Support for the Common Currency'. *European Journal of Political Research*, Vol. 42, No. 5, pp. 685–703.

Banducci, S.A., Karp, J.A. and Loedel, P.H. (2009). 'Economic Interests and Public Support for the Euro'. *Journal of European Public Policy*, Vol. 16, No. 4, pp. 564–581.

Bordo, M.D. and Jonung, L. (2000). *Lessons for EMU from the History of Monetary Unions*, with an introduction by Robert Mundell, IEA, Readings 50, London.

Bordo, M.D. and Jonung, L. (2003). 'The Future of EMU: What Does the History of Monetary Unions Tell Us?'. In Capie, F. and Woods, G. (eds.) *Monetary Unions, Theory, History, Public Choice* (London: Routledge), pp. 42–69.

Deroose, S., Hodson, D. and Kuhlmann, J. (2007). 'The Legitimation of EMU: Lessons from the Early Years of the Euro'. *Review of International Political Economy*, Vol. 14, No. 5, pp. 800–819.

European Commission (2018). 'Standard Eurobarometer Nos. 51–90'.

Frieden, J. and Walter, S. (2017). 'Understanding the Political Economy of the Eurozone Crisis'. *Annual Review of Political Science*, Vol. 20, pp. 371–390.

Guiso, L., Sapienza, P. and Zingales, L. (2016). 'Monnet's Error?'. *Economic Policy*, Vol. 31, No. 86, pp. 247–297.

Hobolt, S.B. and Leblond, P. (2014). 'Economic Insecurity and Public Support for the Euro: Before and During the Financial Crisis'. In Bermeo, N. and Bartels, L.M. (eds.) *Mass Politics in Tough Times* (Oxford: Oxford University Press), pp. 128–147.

Hobolt, S.B. and Wratil, C. (2015). 'Public Opinion and the Crisis: The Dynamics of Support for the Euro'. *Journal of European Public Policy*, Vol. 22, No. 2, pp. 238–256.

Kaltenthaler, K. and Anderson, C. (2001). 'Europeans and Their Money: Explaining Public Support for the Common European Currency'. *European Journal of Political Research*, Vol. 40, No. 2, pp. 139–170.

Mundell, R. (1961). 'A Theory of Optimum Currency Areas'. *American Economic Review*, Vol. 54, No. 4, pp. 657–665.

Roth, F. (2015). 'Political Economy of EMU: Rebuilding Systemic Trust in the Euro Area in Times of Crisis'. *DG ECFIN's European Economy Discussion Paper 16*.

Roth, F., Baake, E., Jonung, L. and Nowak-Lehmann, F. (2019). 'Revisiting Public Support for the Euro: Accounting for the Crisis and the Economic Recovery, 1999–2017'. *Journal of Common Market Studies*, Vol. 57, No. 6, pp. 1262–1273.

Roth, F., Jonung, L. and Nowak-Lehmann, F. (2016). 'Crisis and Public Support for the Euro, 1990–2014'. *Journal of Common Market Studies*, Vol. 54, No. 4, pp. 944–960.

Stiglitz, J.E. (2016). *The Euro* (London: Penguin Books).

Verdun, A. (2016). 'Economic and Monetary Union'. In Cini, M. and Borragan, N. (eds.) *European Union Politics* (Oxford: Oxford University Press), pp. 295–307.

Appendix

Table 8.A1 Changes in net support for the euro, EA19, 2018–2008, 2013–2008 and 2018–2013

Country	CR-RE	euro	ECB	NG	CR	euro	ECB	NG	RE	euro	ECB	NG
Austria	18–08	8	−8	20	13–08	−3	−17	11	18–13	11	9	9
Belgium	18–08	2	−29	22	13–08	−15	−38	14	18–13	17	9	8
Cyprus	18–08	28	−69	−82	13–08	−22	−120	−92	18–13	50	51	10
Germany	18–08	25	−25	37	13–08	−4	−44	19	18–13	29	19	18
EA19	18–08	15	−33	3	13–08	−8	−50	−25	18–13	23	17	28
Estonia	18–08	−	−	−	13–08	−	−	−	18–13	25	8	47
Greece	18–08	35	−51	−39	13–08	22	−63	−50	18–13	13	12	11
Spain	18–08	20	−67	−77	13–08	−26	−100	−103	18–13	46	33	26
Finland	18–08	7	2	−7	13–08	−8	−30	−7	18–13	15	32	0
France	18–08	3	−28	−5	13–08	−16	−32	−11	18–13	19	4	6
Ireland	18–08	−4	−37	2	13–08	−32	−72	−46	18–13	28	35	47
Italy	18–08	9	−34	21	13–08	2	−48	−12	18–13	7	14	33
Lithuania	18–08	−	−	−	13–08	−	−	−	18–13	−	−	−
Luxembourg	18–08	10	−20	18	13–08	−10	−19	5	18–13	20	−1	13
Latvia	18–08	−	−	−	13–08	−	−	−	18–13	−	−	−
Malta	18–08	4	5	18	13–08	−10	−9	14	18–13	14	14	4
Netherlands	18–08	0	−35	29	13–08	−23	−56	−11	18–13	23	21	40
Portugal	18–08	40	−20	19	13–08	−5	−70	−49	18–13	45	50	68
Slovenia	18–08	−7	−58	−17	13–08	−26	−64	−45	18–13	19	6	28
Slovakia	18–08	−	−	−	13–08	−	−	−	18–13	4	−3	11

Notes: CR-RE = Crisis-Recovery. CR = Crisis. RE = Recovery. EA = Euro Area.

Sources: EB69–EB90.

Table 8.A2 Summary statistics for the macro analysis, EA19 countries, 1999–2018

Variable	N	Mean	Std. dev.	Min.	Max.
Net support for the euro	578	47	18.7	−9	85
Net trust in the European Central Bank	578	14.3	27.1	−69	70
Net trust in the national government	533	−17.4	32.4	−85	61
Unemployment rate	578	8.8	4.5	1.9	27.7
Inflation	578	0.8	1.0	−3.7	5.2
GDP per capita growth	578	0.7	1.8	−7.4	17.0

Notes: N = Number of observations. Std. dev. = Standard deviation. Min. = Minimum. Max. = Maximum.

Sources: EB51–EB90 and Eurostat.

Table 8.A3 Pesaran's CADF panel unit root tests, EA19 countries

Variable	Observations	CADF-Zt-bar	Probability
Net support for the euro	562	2.05	0.98
Net trust in the ECB	562	−1.06	0.15
Net trust in the national government	517	−0.18	0.43
Unemployment	562	2.72	0.99
Inflation	562	0.77	0.78
GDP per capita growth	562	0.62	0.73

Notes: H_0: series has a unit root (individual unit root process). H_a: at least one panel is stationary. Table 8.A3 shows that all series have a unit root. A time trend and two lagged differences were utilised. Three lagged differences were utilised for Inflation, GDP per capita growth and Net trust in the ECB. Latvia and Lithuania were not included due to the brevity of their time series.

Table 8.A4 Kao's residual cointegration test, EA19 countries

Cointegration between the following set of variables	Number of included observations	ADF-t-statistic	Probability
Net support for the euro, unemployment, inflation, GDP per capita growth	579	−1.8	0.034
Net trust in the ECB, unemployment, inflation, GDP per capita growth	579	−1.3	0.090
Net trust in the national government, unemployment, inflation, GDP per capita growth	579	−1.7	0.041

Notes: H_0: no cointegration. Table 8.A4 shows that the series are cointegrated and thus stand in a long-run relationship.

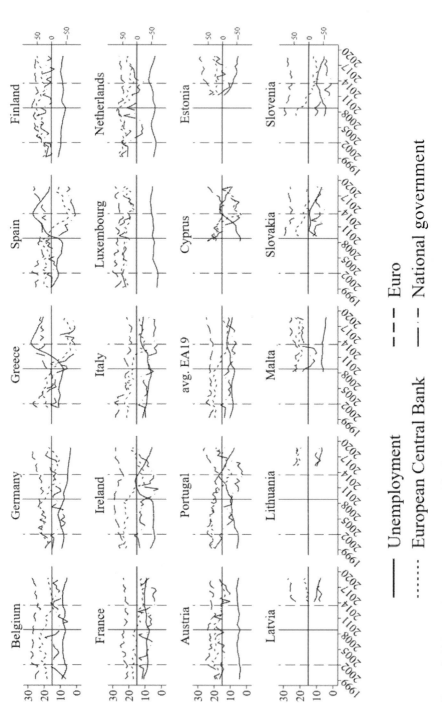

Figure 8.A1 Unemployment and net support for the euro and net trust in the ECB and in the national government, EA19, 1999–2018

Sources: EB51–EB90 and Eurostat.

9 Debt restructuring for the eurozone

Dimitrios P. Tsomocos and Xuan Wang

1 Introduction

The eurozone Debt Crisis has rekindled the debate on the nexus between currency areas and fiscal sovereigns. Goodhart (1997, 1998) presents a wide range of historical evidence on the intertwining relationship between the monetary arm and the fiscal arm of the government. That is, very rarely were fiscal sovereigns and monetary authorities majorly decoupled. Shedding light on the creation of euro, Goodhart (1998) argues that the creation of common currency in Europe begs the question of what would constitute the common fiscal entity. In a similar spirit, but perhaps with a much more pessimistic tone, Friedman (1997) feared that the creation of a common currency in Europe would eventually lead to political disunity, the very situation that those creating the euro wishfully designed to avoid.

Perhaps, the euro crisis vindicated these author's arguments and concerns. After the crisis, much of the intellectual and political debate has been on the benefit of a fiscal union, the idea of creating a common fiscal entity that is well equipped to make state-contingent cross-country transfers within the eurozone. For example, in Farhi and Werning (2017), the authors build a small open economy model of a currency union, and they show even if financial markets within the currency union are highly sophisticated (i.e. markets are complete), with nominal rigidities present, privately optimal risk sharing fails to obtain in equilibrium. Therefore, a role naturally emerges for a fiscal union to implement constrained efficient state-contingent tax transfers within a currency union. In our view, the design of the series of state-contingent tax transfers at the core points to the creation of a union-wide safe assets, the design and implementation of which are more nuanced.

Although the role of a benevolent fiscal union can in theory be welfare-improving for a currency union, even if we suppose a fiscal union could turn out benevolent in reality, it is understood that this is a highly politically constrained option, particularly in the eurozone. The presence of fiscal union is partially based on the US or China model. In the US, different states share the same US dollar, but a federal government is in place to make transfers across states if need be. Similarly, in China, different provinces differ in economic fundamentals, and labour is arguably much less mobile than that in the US or Europe, but the Chinese central government is in the position capable of making fiscal transfers across provinces.

These institutional arrangements are difficult to implement in the eurozone, for political, cultural and historical reasons. Given this constraint, in this chapter, we take the implausibility of fiscal union as given, and argue that debt restructuring can be a substitute to a fiscal union, leading to welfare improvement. In contrast to a fiscal union that resorts to the government's *visible* hand to move nominal resources across countries, the debt restructuring plan designs the bankruptcy rules, but it allows the *invisible* hand of the markets to make the choice based on context-dependent incentives (see Wang 2019).

There is an emerging body of literature that investigates debt restructuring in the context of currency union (see Adam and Grill 2017; Goodhart et al. 2018; Wang 2019). Much of the insight in this chapter originates from Goodhart et al. (2018) and Wang (2019). Conventionally, the debate on the costs and benefits of default and debt restructuring has primarily focused on the debtor, and the effects on the creditors have been largely ignored or assumed to be negative. However, in Goodhart et al. (2018), the authors build a structural model of Greece and Germany and show that debt restructuring for Greece can actually benefit both the debtor (Greece) and the creditor (Germany), given a hard government budget constraint. This is because debt forgiveness lowers the volatility of both German and Greek consumption whereas demanding higher recovery rates has the opposite effect. Under certain conditions, the authors demonstrate that the short-term loss of Germany being more forgiving on Greek debt restructuring would be matched by long-term higher returns from their remaining investments in Greece. This leads to an overall lower volatility of German consumption and welfare improves.

In a similar spirit, Wang (2019) provides a specific rationale why debt restructuring is particular vital in a currency union. Wang (2019) develops a two-country international finance model with uncertainty in a currency union. In this paper, four regimes are considered: (1) a currency union with no fiscal union and a harsh union-wide bankruptcy code; (2) a currency union with a fiscal union and a harsh union-wide bankruptcy code; (3) a currency union with no fiscal union and with a lenient union-wide bankruptcy code, i.e. lenient cross-border debt restructuring terms; and (4) national currencies with no fiscal union and a harsh international bankruptcy code. The model shows the allocation efficiency, risk sharing and asset price dynamics in these four regimes and suggests that debt restructuring (Regime 3) can *mostly* substitute fiscal union (Regime 2) and is welfare-improving *particularly* in a currency union. To clearly illustrate the point that cross-country debt restructuring can compensate for the loss of credible floating exchange rate, the author abstracts away from moral hazard issues from national governments, such that the need for debt restructuring purely stems from the loss of credible floating exchange rate. In the following sections, we shall discuss the conceptual framework, intuition and rationale in more detail.

In Section 2, we review the theoretical argument for the benefit of default; section 3 provides the conceptual framework of international finance with money and default that can be easily extended to analyse currency union issues. Using this conceptual framework, in section 4 we discuss why debt restructuring is particularly important in a currency union. In section 5, we explain how to design bankruptcy codes such that debt restructuring improves resource allocation and risk sharing in a currency union. Section 6 concludes.

2   The role of default for welfare improvement

Policy arena tends to associate default or debt restructuring with disequilibria and mis-allocation, and equally, academic literature traditionally tends to emphasise the *ex post* cost of default and the inefficiency associated with debt restructuring. However, this does not mean the welfare property of default and debt restructuring is not worth studying, nor does it mean default and debt restructuring are inconsistent with the orderly function of markets. As a matter of fact, in "Default and Punishment in General Equilibrium" by Dubey et al. (2005), the authors prove in general equilibrium with incomplete markets, that under very general conditions, refined equilibrium with default always exists in the model, and under some conditions, default can be welfare-improving, despite its social cost.

The idea that default or debt restructuring could be welfare enhancing despite its social cost may seem surprising, but the mechanism is well understood in the general equilibrium literature with incomplete markets. In Dubey et al. (2005), the authors illustrate with an example that features incomplete markets, and they show the tolerance for intermediate default leads to Pareto improvement. This is because default is a choice variable and with an intermediate penalty, it endogenises the asset payoffs. With incomplete markets, default increases the asset span and obtains greater risk sharing. In a similar spirit, Adam and Grill (2017) applies this insight to sovereign default in a currency union. The authors show that with idiosyncratic domestic production risk and non-contingent government debt, it is *ex ante* optimal to occasionally deviate from the legal repayment and default partially. Moreover, a careful quantitative analysis is conducted in this paper, suggesting the Greek debt restructuring in 2012 was not sufficient.

However, given the "diabolic" loop between the government debt and private debt (Brunnermeier et al. 2016) and the sophistication of financial markets to hedge risks, the assumption of non-contingent debt seems strong. In particular, as Kehoe and Pastorino (2017) suggest, if financial markets are complete, it is not clear why optimal risk sharing would not be attainable in a currency union. We argue even if the international financial markets in a currency union are highly sophisticated, i.e. a complete set of financial securities are available for trade vis-à-vis the number of states of uncertainty, optimal risk sharing does not obtain in a currency union in the presence of credit risks. Section 3 sets out the framework for understanding the underlying rational, and the theoretical proof can be found in Wang (2019) by relating endogenous credit risks with (the loss of) floating exchange rate.

3   International finance with money and liquidity

To appreciate why debt restructuring is particularly vital in a currency union, one needs to understand the issuing process of fiat money and the exact relationship between money and credit. Although the benefit of entering the currency union (e.g. reducing transaction cost, removing exchange rate risks, controlling inflation) is well understood, the cost of joining the union seems downplayed. In this section, we start by looking at the relationship between money and credit, then detail the process of fiat money issuance via the banking sector, and then provide the theoretical argument for the nexus between currency areas and fiscal sovereigns. By understanding the nature of fiat money, we should be able to trace the root of the problem and see how the removal of a credible exchange rate can transfer credit risks into the banking sector at the national level.

3.1   Money, credit and banking

Modern monetary and banking systems operate via fiat money. Fiat money, different from commodity money, is a special type of credit and does not serve direct utility values. Its supply, rather than being fixed or exogenous as in the commodity money case, can be elastic depending on the monetary policy rate and financial conditions. In practice, when a borrower applies for loans from a commercial bank, this commercial bank credits deposits to the borrower's bank account simultaneously. When deposits are withdrawn or moved across banks, then commercial banks swap safe assets with central bank reserves subject to a transaction cost, i.e. policy rate. The central bank acts as a settlement bank connecting all the private commercial banks, extending liquidity in its currency as the ultimate issuer of fiat money (see McLeay et al./Bank of England 2014). This operational fact was extensively written about by early economists when the banking sector just started booming (see Macleod 1866; Wicksell 1906; Hahn 1920; Hawtrey 1919; Schumpeter 1934, 1954; Keynes 1931). What lies at the heart of this operation, i.e. fiat money issued against bank credit, is the IOU nature of money.

However, it is understood that many recent micro-founded monetary models abstract money completely away from banking and credit and that these models tend to have very limited scope to provide insight on the nominal forces and their impact on the real economy and debt crisis (see discussions in Tsomocos 2003; Piazzesi and Schneider 2018; Goodhart, Tsomocos and Wang 2019). Thus, to meaningfully model and provide the scope for policy in the context of the eurozone Debt Crisis, we purposefully resort to the general equilibrium theory of money that has rigorously incorporated the credit nature of money (see Grandmont and Younes 1972, 1973; Shubik and Wilson 1977; Shubik (1999); Dubey and Geanakoplos 2003a, 2003b, 2006; Drèze and Polemarchakis 2001; Tsomocos 2003). In this body of literature, money issued against an offsetting debt obligation whose repayment guarantees money's exit from the economic system is termed as *inside money*, and money clear of debt obligation is referred to as *outside money*. One insight from these works is that an important role for banks is to provide the value of fiat money (Dubey and Geanakoplos 1992). Extending this framework to an international finance model, both the value of fiat money and the exchange rate determination can be studied alongside banking. We view an international finance model that incorporates inside money and banking liquidity as a natural laboratory to study currency union debt sustainability and debt restructuring.

To the best of our knowledge, the seminal works that incorporates inside money and banking liquidity in an international finance framework are Geanakoplos and Tsomocos (2002), Tsomocos (2008) and Peiris and Tsomocos (2015), on which the currency union model in Wang (2019) is based. In section 3.2, we summarise the key ingredients and insights of this suite of models. Sensible modifications of these models can establish a tractable analytical framework suited to investigate eurozone debt restructuring (section 4).

3.2 Modelling framework

Key features

We synthesise the key features of Geanakoplos and Tsomocos (2002), Tsomocos (2008), Peiris and Tsomocos (2015) and Wang (2019). The summary is provided as follows.

•   Inside money issued against bank credit

   Fiat money is the stipulated means of exchange in this economy, and inside money is issued against an offsetting bank credit which carries credit risks. Money also serves as a store of value and flows across and through budget constraints. Agents need to use fiat money for transactions, asset payoffs and loan repayment.

•   Value of money, price of money, exchange rate, and interest rate

   Modelling inside and outside money in a general equilibrium with incomplete markets establishes equilibrium existence and achieves both real and nominal determinacy. In particular, without appealing to nominal rigidity, price-level determinacy allows us to relate inflation to borrowers' credibility and bankruptcy procedure. The following definitions relating to money are coherently and precisely depicted in the model: (1) value of money refers to the inverse of price level, i.e. how much is a unit of money worth in terms of real goods – it is the relative price between money and goods; (2) price of money is the relative price between money and money itself (by Walras' Law, it is one); (3) exchange rate is the relative price between one type of money and another type of money; and (4) interest rate is the relative price between bank credit and money.

•   Idiosyncratic and aggregate risks

   Both idiosyncratic income risks and aggregate endowment risks can be captured because the model is general enough to include multiple types of goods and uncertainty relating to multiple types of endowments. These fundamental risks can translate into credit risks when borrowers evaluate the state-dependent marginal benefit of default and the marginal cost of default.

- Incomplete risk sharing and nominal assets

  There are multiple nominal assets available to hedge the risks, but the assets do not need to fully span the states of uncertainty. In the case when the assets do not fully span, markets are incomplete, giving rise to a non-trivial role for policy to improve welfare. Particularly, assets payoffs are in terms of fiat money, rather than consumption goods or goods bundles, and the monetary payoff eventually flows back to the banking sector to (partially) extinguish the loans. This is not only important for evaluating the bankruptcy conditions of the banking sector, it is also key to appreciating the viability of a currency union. This is because asset payoffs are in terms of fiat money currencies, and the exchange rate or the removal of exchange rate between different currencies could alter asset span in the presence of credit risks, generating additional nominal and real effects.

- Inter-temporal decision for consumption smoothing

  The standard consumption smoothing can be carried out via money or nominal assets. The state prices or the Euler equation is thus affected by agent heterogeneity, liquidity premia and credit risk premia. The implication of financial intermediary, liquidity and default on asset pricing can be studied simultaneously.

- Endogenous default

  Strategic default is modelled a la Shubik and Wilson (1977) and Dubey et al. (2005). A default penalty parameter λ is assumed that can be interpreted as the harshness of the terms for debt restructuring. And the total cost of default is non-pecuniary and increases with the real value of the defaulted amount. Thus, the model produces the classic Fisherian debt deflation mechanism via money and default (Fisher 1933). In our view, this modelling approach is comprehensive enough to capture a wide range of default punishment that could go beyond direct market/credit exclusion and pecuniary costs. Indeed, as Wang (2019) argues, particularly in the case of currency union debt crisis, a harsh non-pecuniary default could result in austerity tax and internal devaluation. However, the cost of austerity tax and internal devaluation go beyond a direct pecuniary penalty because these costs are not a direct deadweight loss in the budget sets.

Basic economic environment

Geanakoplos and Tsomocos (2002), Tsomocos (2008), and Peiris and Tsomocos (2015) build a general framework for international finance models in which trade, monetary forces and financial frictions can be studied simultaneously. Here we describe a two-period general equilibrium with incomplete markets (GEI) augmented with money, liquidity and default to synthesise these three papers and to summarise the basic economic environment. There are multiple countries in this economy, and in each country, there are many households that can differ in their endowments and preferences. A variety of perishable goods are also modelled but they cannot be inventoried between periods. Each good is associated with a single country. Every good is assumed to be present in international trade, and no household has the null endowment of goods in any time period. In the second period, there are a finite number of states relating to households' endowment structure, and a set of nominal financial securities are available for trade in the first period for risk sharing.

Each country has a central bank to issue national currencies (inside money) against loans, and exchange rate can be determined via foreign exchange rate markets. Various frictions of the foreign exchange markets and exchange rate regimes (e.g. managed floating, currency board system, central bank sterilisation) can be incorporated to analyse their implications for economic allocation and asset prices. To model a currency union, Wang (2019) removes the foreign exchange markets and only models one central bank as the ultimate lender of last resort in the open economy. Moreover, borrowers in this economy are subject to default penalties, and choose asset deliveries and loan repayments.

3.3 Main insight

In this suite of models, we can prove equilibrium existence and determinacy (see the theorems in Geanakoplos and Tsomocos 2002; Tsomocos 2008). Price-level determinacy obtains due to seigniorage transfer and/or default. Given that exchange rate is the relative price between different currencies, exchange rate is also determined in this suite of models due to seigniorage transfer and/or default.

This is particularly important to our understanding of many modern monetary phenomena. To help pin down inflation determinacy in monetary and international finance modelling, we do not need sticky prices, a priori that exogenously decouples price stability from borrowing and default. However, a glimpse into a myriad of historical episodes of hyperinflation and currency crises can tell us that price stability and capital flight are sensitive to financial conditions, but not so much to exogenous inflexibility of adjusting goods prices and wages.

Another main result is the general non-neutrality of money and its implication for banking insolvency in a currency union. In this suite of models, the change of monetary policy alters inflation, default risks and real allocation, and the reason is purely financial. This is because monetary policy rate serves as a transaction cost that enters agents' financing decision as a marginal cost of financing. A rise in monetary policy rate increases borrowing cost and the marginal cost of financing, which can stifle trade and production, and lead to a contraction of endogenous money supply. The fall in price level increases the debt burden, hence, the marginal cost of default, causing further default and non-performing loans, which may result in banking insolvency. This has second round effect to the borrowing cost in the economy because the term structure of the interest rate includes default risk premia and is likely to further drive up the borrowing cost.

Following this line of logic, monetary policy is naturally tied to the liquidity condition or even the solvency condition of the domestic banking system. In a currency union, a union-wide monetary policy is constrained from fulfilling the liquidity demand of various national-level banks. Therefore, it does not seem all that surprising that some national banks inevitably run into solvency issues in the currency union.

4   Why debt restructuring is particularly vital in currency unions

So far, the theory suggests that seigniorage transfer and/or default achieves price-level determinacy, money has value, and that exchange rate is determined in equilibrium. In this section we argue, once a regime such as currency union fixes the exchange rate to one at all times, this nominal friction will eventually bite the domestic banking system. Without debt restructuring, national government needs to resort to austerity tax and interval devaluation to bail out banks, giving rise to a divergent growth pattern within the currency union.

4.1   Seigniorage, inflation and credibility

To illustrate our points precisely, we use Equations 1 and 2 that are different versions of the Quantity Theory of Money obtained from the previously mentioned suite of models. These equations could also help us understand the economic reason why some countries chose to join the eurozone in the first place. Although the precise form of the expressions can vary depending on the specific structural assumptions, the gist remains.

$$\sum_{\{h\in H\}}\sum_{\{l\in L\}} p_l q_l^h +\sum_{\{h\in H\}}\sum_{\{m\in S\}} \pi_m \theta_m^h = M +\sum_{\{h\in H\}} m^h \tag{1}$$

$$\sum_{\{h\in H\}}\sum_{\{l\in L\}} p_l q_l^h +\sum_{\{h\in H\}}\sum_{\{m\in S\}} \pi_m \theta_m^h = M +\sum_{\{h\in H\}} d^h \tag{2}$$

Equation 1 relates price-level determinacy and inflation dynamics to seigniorage transfer, which is the nexus with the fiscal sovereign. l indexes the type of perishable good that belongs to the set of all types of goods L, h indexes the household that belongs to the set of all households H and m indexes the financial asset that belongs to the set of all financial assets S. p denotes the price of goods, q denotes the quantity of goods trade, π denotes asset prices and θ denotes asset positions. Particularly, M is the aggregate amount of inside money issued against bank credit. In modern monetary and banking architecture, central banks do not set M but decide on the policy rate. In the model, given the policy rate, M is endogenously determined in equilibrium. m^h is any monetary endowment or outside money held by household h and can be infinitesimally small. Along with inside money, it is used to facilitate transactions. The total amount of ε flows through the budget constraints and contributes to interest payment, and it eventually becomes the government's seigniorage.

The key to establishing price-level determinacy is that the seigniorage collected by the government through interest rate payments are not reinjected to the economy in the same period. Thus, the government budget constraints need not be satisfied in very period and in this sense fiscal policy is non-Ricardian (Buiter 1999; Sims 1994). Indeed, as Goodhart (1997) argues, seigniorage can be considered as part of government's taxation plan, and as Shubik put it, it is the "institutionalised symbol of trust". In our view, seigniorage is the nexus between currency areas and fiscal sovereigns, supported by the empirical regularity that a well-functioning state has its own monetary power, despite the fact that the monetary authority and the fiscal authority are operationally separate. As Wang (2019) shows, part of the economic issue of a currency union is the split of seigniorage, as it is collected by a union-wide central bank, rather than by national central banks that could coordinate with their own national governments.

The difference between Equation 2 and Equation 1 is that Equation 2 replaces seigniorage with the aggregate default $\sum_{\{h \in H\}} d^h$. As Lin et al. (2016) prove, even without outside money, positive default in every state of the world on some long-term loan endogenously creates positive liquid wealth that supports positive interest rates and both nominal and real determinacy obtains. A non-Ricardian policy across loans markets allows the central bank to earn seigniorage to compensate for any losses. In other words, a credible and consistent bankruptcy procedure establishes the institutionalised symbol of trust of fiat money. The takeaway of this presentation of the Quantity Theory of Money is that price-level determinacy and inflation dynamics depend on aggregate default, and that a bankruptcy procedure that lacks consistency and credibility can lead to hyperinflation.

To see the intuition, suppose a country over borrows either publicly or privately but lacks a credible bankruptcy procedure that does not tolerate a hard default and enforce debt discipline. The only way the country could achieve that is through further borrowing. As we have discussed, fiat money is issued against credit, and if the credit does not offset, then money accumulates in the system and leads to hyperinflation. In this sense, inflation is also sometimes referred to as "soft default". This takeaway is especially relevant to the currency union, because one of the most powerful arguments for some countries to join the eurozone was to shield those countries from high inflation in their domestic economy.

4.2 *Exchange rates, credit risks and failing banks*

Nevertheless, history presents ample evidence that suggests entering a fixed exchange rate regime to tackle domestic inflation is merely delaying the issue and can cause severe currency crises. Similarly, we argue that using a currency union to shield countries from domestic inflation is also just a temporary solution and can lead to a severe "currency crisis", disguised as a debt crisis. An ancient Chinese idiom sums it up perfectly: it is better to teach fishing to someone than to give them fish. The cause of hyperinflation has deep institutional roots relating to bankruptcy and default penalty, solving hyperinflation would require implementing a consistent and credible bankruptcy procedure and enforcing debt discipline.

However, solving it simply by fixing the exchange rate or removing the domestic currency altogether seems all too "easy", and more often than not, brutal force has its consequences.

So, what are the consequences? Suppose a country has limited capability for debt enforcement and the government also does not wish to see prevalent hard default. Inflation is a natural way to smooth hard default and digest the credit risks, but inflation brings its own set of social cost. To avoid the social cost of inflation, this country joins a currency union. When a negative income shock hits, this country will see a reduction in both exports and imports; however, given the credit risks in its domestic loans, the tendency to reduce export would be larger than the tendency to reduce imports, because when the negative income shock hits, the marginal benefit of default increases due to higher marginal utility of consumption, and households end up defaulting more on the domestic loans. This implies that a negative income shock actually results in the country's current account deficit. In a hypothetical world of competitive floating exchange rate, the pressure of current account deficit would drive up the demand for foreign currency and lead to an expected depreciation of domestic currency, thus, the domestic debt burden decreases in the future such that there is enough liquidity going around to repay domestic bank loans eventually. The domestic banking system would have been fine. Now we are in the currency union world, the market-based currency depreciation is simply not an option, hence, domestic debt burden increases compared to the hypothetical case of floating exchange rate, leading to less liquidity to repay domestic loans. If the shock is big enough, a current account deficit can easily translate into a domestic banking crisis.

In short, both inflation and exchange rates are price mechanisms to digest credit risks and smooth out hard default, and once these prices are constrained, the credit risks simply show up somewhere else in the economic system. In the currency union case, the credit risks are in essence "transferred" to the national banks. If we could take the liberty to use an analogy, a currency union for some member countries is isomorphic to going back to the "gold" standard, the supply of which is inelastic to its domestic fundamentals. And when the economy needs to grow and capital needs to accumulate, a gold standard is expected to witness a chain of default and banking insolvency.

This narrative seems to fit well with the eurozone Debt Crisis. Mindful of the high social cost of banking insolvency, national governments in the periphery countries have resorted to bailing out domestic banks, but the sovereign instead take on the default stress. Given harsh bankruptcy terms for cross-country borrowing within the union, national governments are left with limited options except austerity measures and internal devaluation to pay back the debt.

In Wang (2019), this equilibrium is characterised in Regime (A), a currency union with no fiscal union and a harsh bankruptcy penalty for cross-border debt. In this Regime, the domestic banking system at the bad state runs into insolvency due to the loss of floating exchange rate in the presence of credit risks. And to avoid the high social cost of systemic bank failure, the national government levies tax to bailout the domestic banks. This bailout tax distorts the economic allocation, prices and asset prices, and is equivalent to austerity measures that give rise to internal devaluation. To see this, Wang (2019) derives the following propositions.

- The bailout tax distorts the Fisher effect and causes the "internal devaluation" effect.

  That is, the domestic nominal interest rate is approximately equal to the real interest rate plus inflation premium adjusted by the bailout tax rate. Given the nominal interest rate, the higher the bailout tax rate, the lower the inflation and the real interest rate. In this regime of a currency union, credit risks and the viability of the national banking systems push down union-wide inflation and real interest rate, generating the "internal devaluation" effect.

- The bailout tax distorts allocation efficiency within state and risk sharing between countries.

  In this regime, with an intolerance of cross-country debt restructuring, the marginal rate of substitutions of domestic and foreign goods between countries within the same state of nature do not equate, as they are distorted by the bailout tax. Moreover, the marginal rate of substitutions across states do not equate, as the bailout tax prevents optimal risk sharing.

- The bailout tax affects asset prices through affecting the stochastic discount factor.

  The implication of these analytical results is that the bailout tax generates fiscal austerity and internal devaluation for the periphery countries in the eurozone and could drive the divergence of growth and financial risk profiles within the currency union. Hence, it is vital to use debt restructuring as one approach to alleviate the domestic banking stress in the eurozone. In section 5, we argue for the use of debt restructuring to remove the need for fiscal austerity and internal devaluation, and the result is welfare enhancing via both prices and quantities.

5 Bankruptcy codes and credit risks in a currency union

As we have argued, creating a currency union in Europe to shield member countries from domestic inflation problems is not solving the inflation problem at its root, and can eventually lead to a currency union "currency crisis", disguised as a "debt crisis" with fiscal implications. In the absence of fiscal union, one way to address this currency-debt crisis is to use capital markets to shoulder part of the default cost and relieve the banking system from insolvency. As Wang (2019) shows, the tolerance of cross-country partial default and debt restructuring can achieve this aim. In this sense, we are arguing for the benefit of default, in a similar spirit to Dubey et al. (2005) and Adam and Grill (2017). However, the one step forward of our argument and that of Wang (2019) is that the financial markets are assumed highly sophisticated. That is, for the international financial markets within the currency union, a complete set of financial securities conditional on states of nature is available for trade *ex ante*. Hence, the benefit of default in our argument stems purely from credit risks and the loss of exchange rate, a currency union specific friction, rather than *ex ante* market incompleteness.

Taking this argument one step further, Goodhart et al. (2018) incorporate non-trivial production sectors in a two-country dynamic stochastic general equilibrium model. Calibrating with the German and Greek data, the authors show that debt restructuring not only is beneficial for the debtor alone but also is conducive to the creditor's welfare improvement given a hard government budget constraint. This is because the short-term cost of debt restructuring for the creditor would be outweighed by the long-term benefit of maintaining investments in Greece, such that the Germany's consumption volatilities decrease.

5.1 Implications of debt restructuring in the eurozone

With suitable lenient terms for cross-country debt restructuring within the currency union, the default stress on the domestic banking system can be much alleviated and, instead, the financial markets absorb the credit risks that cannot be digested due to the loss of exchange rate. The punchline of our analysis is that debt restructuring can be a plausible way to compensate for the loss of credible exchange rates. Figure 9.1 illustrates one numerical result of Wang (2019). Country I resides in a

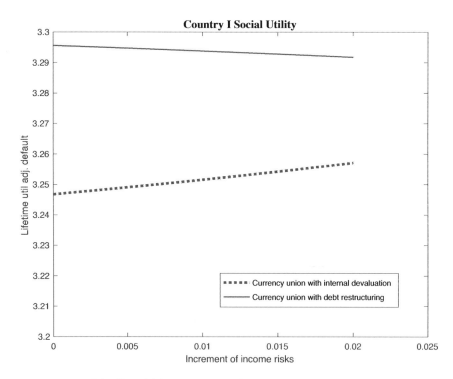

Figure 9.1 Social utility with internal devaluation and with debt restructuring

Source: Wang (2019).

currency union. The vertical axis is the lifetime utility of the households in Country I consuming both foreign and domestic goods, minus the social cost of default (if any), and the horizontal axis is the increment of income shocks to the baseline calibration. The dotted line illustrates the numerical solution of the equilibrium when the currency union has a harsh bankruptcy procedure for cross-country borrowing and needs to resort to internal devaluation to render the system viable; the solid line shows the numerical solution of the equilibrium when the currency union allows for debt restructuring of cross-country borrowing. We can see that debt restructuring in a currency union can bring sizable welfare improvement. As Wang (2019) shows, this welfare improvement is Pareto improving in the currency union.

Analytically, the following propositions from Wang (2019) explain the driving force behind the welfare improvement.

• Debt restructuring for cross-country borrowing saves domestic banks.

That is, financial markets have the capacity to absorb credit risks if debt restructuring is allowed, and it alleviates the default stress from the domestic banking system that would have otherwise failed. In other words, debt restructuring in a currency union removes the need for bailout tax and internal devaluation.

• Allocation efficiency and risk sharing both improve.

In this regime, with cross-country debt restructuring, the marginal rate of substitutions of domestic and foreign goods between countries within the same state of nature are not distorted by the bailout tax. Moreover, the marginal rate of substitutions across states are not distorted by the bailout tax. Although Pareto optimality still does not obtain due to the positive borrowing cost and default premia, the distortion with debt restructuring is less than the case without.

5.2 Implementation

A noteworthy advantage of debt restructuring of cross-country borrowing within the currency union is that it can leverage the invisible hand of the financial markets. Dubey et al. (2005) prove that orderly default on financial securities – in other words, the possibility of debt restructuring – is consistent with the existence of equilibrium and the orderly function of the markets. The intuition is that if the cost and the terms of debt restructuring are well understood by the markets, the markets will ask for a suitable credit risk premium of the underlying financial assets as a compensation. If the terms of debt restructuring are lenient, the default risk would increase, driving down the price of the asset, and if the price is low enough, there can be buyers. Indeed, Wang (2019) shows that with suitable terms of debt restructuring, the defaultable financial assets in the currency union are traded. Unlike the visible hand of a fiscal union that can move nominal resources between countries in the currency union, debt restructuring leaves the transfer of nominal resources to the markets via market participants' own choice of default.

For eurozone debt restructuring to work, i.e. compensating for the loss of a credible floating exchange, the terms of debt restructuring should be consistent and *ex ante* well understood by market participants. This requires a credible bankruptcy law for cross-country borrowing in the currency union, such that the market participants can properly price in the credit risks of the financial assets. Therefore, it is important to note that the debt restructuring we argue in this chapter is not an *ex post* discretionary debt restructuring that few markets participants could rationally anticipate. Thus, the usual argument against debt restructuring that it is "unfair" to the lenders does not go through, because in our scenario, the credit risks are correctly priced in, and no one is forcing market participants to buy or sell the defaultable financial assets.

6   Conclusions

In this chapter, we have argued for the role of debt restructuring in the eurozone as a plausible way to compensate for the loss of exchange rates in the presence of credit risks. Debt restructuring is particularly relevant and vital in the eurozone because the cross-country fiscal backstop is still highly incomplete, and a fully fledged fiscal union is understood to be a politically constrained option. We started by reviewing the theoretical argument for the benefits of default and debt restructuring. We noted that our argument need not reply to the incompleteness of the financial markets and that the need for debt restructuring purely stems from currency union specific frictions. Then we introduce a suite of international finance models with money and liquidity, suitable to structurally study the debt restructuring issue of a currency union. To appreciate that the eurozone Debt Crisis is partially a disguised classic "currency crisis" due to fixing the exchange rate, we borrow the conceptual advance from the general equilibrium theory of money and default and emphasise the credit nature of fiat money and its interlinkages with the financial system. Then we relate credit risks to exchange rate and argue why debt restructuring is particularly vital for the eurozone. Finally, we compare and contrast the scenarios with and without debt restructuring in the eurozone.

Much of the insight in this chapter is based on the theoretical arguments in Goodhart et al. (2018) and Wang (2019). Going forward, it is of significance to extend Wang (2019) to a dynamic setting and calibrate it with the eurozone data, allowing us to carefully evaluate the quantitative impact of debt restructuring in the eurozone. A wider implication of this chapter is that for the understanding of modern monetary and financial phenomena, particularly the viability of a currency union, we simply cannot ignore the credit nature of fiat money and the interplay of liquidity and default, which matter not only for price stability but also for financial stability, in both a closed economy and an open economy such as the eurozone. For that, we owe it to the intellectual legacy from Keynes, Minsky, Shubik and Grandmont and Younes.

Acknowledgement

We wish to acknowledge Juan E. Castañeda for his helpful comments and suggestions.

References

Adam, K. and M. Grill (2017), "Optimal Sovereign Default", *American Economic Journal: Macroeconomics*, 9(1), 128–164.

Brunnermeier, M. K., L. Garicano, P. R. Lane, M. Pagano, R. Reis, T. Santos, D. Thesmar, S. van Nieuwerburgh and D. Vayanos (2016), "The Sovereign-Bank Diabolic Loop and ESBies", *American Economic Review*, 106(5), 508–512.

Buiter, W. H. (1999), "The Fallacy of the Fiscal Theory of the Price Level", NBER Working Paper No. W7302, Cambridge, MA.

Drèze, J. H. and H. M. Polemarchakis (2001), "Monetary Equilibria", In Debreu, Neuefeind and Trockel (eds.): *Economic Essays*, 83–108, Berlin, Heidelberg: Springer.

Dubey, P. and J. Geanakoplos (1992), "The Value of Money in a Finite Horizon Economy: A Role for Banks", *Cowles Foundation Paper*, 901. New Haven, Connecticut.

Dubey, P. and J. Geanakoplos (2003a), "Inside and Outside Fiat Money, Gains to Trade, and IS-LM", *Economic Theory*, 21(2–3), 347–397.

Dubey, P. and J. Geanakoplos (2003b), "Monetary Equilibrium with Missing Markets", *Journal of Mathematical Economics*, 39(5–6), 585–618.

Dubey, P. and J. Geanakoplos (2006), "Determinacy with Nominal Assets and Outside Money", *Economic Theory*, 27(1), 79–106.

Dubey, P., J. Geanakoplos and M. Shubik (2005), "Default and Punishment in General Equilibrium", *Econometrica*, 73(1), 1–37.

Farhi, E. and I. Werning (2017), "Fiscal Unions", *American Economic Review*, 107(12), 3788–3834.

Fisher, I. (1933), "The Debt-Deflation Theory of Great Depressions", *Econometrica*, 1(4), 337–357.

Friedman, M. (1997), "The Euro: Monetary Unity to Political Disunity", *Project Syndicate*, 28.

Geanakoplos, J. and D. P. Tsomocos (2002), "International Finance in General Equilibrium", *Research in Economics*, 56(1), 85–142.

Goodhart, C. A. (1997), "Two Concepts of Money, and the Future of Europe", *Optimum Currency Areas-New Analytical and Policy Developments*, 89–96.

Goodhart, C. A. (1998), "The Two Concepts of Money: Implications for the Analysis of Optimal Currency Areas", *European Journal of Political Economy*, 14(3), 407–432.

Goodhart, C. A., M. U. Peiris and D. P. Tsomocos (2018), "Debt, Recovery Rates and the Greek Dilemma", *Journal of Financial Stability*, 35, 192–214.

Goodhart, C. A., D. P. Tsomocos and X. Wang (2019), "Bank Credit and Default in Infinite Horizon", Available at SSRN 3491217.

Grandmont, J.-M. and Y. Younes (1972), "On the Role of Money and the Existence of a Monetary Equilibrium", *The Review of Economic Studies*, 39(3), 355–372.

Grandmont, J.-M. and Y. Younes (1973), "On the Efficiency of a Monetary Equilibrium", *The Review of Economic Studies*, 40(2), 149–165.

Hahn, A. (1920), *Volkswirtschaftliche Theorie des Bankkredits*, Tubingen: J.C.B. Mohr.

Hawtrey, R. G. (1919), *Currency and Credit*, London: Longmans.

Kehoe, P. J. and E. Pastorino (2017), "Fiscal Unions Redux", *Economic Theory*, 64(4), 741–776.

Keynes, J. M. (1931/2010), "The Consequences to the Banks of the Collapse of Money Values", in *Essays in Persuasion*, 150–158, Springer.

Lin, L., D. P. Tsomocos and A. P. Vardoulakis (2016), "On Default and Uniqueness of Monetary Equilibria", *Economic Theory*, 62(1–2), 245–264.

Macleod, H. D. (1866), *The Theory and Practice of Banking: With the Elementary Principles of Currency, Prices, Credit, and Exchanges*, Volume 1, Longman.

174   *Dimitrios P. Tsomocos and Xuan Wang*

McLeay, M., A. Radia and R. Thomas (2014), "Money Creation in the Modern Economy", *Bank of England Quarterly Bulletin*, London Q1.

Piazzesi, M. and M. Schneider (2018), "Payments, Credit and Asset Prices", Working Paper.

Peiris, M. U. and D. P. Tsomocos (2015), "International Monetary Equilibrium with Default", *Journal of Mathematical Economics*, 56, 47–57.

Schumpeter, J. A. (1934), *The Theory of Economic Developments: An Inquiry Into Profits, Capital, Credit, Interest, and the Business Cycle*, Piscataway: Transaction Publishers.

Schumpeter, J. A. (1954), *The Theory of Money and Financial Institutions*, Volume 1, Cambridge, MA: MIT Press.

Shubik, M. (1999), *The Theory of Money and Financial Institutions*, Volume 1, Cambridge, MA: MIT Press.

Shubik, M. and C. Wilson (1977), "The Optimal Bankruptcy Rule in a Trading Economy Using Fiat Money", *Zeitschrift fur Nationalokonomie*, 37(3–4), 337–354.

Sims, C. A. (1994), "A Simple Model for Study of the Determination of the Price Level and the Interaction of Monetary and Fiscal Policy", *Economic Theory*, 4(3), 381–399.

Tsomocos, D. P. (2003), "Equilibrium Analysis, Banking and Financial Instability", *Journal of Mathematical Economics*, 39(5–6), 619–655.

Tsomocos, D. P. (2008), "Generic Determinacy and Money Non-Neutrality of International Monetary Equilibria", *Journal of Mathematical Economics*, 44(7–8), 866–887.

Wang, X. (2019), "When Do Currency Unions Benefit From Default?", Job Market Paper, Saïd Business School, Oxford University, Oxford, United Kingdom, 15.

Wicksell, K. (1906), *Lectures on Political Economy, Volume Tow: Money*. Lionel Robbins, ed., London: Routledge and Sons, Ltd.

10 The rationale for a safe asset and fiscal capacity for the eurozone

Lorenzo Codogno and Paul van den Noord

1 Introduction

With the ongoing surge in populism and drive to recover national sovereignty, market discipline appears as the most effective means to prevent irresponsible policies and free riding in the eurozone. Unfortunately, this also leaves it vulnerable to shocks and instability. In those parts of the eurozone with high legacy debt and a poor quality of banks' balance sheets, fiscal stimulus could reignite the bank-sovereign doom-loop, overstretch the eurozone's fiscal framework and pose existential threats. Not using the fiscal lever, however, would result in welfare losses as well, not least since shock absorption by monetary policy is heavily constrained by the zero lower bound (ZLB).

We strongly agree on the need to have unity of liability and control, i.e. a full fiscal and political union that is underpinned by democratic legitimacy. Otherwise, sharing liabilities across eurozone nations remains elusive. We also strongly agree on the need to preserve market discipline and avoid moral hazard, not only once financial and fiscal integration of the eurozone is complete but also in the transition. Ultimately, countries must be allowed to default. However, we think it is in nobody's interest to put macroeconomic stability – and indeed the very existence of the eurozone – at risk each time the economy is hit by an exogenous shock.

Two potential tools to secure macroeconomic stability in the eurozone have gained prominence in recent years: the creation of a eurozone "fiscal capacity" and the creation of a eurozone "safe asset". Both devices aim to ease some of the burden of stabilisation policies from the national sovereigns and the European Central Bank (ECB).

Specifically, the purpose of a eurozone safe asset is to provide banks in the eurozone with a bond, guaranteed jointly by the sovereigns, they can use as collateral for inter-bank loans and ECB repos. Unlike the use of national sovereign debt for these purposes, the risk of haircuts associated with fiscal stress hitting the national government would be small as this risk is "shared" across the eurozone, and eventually backstopped by the ECB. This would strengthen the transmission of monetary policy – as banks' lending activities would be less exposed to national sovereign risk and fiscal stress – as well as create new fiscal space as national sovereigns would be less exposed to credit risk in their national banking systems.

The purpose of a eurozone fiscal capacity is two-pronged. First, it would help national sovereigns to absorb "asymmetric shocks", to the extent the capacity is allowed to allocate funding across member states according to their specific cyclical needs at any point in time. An example of such a device would be a eurozone unemployment insurance or the provision of eurozone conditional loans to national sovereigns in case of cyclical distress. Second, it could be used to absorb "common shocks", by adjusting the eurozone aggregate fiscal policy stance, as required, in support of ECB monetary policy, via for instance a eurozone public works programme.

These two devices – safe asset and fiscal capacity – are conceptionally intertwined, even if not necessarily perceived that way in policymaking circles. Specifically, the creation of fiscal capacity at the centre, to the extent it is allowed to run temporary deficits funded by the issuance of a supranational bond, ultimately backstopped by the ECB, inevitably entails the creation of a safe asset. This is true even if initially perhaps the safe asset may not be issued in a sufficient quantity to satisfy all of the demand for such an asset by banks. Conversely, once a safe asset has been created, it is technically (though perhaps not politically) possible to use it for funding purposes, i.e. create fiscal capacity at the centre.

Both devices also come with constraints, such as the need to secure political support for the inevitable sharing of financial risk and – in some scenarios – fiscal redistribution across member states. These concerns need to be tackled upfront through the enforcement of strict conditionality, such as full compliance with the EU fiscal rules and a strong commitment to structural reforms. Otherwise, there is no point moving ahead with these devices. We provide evidence that, if moral hazard is sufficiently contained (but not to an extent where exogenous shocks would be lethal), these devices can be welfare enhancing for all participants.

Against this backdrop, this chapter aims to assess the macroeconomic stabilisation properties of the proposed devices according to certain criteria – such as smoothing the aggregate cycle or minimising the cyclical divergencies between countries – in a tractable format. This assessment makes use of a simple Mundell-Fleming framework, adapted to the features of a closed monetary union. This framework has been routinely used in the past to assess, for instance, the role of fiscal rules or the impact of structural reforms on the effectiveness of fiscal automatic stabilisers (see e.g. Buti et al. 2002, 2003). However, it has so far not been used to assess the role of fiscal capacity and safe assets. Before delving into this analysis, the chapter starts with a brief review of the specifics of the proposed devices.

2   The proposals

2.1   *Broad objectives*

Before the financial and sovereign debt crises hit the eurozone in 2008, the predominant conundrum was the lack of mechanisms to absorb asymmetric shocks. It was argued that monetary policy, being conducted at the central level, could never absorb such shocks ("one size cannot fit all"), while fiscal policy, conducted at the national level, was heavily constrained by strict fiscal rules. Meanwhile, so-called alternative adjustment mechanisms, such as cross-border labour migration or international risk sharing via the financial markets, were seen as underdeveloped in the eurozone.

The upshot was that asymmetric shocks would unavoidably lead to temporary economic divergence. However, more importantly – once "hysteresis" kicks in – it would contribute to persistent economic divergence, thus potentially undermining the cohesion of the eurozone. The standard policy prescriptions to address this issue were (1) reinforcing the EU "Internal Market" for labour and capital so as to bolster the "alternative adjustment mechanisms", (2) pursuing product and labour market reform at the national level to rein in hysteresis and (3) speeding up fiscal consolidation so as to create buffers to allow the operation of "automatic stabilisers" within the limits set by the fiscal rules.[1]

Since the onset of the financial and sovereign debt crises in 2008, however, the challenges indicated have become all but more severe. Specifically:

1   The sovereign debt crisis in the eurozone gave birth to a "doom loop" – the vicious circle of a sovereign under stress prompting haircuts on sovereign bonds on banks' balance sheets, thereby raising their funding cost and interest rates on loans, driving the economy into a recession, causing more fiscal stress, and so on. First steps towards a "Banking Union" in the wake of the acute phase of the crisis served to mitigate the doom loop to some extent. However, the Banking Union is far from complete. For instance, a single European Deposit Insurance and a full-blown single banking resolution fund, backstopped by the joint sovereigns, are still missing.

2   Looking ahead, restructuring risk may become an additional source of instability. The financial and sovereign debt crisis led to the creation of a number of rescue mechanisms with the European Stability Mechanism (ESM) playing a pivot role. The ESM is still evolving, and the latest innovation is the strengthening of the requirement that sovereign debt needs to be sustainable (and therefore restructured) before a country can apply for a rescue program of the ESM.[2] In some sense, this is a welcome development: it protects the taxpayer against undue support for investors in sovereign bonds of countries in distress and bolsters market discipline. However, it also implies that as investors fear a haircut the risk of a sell-off once a country is hit by an adverse shock increases quickly, which in turn would severely affect the banks established in the jurisdiction concerned. Hence, the approach chosen for ESM financial assistance may also become a de facto source of financial risk, even if the (in)solvency of the country's debt — not ESM conditionality — is the true culprit.

3   Monetary policy continues to edge at the brink of a de facto ZLB. The ECB's massive asset purchase programme has helped to push the implied, effective or "shadow" policy rate into negative territory, but there are limits to that policy as well – be it technical or political. We would argue that this limit has probably been reached as well. Net asset purchases by the ECB

stopped at the beginning of 2019 and, even if it is restarted or new tools are introduced, there is only limited monetary policy space left. This renders the eurozone very vulnerable to symmetric shocks. We have moved from "one size does not fit all" to "one size fits nobody".

2.2 Proposals for a safe asset

The general purpose of a "safe asset" for the eurozone is to create a security that banks could buy to serve as collateral for inter-bank loans and repos and ECB funding, instead of national sovereign bonds. Its advantage is that it would break the "banks-sovereign doom loop" mentioned earlier. By no means do we have the ambition to provide a detailed and exhaustive literature overview on the safe asset, but instead we want to characterise what we consider the main proposals regarding their mechanics and governance implications.

Specifically, we distinguish two main classes:

1   *ESBies*. These bonds would be issued at the centre against national sovereign bonds purchased in the secondary market in quantities corresponding to the "capital key" of the ECB (i.e. broadly in proportion to the national GDP and population size of each member state). On the specifics:

   a   The purchases would typically be capped at 60% of national GDP, in line with the Maastricht debt criteria. Hence, a member state wishing to issue debt over and above 60% of GDP would pay a risk premium, keeping market discipline intact.

   b   ESBies are less risky than the underlying sovereign bonds owing to diversification (generally not all sovereigns would go bust at once). Also, it is proposed to create junior and mezzanine bonds alongside the ESBies, which would absorb most, if not all, of the losses, at default of the underlying sovereign debt. As a result, ESBies would be automatically rated triple-A.

   c   ESBies would be traded in the bond market and could be purchased by banks to serve as collateral and for repos. These purchases could be encouraged, for instance, by exempting ESBies from risk weighting to assess banks' capital requirements.

2   *E-bonds*. These bonds would be issued by an existing or newly created triple-A issuer at the centre with a joint guarantee from the sovereigns.[3]

   a   Unlike ESBies, the money raised in the market would not be used to purchase national sovereign bonds in the secondary market but instead to provide "soft" loans to national sovereigns. These loans would not be used to fund government deficits, but rather to replace sovereign debt in circulation as it matures, hence would be phased in gradually.

   b   Again, in most proposals, these loans would be capped at 60% of national GDP, in line with the Maastricht debt criteria. Hence, a member state wishing to issue debt over and above 60% of GDP would have to turn to the market and pay a risk premium.

c   These soft loans could be issued in the form of bonds with a guarantee from the joint sovereigns, sometimes labelled "blue bonds" (as opposed to "red bonds" issued without such a guarantee). Otherwise, E-bonds serve the same purpose as ESBies.

A potential drawback of the E-bonds proposal is that there is a relatively long transition period in which unprotected sovereign bonds are gradually replaced with blue bonds as they mature. Eurozone stability in the meantime would be vulnerable as the new sustainability requirements of the ESM, as noted earlier, potentially add fuel to the banks-sovereign doom loop via the threat of restructuring. For some years, the current situation would effectively not change. One proposal to address this is to exempt sovereign debt from this requirement up to a certain amount that corresponds to the debt cap enshrined in the Fiscal Compact.[4]

Other proposals have been floated, but these can generally be seen as variants of the devices mentioned. For instance, the European Commission has floated a proposal for "Stability Bonds" which refers to the joint issuance of sovereign bonds at the centre with a joint guarantee, with the proceeds allocated to the member states according to the capital key (European Commission 2011). This is similar to the E-bonds proposal.[5]

A concern with regard to these safe assets is that their safety ultimately rests on financial engineering while the underlying risk (of sovereign default) does not change (see e.g. De Grauwe and Ji 2018). We would argue that a safe asset in the eurozone would only be genuinely safe when ultimately backstopped by the ECB, with fiscal backstops and risk sharing serving as the first line of defence.

2.3   *Proposals for fiscal capacity at the centre*

The key tenet of proposals for fiscal capacity is to create a central fiscal authority, which can issue debt that in turn serves to fund new expenditure, either at the centre or at the national level. As a result, it directly affects the fiscal policy stance either at the national level or in aggregate (or both). This property distinguishes it from the safe asset proposals, which a priori do not affect the fiscal stance as they only aim to securitise in some shape or form already existing sovereign debt. Even so, fiscal capacity proposals generally entail (or at the minimum prepare the ground for) the creation of a single eurozone "sovereign" bond which could serve as a safe asset for banks.

We distinguish three strands of proposals.

1   *Loans from the centre.* This is the least radical option – actively promoted by the European Commission – which entails the provision of loans from a newly created fiscal capacity to member states in recession, subject to conditionality (for instance they need to respect their commitments under the EU fiscal rules). Such a fiscal capacity could borrow at better terms, i.e.

lower rates than the national sovereign could, and as such is welfare enhancing. This device is distinct from emergency loans extended by the ESM,
which are not meant to be used for fiscal stimulus purposes at all. ESM
loans are subject to the member state concerned adopting an adjustment
programme (implying fiscal restraint) and presumably restructuring their
sovereign debt. However, the funding mechanism, i.e. the issuance of bonds
at the centre to finance top-down loans, is similar, and so is the principle
that the loans will have to be repaid in full. E-bonds follow this approach
as well.

2   *Public works at the centre and top-down grants.* One step further in the
    direction of a full "fiscal union" would be to create an entity at the centre
    that can raise its own tax, for instance, a eurozone VAT surtax, and raise
    capital through bonds issued against future tax proceeds. The capital thus
    raised could be spent on, for example, public works that transcend national
    interests (or much more controversially a European army) or handed out as
    grants (as opposed to loans) to the national sovereigns in accordance with
    the capital key. In principle endowing a fiscal capacity with power to raise
    tax would not entail a redistribution of fiscal means across member states
    as long as the tax base is close enough to the capital key, but it would entail
    fiscal stimulus when bonds are issued (or fiscal restraint when grants and
    bond issuance are rolled back) at the centre.

3   *Horizontal transfers.* The next step towards fiscal union is to allow the
    fiscal entity at the centre to spend tax proceeds and capital raised in the
    bond market on public (welfare or other) programmes in the member
    states, according to their "cyclical" needs. The most well-known example
    would be the creation of a eurozone unemployment insurance, which
    could not only run deficits or surpluses at the centre (and hence affect
    the aggregate eurozone fiscal stance) but could also run deficits in some
    member states and surpluses in others at any point in time. These deficits
    and surpluses would have to be purely cyclical in nature, i.e. they would
    cancel out both over time and across countries. Obviously for this "neu-
    trality" principle to hold, it is required that shocks in all countries are
    drawn from the same distribution and that the rules (for instance unem-
    ployment benefit rules), and their implementation, are identical across
    countries and over time.[6]

Each of these devices has consequences for eurozone governance. A safe asset
without fiscal capacity at the centre will not influence the aggregate fiscal stance
and macroeconomic policy mix, and since for new deficit spending the member state has to turn to the market, the incentives for fiscal discipline would
not change much.[7] As a result, while tighter surveillance of national fiscal policy may be welcome in its own right, there is little in this device that would
call for even more fiscal surveillance. On the other hand, a change in financial regulation would be required to encourage the use of safe bonds by banks
instead of national sovereigns, such as the still hotly debated introduction of risk

weighting. More generally, financial risk stemming from the banking system would be reduced, thus facilitating financial surveillance by the single supervisor and national supervisors. Finally, the transmission of monetary policy would be facilitated. Even so, to the extent that the safe asset is ultimately backstopped by the ECB, the risk of fiscal dominance needs to be contained by reasserting its independence.

The creation of fiscal capacity, because it would enable a centralised fiscal policy, entails an even larger risk of fiscal dominance. This is much less the case if all fiscal capacity could do is extending loans to stopgap national sovereigns, funded by centrally issued debt. However, fiscal capacity that can accord debt-funded grants to member states is subject to credit risk and could be susceptible to exerting pressure on the European Central Bank to keep policy rates low. If the central entity enjoys taxing power, it could also be susceptible to squeezing national tax bases. Therefore, it could be argued that a fiscal capacity of that kind would need to be subject to democratic control at the eurozone level. This is, arguably, even more the case if the fiscal capacity has the power to redistribute fiscal resources across member states. Barring such democratic control, strict conditionality for access to loans extended by the fiscal capacity would be crucial.

3 Assessing the proposed devices: an analytical framework

To assess the macroeconomic stabilisation properties of the proposed devices, we make use of a standard Mundell-Fleming model, adapted to the features of a closed monetary union (a single supra-national monetary policy with multiple national fiscal policies). We adopt a two-country setting comprising a "core" country and a "periphery" country.[8] The periphery country differs from the core country in only one aspect, which is its smaller fiscal policy space, due for instance to a higher public debt burden accumulated in the past and a comparatively poor reputation in the financial markets, reflected in a higher sensitivity of sovereign bond yields to fiscal expansions. Otherwise, we assume the two economies to be identical.

Alongside the two national sovereigns, we include a supra-national entity (dubbed "fiscal capacity") which can issue a single bond with a guarantee from the national sovereigns, and backstopped by the central bank. It can earmark the money raised to either purchase existing sovereign bonds in the secondary market, or issue new loans (over and above existing debt) to the national sovereigns. In the former case, the single bond solely serves as a safe asset for banks to replace existing sovereign debt on their balance sheet, whereas in the latter case it serves to fund a supra-national fiscal expansion (a fiscal capacity proper). The money raised in the latter case is distributed to the national sovereigns according to a simple rule, for which we examine two alternatives. In the first alternative, the funds are allocated to minimise the aggregate output loss in the wake of an adverse shock, whereas in the second alternative the allocation of funds is geared to minimising the difference in output losses between the two countries. We will show that these are mutually incompatible goals, notably when shocks are asymmetric.

3.1   The real economy

As noted, we use a standard Mundell-Fleming approach, adapted to the features of a closed monetary union.[9] The aggregate demand equations read:

$$y^d = -\phi_1\left(r - \pi^e\right) + \phi_2\left(d + f\right) - \phi_3\left(\pi - \pi^*\right) - \phi_4\left(y - y^*\right) + \varepsilon^d$$
$$y^{*d} = -\phi_1\left(r^* - \pi^e\right) + \phi_2\left(d^* + f^*\right) + \phi_3\left(\pi - \pi^*\right) + \phi_4\left(y - y^*\right) + \varepsilon^{*d} \tag{1}$$

An asterisk (*) indicates the periphery country. In each country aggregate demand, y^d and y^{*d}, is determined by the real interest rate $r - \pi^e$ and $r^* - \pi^e$ (where π^e denotes "expected inflation", which is assumed to be uniform across the monetary union), the primary fiscal deficit (d and d^*) and cross-border trade. The latter is a function of the inflation differential ($\pi - \pi^*$), and the relative pace of economic growth ($y - y^*$). In addition, we include the fiscal multiplier effect of transfers from the fiscal capacity, denoted by f and f^*. For simplicity, we assume the fiscal multipliers to be the same for national and supra-national fiscal expansions (or contractions). Finally, ε^d and ε^{*d} are demand shocks.

Aggregate supply y^s and y^{*s} is determined via an inverted Phillips-curve type of equation, including the inflation "surprises" $\pi - \pi^e$ and $\pi^* - \pi^e$ and supply shocks ε^s and ε^{*s}:

$$y^s = \left(\pi - \pi^e\right)/\omega + \varepsilon^s$$
$$y^{*s} = \left(\pi^* - \pi^e\right)/\omega + \varepsilon^{*s} \tag{2}$$

The parameter ω captures the slope of the Phillips-curve. All variables are defined as deviations from a not specified steady state and, accordingly, expected inflation is assumed to be nil $\pi^e = 0$ and all shocks are normally distributed around nil.

The interest rates r and r^* can be seen as the rate charged on bank loans, which we assume to carry a risk premium over and above the monetary policy rate i, induced by fiscal developments. Specifically, as sovereign debt serves as collateral for inter-bank loans and repos, a deterioration in the fiscal position will raise the funding cost for banks (who are facing a bigger haircut on their collateral), which will be passed through onto higher interest rates on domestic loans. The degree to which this mechanism is at play depends on the initial balance sheet situation of banks and the sovereign: if banks carry a lot of non-performing loans and/or their initial sovereign debt portfolios are sizeable relative to their capital, the impact of a deterioration of the fiscal position on domestic interest rates will be stronger. This aims to capture the doom loop that hit the periphery more so than the core and may further increase with the new requirement that sovereign debt needs to be sustainable (and therefore restructured) before a country can apply for a rescue programme of the ESM.[10]

Given that we consider the core country to have a fiscally prudent history and the periphery country a profligate one, we assume that only the periphery country's bank lending rate carries a risk premium,[11] so:

$$r = i$$
$$r^* = i + \eta d^* \tag{3}$$

The variables f and f^* do not enter Equation 3 since these do not add to the market debt of the national sovereigns (as these are grants or loans from fiscal capacity in exchange for IOUs), they will not lead to haircuts on banks' collateral.

The primary fiscal deficits d and d^* are partly endogenous on the account of automatic stabilisers (e.g. variations in tax proceeds or social security outlays as a function of cyclical economic activity), so:

$$d = -\tau y + g$$
$$d^* = -\tau y^* + g^* \tag{4}$$

where g and g^* denote the stance of the "structural" or "discretionary" (as opposed to the "cyclical" or "induced") component of the fiscal deficit in each country and τ roughly corresponds to the size of the government sector relative to aggregate output, in each country.

The model is perfectly symmetric across the countries with regard to all parameters, with one exception, which is that $\eta > 0$, to capture the banks-sovereign doom loop in the periphery. However, as discussed in more detail in section 4, once a safe asset is introduced and has replaced the national sovereign bonds as collateral for banks, this asymmetry will disappear and hence $\eta = 0$ and the rates on bank loans are identical and equal to the policy rate. We assume that the safe asset is backstopped by the central bank such that the sovereign risk is nil, while for simplicity we also abstract from duration and inflation risk. It is important to note also that the assumption of zero sovereign risk does not apply to the national sovereign bonds, which continue to be issued without a backstop from the central bank. However, these bonds no longer figure on banks' balance sheets.

Reduced form equations for output and inflation may be derived from Equations 1–4 assuming that $y^d = y^s = y$, $y^{*d} = y^{*s} = y^*$ We assume, for convenience, that $\pi^e = 0$. The math is quite cumbersome, so we resort to shorthand notation (signs of first derivatives are indicated above variables):

$$y = y\overset{- + ? \ + \ + \ + \ + \ \ + \ -}{\left(i, g, g^*, f, f^*, \varepsilon^d, \varepsilon^{*d}, \varepsilon^s, \varepsilon^{*s} \right)} \tag{5}$$

$$y^* = y^*\overset{- + ? \ + \ + \ + \ + \ \ + \ -}{\left(i, g, g^*, f, f^*, \varepsilon^d, \varepsilon^{*d}, \varepsilon^s, \varepsilon^{*s} \right)} \tag{6}$$

$$\pi = \pi \overset{-+?\ +\ +\ +\ +\ \ +\ -}{\left(i,g,g^*,f,f^*,\varepsilon^d,\varepsilon^{*d},\varepsilon^s,\varepsilon^{*s}\right)} \tag{7}$$

$$\pi^* = \pi^* \overset{-+?\ +\ +\ +\ +\ \ +\ -}{\left(i,g,g^*,f,f^*,\varepsilon^d,\varepsilon^{*d},\varepsilon^s,\varepsilon^{*s}\right)} \tag{8}$$

From these reduced-form equations, the following can be inferred:

1   Fiscal expansions in the core boost output and inflation in both countries. This is a priori not clear for fiscal expansions in the periphery. Only if in the periphery the negative feedback via costlier bank lending falls short of the standard multiplier effect of fiscal policy will the net impact be positive. This requires that $\eta < \phi_2 / \phi_1$, a condition that is satisfied by mainstream empirical estimates (in our numerical examples we assume that $\eta = 0.2$, $\phi_1 = 1$ and $\phi_2 = 0.5$).[12] Even so, the overall output impact of fiscal expansions in the periphery is muted by the bank lending channel.

2   Fiscal expansions conducted by the fiscal capacity are unambiguously positive for output and inflation in both countries as this does not impinge on the bank lending channel. Similarly, monetary policy easing is unambiguously positive for output and inflation in both countries, and so are (positive) demand shocks (and vice versa for adverse demand shocks).

3   For supply shocks, the impact is more diverse than for demand shocks. Domestic supply shocks have an unambiguously positive impact on domestic output and a negative impact on domestic inflation. However, positive supply shocks abroad have a negative impact on output at home due to a loss of competitiveness. Supply shocks have an unambiguously negative impact on inflation at home and abroad.

The monetary and discretionary fiscal policy variables in our model (i,g,g^*,f,f^*) are endogenously determined via a set of policy reaction functions. However, rather than postulating these reaction functions (e.g. a Taylor rule for monetary policy) we will derive these from welfare loss minimising behaviour by the relevant actors (the central bank, the national governments and the fiscal capacity). We will now turn to each of these policy instruments separately.

3.2   Monetary policy

The central monetary authority is assumed to minimise the welfare loss $L_{\bar\pi}$ associated with aggregate inflation $\bar\pi$ measured against targeted inflation (assumed to be nil). Monetary policy may be subject to "inertia", i.e. the monetary authority tolerates some deviation from targeted inflation in order to avoid socially costly swings in the interest rate:

$$\min_i L_{\bar{\pi}} = \frac{1}{2}\bar{\pi}^2 + \alpha\frac{1}{2}i^2$$

$$\bar{\pi} = \frac{1}{2}\pi + \frac{1}{2}\pi^*$$

(9)

where α measures the welfare cost of interest rate volatility relative to that of missing the inflation target. The monetary policy reaction function then reads:

$$i = i\Big(\overset{+}{g},\overset{?}{g^*},\overset{+}{f},\overset{+}{f^*},\overset{+}{\varepsilon^d},\overset{+}{\varepsilon^{*d}},\overset{-}{\varepsilon^s},\overset{?}{\varepsilon^{*s}}\Big)$$

(10)

The signs of the impact responses are unambiguous and straightforward, except in the cases of fiscal expansion in the periphery and a supply shock in the periphery. The reason for the former is again that a priori it cannot be ruled out that a fiscal expansion in the periphery ends up being contractionary due to the predominance of the bank lending channel. For supply shocks in the periphery the reason is similar: a priori a positive supply shock would reduce inflation and trigger an easing of monetary policy (like in the core country). However, in the periphery country, the bank lending channel acts as an accelerator that, via the automatic fiscal stabilisers, improves the fiscal situation, reduces the cost of credit and thus triggers a tightening of monetary policy.

3.3 National fiscal policies

The national governments in both countries are assumed to minimise the welfare loss L_g or L_{g^*} associated with variations in their output gap (the deviation of output from its steady state equilibrium). Akin to monetary policy, fiscal policy is subject to inertia due to adjustment costs associated with a change in policy:

$$\min_g L_y = \frac{1}{2}y^2 + \beta\frac{1}{2}g^2$$

$$\min_{g^*} L_{y^*} = \frac{1}{2}y^{*2} + \beta\frac{1}{2}g^{*2}$$

(11)

where β represents the cost of changing the budget relative to excess demand or supply. Minimisation of these welfare losses yields reaction functions for fiscal policy in both countries, which in short-hand notation read:

$$g = g\Big(\overset{+}{i},\overset{?}{g^*},\overset{-}{f},\overset{-}{f^*},\overset{-}{\varepsilon^d},\overset{-}{\varepsilon^{*d}},\overset{-}{\varepsilon^s},\overset{+}{\varepsilon^{*s}}\Big)$$

(12)

$$g^* = g^* \left(\overset{+}{i}, \overset{-}{g}, \overset{-}{f}, \overset{-}{f^*}, \overset{-}{\varepsilon^d}, \overset{-}{\varepsilon^{*d}}, \overset{+}{\varepsilon^s}, \overset{-}{\varepsilon^{*s}} \right) \tag{13}$$

Similar to the earlier policy reaction functions, there is ambiguity with regard to the impact of fiscal expansion in the periphery, and for the same reasons as discussed previously (possible predominance of the bank lending channel of fiscal policy). Otherwise, the impulse responses are straightforward in light of the earlier discussion, with again supply shocks abroad triggering fiscal expansions at home to offset the loss of competitiveness.

3.4 The fiscal capacity

While the welfare loss functions as formulated for monetary and national fiscal policies are relatively straightforward, it is not a priori clear what objectives the fiscal capacity should pursue. In very general terms, its goal could be to "promote the stability of the monetary union", but stability has at least two dimensions:

1   "Stability" could refer to the need to stem the cyclical fluctuations in the aggregate output of the monetary union as a whole. The fiscal capacity's role would then be to support monetary policy in the pursuit of its aggregate inflation goal. As such, it would ease some of the burdens of monetary policy and help to establish a more balanced (fiscal-monetary) policy mix for the monetary union as a whole. This could be desirable if monetary policy is over-stretched (as some would argue is currently the case in European Monetary Union [EMU]), i.e. its effectiveness is constrained by the zero lower bound.
2   However, "stability" could also refer to the "cohesion" of the monetary union: too much cyclical divergence between the members of the monetary union potentially undermines its cohesion and the role of the fiscal capacity would be to minimise this divergence. As such, the fiscal capacity, rather than relieving pressure on monetary policy, would then support or ease the burden for national fiscal policies. This could be particularly welcome where fiscal policy in the periphery is constrained by the banks-sovereign doom loop.

If we take the first objective as our guide, the welfare-loss function, the fiscal capacity aims to minimise would read:

$$\min_{f,f^*} L_{\bar{y}} = \frac{1}{2}\bar{y}^2 + \gamma\frac{1}{2}\left(f^2 + f^{*2}\right)$$

$$\bar{y} = \frac{1}{2}y + \frac{1}{2}y^* \tag{14}$$

where the parameter γ captures the adjustment cost associated with supra-national fiscal policy relative to cyclical fluctuations in the aggregate output gap. The

adjustments cost could stem from the political capital that is "consumed" whenever the fiscal capacity intervenes as there will probably always be latent – if not
overt – political opposition. This gives rise to the following reaction functions:

$$\overset{+ \ - \ - \ ? \ - \ - \ + \ -}{f = f\left(i, f^*, g, g^*, \varepsilon^d, \varepsilon^{*d}, \varepsilon^s, \varepsilon^{*s}\right)} \tag{15}$$

$$\overset{+ \ - \ - \ ? \ - \ - \ + \ -}{f^* = f^*\left(i, f, g, g^*, \varepsilon^d, \varepsilon^{*d}, \varepsilon^s, \varepsilon^{*s}\right)} \tag{16}$$

We see here the same ambiguities with regard to the impact of fiscal expansions in
the periphery and for the same reason. Interestingly, there is a potential asymmetry
about the impact of supply shocks. Positive supply shocks in the core would trigger
a fiscal expansion at the supra-national level (assuming there is fiscal capacity to
begin with) to offset the loss in competitiveness in the periphery that is not neutral
for the monetary union as a whole due to its demand spillover effects via the bank
lending channel. The same reasoning holds for the negative signs on supply shocks
in the periphery in Equations 15 and 16.

   If, however, we take the second objective as our guide, the fiscal capacity may
be expected to minimise the welfare loss stemming from deviations of these fluctuations from one country against the other:

$$\min_{f, f^*} L_{\bar{y}} = \frac{1}{2}\bar{\bar{y}}^2 + \gamma \frac{1}{2}\left(f^2 + f^{*2}\right)$$

$$\bar{\bar{y}} = \frac{1}{2}y - \frac{1}{2}y^* \tag{17}$$

where $\bar{\bar{y}}$ gauges the (standard) deviation of output fluctuations from the mean, as
opposed to the mean of these fluctuations themselves ($\bar{y}$). This gives rise to the
following policy reaction functions:

$$\overset{- + \ - + \ - \ + \ - \ +}{f = f\left(i, f^*, g, g^*, \varepsilon^d, \varepsilon^{*d}, \varepsilon^s, \varepsilon^{*s}\right)} \tag{18}$$

$$\overset{+ + + - \ + \ - \ + \ -}{f^* = f^*\left(i, f, g, g^*, \varepsilon^d, \varepsilon^{*d}, \varepsilon^s, \varepsilon^{*s}\right)} \tag{19}$$

Interestingly, we now find opposing effects of monetary policy, with a monetary
contraction producing a fiscal contraction by the fiscal capacity in the core and
expansion by the fiscal capacity in the periphery. This occurs because a monetary
contraction fuels the banks-sovereign doom loop in the periphery, and therefore
fiscal support in the periphery and fiscal contraction in the core is called for to stem
cyclical divergence. More generally, fiscal policy at the supra-national level tends

to go in opposite directions in one country relative to the other, for a given shock to stem cyclical divergence.

We think this is an important result from our analysis at this point. It goes to show that fiscal transfers from one country to the other are inevitable if fiscal capacity pursues goals other than just the stabilisation of the aggregate business cycle or, as we will show in section 4, if the banks-sovereigns doom loop is active. However, if fiscal capacity is geared towards stabilising aggregate output (regardless of cross-country divergence), such transfers are highly unlikely. We will turn to this again in the next section.

A final observation is in order about the assumed symmetry of the inflation proneness between the periphery versus the core. Before the financial crisis, inflation in the periphery persistently outpaced that in the core. Some of this may be attributable to asymmetric demand and supply shocks associated with the creation of the single currency, such as the removal of exchange rate risk on international capital flows. The latter has been an essential driver of the real estate booms and the associated reallocation of resources to construction activity in parts of the periphery, which in turn may have contributed to an inflation differential between the two blocks. However, there may have been parametric divergences as well, due to supply rigidities in the periphery and differences in inflation expectations, which can be represented by reformulating Equation 2 as:

$$y^s = \left(\pi - \pi^e\right)/\omega + \varepsilon^s$$
$$y^{*s} = \left(\pi^* - \pi^{e*}\right)/\omega^* + \varepsilon^{*s}$$

(2a)

where $\omega^* > \omega$ and $\pi^{e*} - \pi^e = f\left(\pi^* - \pi\right)$. This implies that – all else equal – demand stimulus in the periphery would turn out more inflationary than in the core. This would have two effects, one being a loss in international market share of the periphery to the core (the competitiveness channel) and the other one being a loss of domestic demand in the core relative to the periphery due to a widening of the real interest rate differential (the real interest rate channel). In our view, the net effect of these two channels on the levels of economic activity in the two blocks (as opposed to the split between net exports and domestic absorption in each block), to the extent this is attributable to parametric divergence, is likely to be small and will be ignored for the sake of tractability.

4   Assessing the proposed devices: results

Given that we have identified the relevant policy reaction functions it is possible to solve the model for each of the five policy instruments (i, g, g^*, f, f^*). This solution represents a "Nash equilibrium", i.e. an uncoordinated equilibrium in which all actors pursue their goals independently. Independence in this case has a specific formal meaning, which is that each actor pursues his own welfare loss minimisation goals without considering ex ante how the other actors might respond.

4.1 Numerical calibration of the model

Despite its relative simplicity, the model is still too complex to derive the Nash equilibria analytically so that we will resort to numerical solutions. The assumed baseline values for the parameters are listed in Table 10.1. These values are based on the mainstream literature but are by no means written in stone and are open to discussion. However, we do believe their order of magnitude is broadly correct. We will here briefly discuss the rationales for our picks.

For the responsiveness of the primary fiscal deficit to variations in economic activity gauged by the parameter τ, estimates are available in Girouard and André (2005). The average estimate for the eurozone countries in their sample is 0.48. The difference in their estimates for the averages for the core (0.51) and periphery (0.46) is negligible (the core countries in their sample are Austria, Belgium, Finland, France and the Netherlands, and the periphery countries in their sample are Ireland, Italy, Portugal and Spain). Accordingly, we assume that $\tau = 0.5$.

The parameter gauging the slope of the Phillips-curve ω is based on two studies that estimate, respectively, the semi-elasticity of inflation with regard to the unemployment rate and the semi-elasticity of the unemployment rate relative to real output. Specifically:

1   Ball et al. (2013) provide estimates for the former for a series of advanced economies, including nine eurozone countries for which they on average estimate −0.45. The variation across countries of this estimate is quite limited, and in fact, the averages for the core countries (Belgium, Finland, France, Germany, Netherlands) and periphery countries (Ireland, Italy, Portugal, Spain) in the sample are also −0.45.
2   Conveniently, Llaudes (2005) provides estimates for the latter, including for the same set of eurozone countries covered by Ball et al. (2013). Their average estimate for the eurozone countries is −0.54, with their average estimate for the core at −0.58 and the periphery at −0.49. These are probably not statistically different.

Table 10.1 Numerical calibration of the model[a]

Parameter	Value	Source
τ	0.5	Girouard and André (2005)
ω	0.25	Ball et al. (2013), Llaudes (2005)
η	0.2	Baldacci and Kumar (2010)
ϕ_1	1.0	Clements et al. (2001)
ϕ_2	0.5	Baum et al. (2012), Barrell et al. (2012)
ϕ_3	0.5	Bayoumi et al. (2011), ECB (2013)
ϕ_4	0.5	Bayoumi et al. (2011), ECB (2013)

Note:

a See the explanation in the main text.

Based on these estimates, we assume that $\omega = 0.25$ (very close to the multiple of the two previous estimates, $-0.45 \times -0.54 = 0.24$).

Clements et al. (2001) estimated interest rate multipliers, which for the euro area as a whole are -1.1 after 6 quarters, -1.1 after 8 quarters, and -0.8 after 12 quarters. There are some noticeable differences between countries, but these do not seem to be systematic concerning whether a country is core or periphery.[13] Given this, it looks reasonable to assume that $\phi_1 = 1$.

Baldacci and Kumar (2010) show that an increase in the fiscal deficit by 1 percentage point raises the sovereign yield by 20 basis points on average for a sample of advanced and emerging market countries. This impact can be larger if the initial fiscal position of a country is "poor" (high debt and deficit), up to 60 basis points. However, since this sample includes countries with extremely vulnerable fiscal situations, such as Venezuela, Bolivia and Brazil, we will take the baseline estimate in Baldacci and Kumar (2010) as our guide, and hence assume that $\eta = 0.2$.

For the fiscal multiplier ϕ_2 there is a wide range of estimates available in the literature, with their size depending inter alia on the openness of the economy, due to import leakages. Baum et al. (2012) estimate for the G7 (minus Italy) multipliers in the range of 0.7 to 1.3 for changes in public expenditure and in the range of 0.0 to 0.4 for tax revenues. Barrell et al. (2012) for 18 OECD (Organisation for Economic Co-operation and Development) countries (including EMU countries) estimate multipliers for government consumption of 0.53 in the core (Austria, Belgium, Finland, France, Germany, Netherlands) and 0.66 in the periphery (Greece, Ireland, Italy, Portugal, Spain). For social benefits, they estimate 0.26 for the core, and 0.17 for the periphery. Their tax multipliers are small overall, of the order of 0.1–0.2. So, it would seem that ϕ_2 should be in the range of nil to 0.5, but since our fiscal multiplier is before subtraction of trade leakages (which are modelled separately, see the following), we adopt a value at the upper end of this range, i.e. $\phi_2 = 0.5$.

Estimates for the parameters that capture cross-border trade, ϕ_3 for absorption and ϕ_4 for competitiveness, are available in Bayoumi et al. (2011). They provide separate estimates for the eurozone prior to the creation of the single currency and after its creation, suggesting that the impact of competitiveness has increased. Specifically, their estimate for the price elasticity of intra eurozone exports is around -1 before and -1.5 after the adoption of the euro. Their estimate of the foreign demand elasticity of exports is around 1.5 (both before and after the adoption of the euro). However, since these elasticities arc estimated through export equations, we need to multiply them by the share of intra-area exports in GDP. According to the ECB (2013), these shares average around 40% in the core and 30% in the periphery. We will ignore this difference and multiply the elasticities of Bayoumi et al. (2011) by 0.35, which yields (rounded to the first decimal) $\phi_3 = \phi_4 = 0.5$.

Finally, for the inertia coefficients in the welfare loss functions α, β and γ, we have adopted a value of 0.1, which means that the fiscal and monetary authorities value the cost of deviating from their policy goal ten times as much as the cost of changing their policy instrument variable(s). This is an arbitrary choice, but alternative experiments with our model (not reported here) indicate that significantly higher values of the inertia coefficients do not alter the thrust of the results.

The shocks in our experiments are fixed at, respectively, $\varepsilon^d = \varepsilon^{*d} = -5\%$ (symmetric demand shock), $\varepsilon^d = -\varepsilon^{*d} = 5\%$ (asymmetric demand shock),

$\varepsilon^s = -\varepsilon^{*s} = 5\%$ (symmetric supply shock) and $\varepsilon^s = -\varepsilon^{*s} = 5\%$ (asymmetric supply shock). To facilitate the discussion, the results for each of these sets of shocks are presented in graphical form.

4.2 The current situation

In the current situation, the doom loop is still intact, so we keep the baseline value $\eta = 0.2$. Obviously, there is no fiscal capacity and hence we assume that $f = f^* = 0$. From the impulse responses shown in Figure 10.1 the following can be inferred:

1   After a symmetric demand shock, fiscal stimulus in the periphery lags behind that in the core, as the former is held back by the need to contain the increase

Policy instruments[c]

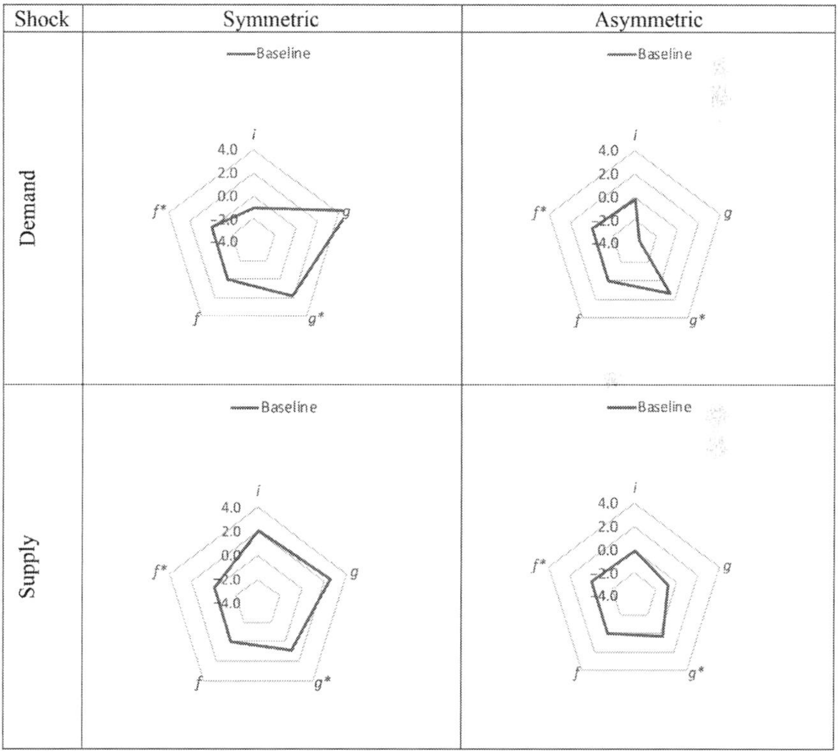

Figure 10.1 Shock responses[a] – baseline[b]

Notes:

a Each diagram shows the shock responses to a specific type of shock (demand or supply, symmetric or asymmetric, see main text). In a situation without shocks all variables are zero.
b Baseline refers to a situation without a safe asset and without fiscal capacity at the centre.
c The policy instruments shown are the monetary policy rate i, the fiscal stance in the core g, the fiscal stance in the periphery g^*, the stance of the fiscal capacity in the core f, and the stance of the fiscal capacity in the periphery f^*.

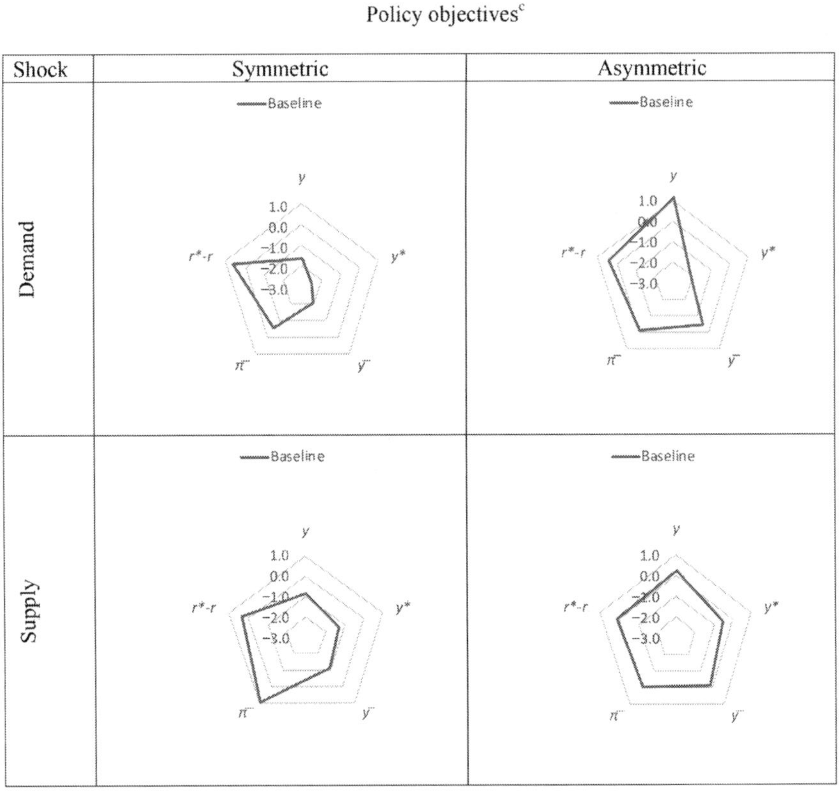

Policy objectives[c]

Figure 10.1 (*cntd.*) Shock responses[a] – baseline[b]

Notes:

a Each diagram shows the shock responses to a specific type of shock (demand or supply, symmetric or asymmetric, see main text). In a situation without shocks all variables are zero.

b Baseline refers to a situation without a safe asset and without fiscal capacity at the centre.

c The policy objectives shown are the levels of output in the core y, in the periphery y, and on aggregate $\bar{y}$, the aggregate rate of inflation $\bar{\pi}$, and the spread between the costs of bank credit in the periphery and in the core $r^* - r$.

in the cost of bank lending. If the demand shock is asymmetric, the core tightens fiscal policy more than the periphery eases it, as may be expected given the need to contain the rise in the cost of loans. Not surprisingly, output stabilisation works out better in the core than in the periphery.

2   After a symmetric supply shock inflation kicks in materially and hence monetary policy is tightened. This is not the case when the supply shock is asymmetric due to the offsetting forces on inflation in the two economies. Either way, fiscal policy in the core responds more strongly than in the periphery for the same reason as given previously.

The upshot is that the asymmetric response of the cost of credit to fiscal develop-ments hampers a commensurate fiscal response in the periphery, which implies an asymmetry also in the impulse response of output. Hence, regardless of the type of shock, the periphery is always worse off in the current situation.

4.3 A safe asset

The introduction of the safe asset removes the doom loop, and hence we assume that $\eta = 0$. With that, the impulse responses of both countries become perfectly symmetric, as is confirmed in Figure 10.2:

1   After a symmetric demand shock, fiscal stimulus is now indeed symmetric, while the yield spread on bank loans disappears. Importantly, the output loss is

Policy instruments[c]

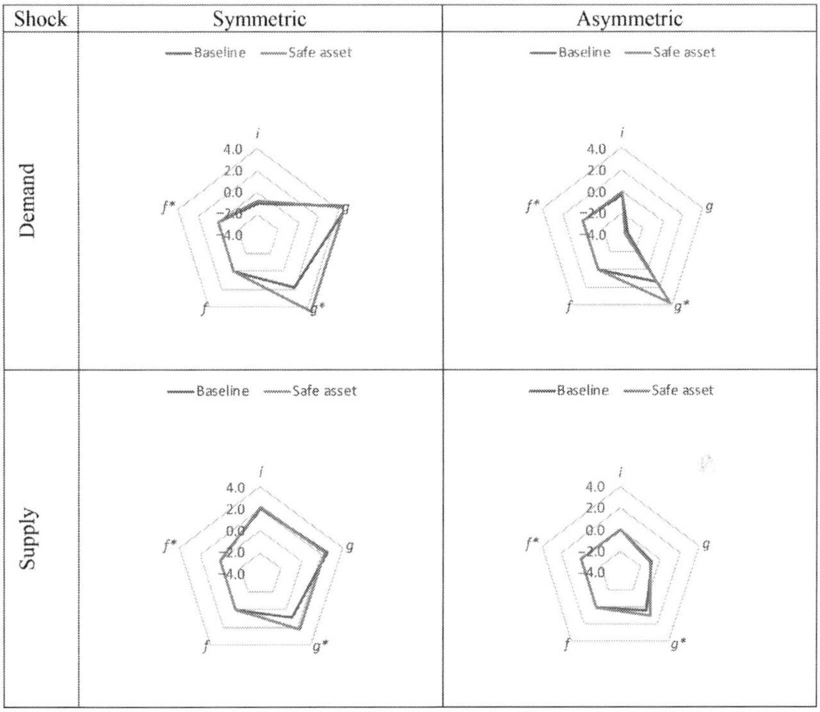

Figure 10.2 Shock responses[a] – baseline and safe asset[b]

Notes:

a   Each diagram shows the shock responses to a specific type of shock (demand or supply, symmetric or asymmetric, see main text). In a situation without shocks all variables are zero.

b   Baseline refers to a situation without a safe asset and without fiscal capacity at the centre.

c   The policy instruments shown are the monetary policy rate i, the fiscal stance in the core g, the fiscal stance in the periphery g^*, the stance of the fiscal capacity in the core f, and the stance of the fiscal capacity in the periphery f^*.

Policy objectives[c]

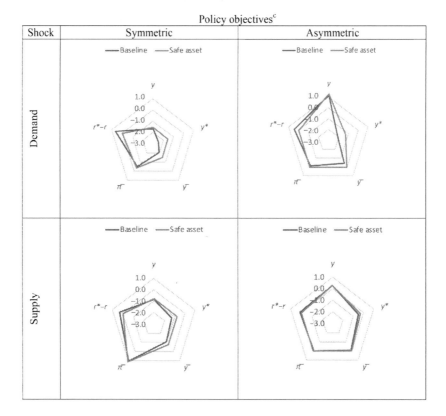

Figure 10.2 (*cntd.*): Shock responses[a] – baseline and safe asset[b]

Notes:

a Each diagram shows the shock responses to a specific type of shock (demand or supply, symmetric or asymmetric, see main text). In a situation without shocks all variables are zero.

b Baseline refers to a situation without a safe asset and without fiscal capacity at the centre.

c The policy objectives shown are the levels of output in the core y, in the periphery y^*, and on aggregate $\bar{y}$, the aggregate rate of inflation $\bar{\pi}$, and the spread between the costs of bank credit in the periphery and in the core $r^* - r$.

smaller for both economies relative to the present situation, indicating that the introduction is a win–win from a macroeconomic stabilisation point of view.

2   After an asymmetric demand shock, the safe asset allows the periphery to ease fiscal policy more and hence to contain the output loss more relative to the current situation. The yield spread on bank loans narrows relative to the current situation, and inflation is somewhat higher.

3   The safe asset creates some space for the periphery to expand its fiscal policy more than in the baseline, also in the case of a symmetric supply shock. The output imbalance diminishes as a result. However, the safe asset is of little significance for the impulse responses to asymmetric supply shocks.

Overall, the introduction of a safe asset improves the stabilisation properties of fiscal policy, from which both countries benefit, especially in the case of symmetric demand shocks.

4.4   Fiscal capacity aimed at macro-stabilisation

We now introduce fiscal capacity able to provide (additional) fiscal impetus, geared towards stabilisation of the aggregate business cycle. We compute the Nash equilibria for cases both without and with the creation of a safe asset to replace sovereign bonds on banks' balance sheets. The main findings are that (see Figure 10.3):

1   The output losses after a symmetric demand shock are smaller relative to the current situation for both countries. Fiscal capacity at the centre provides

Policy instruments[c]

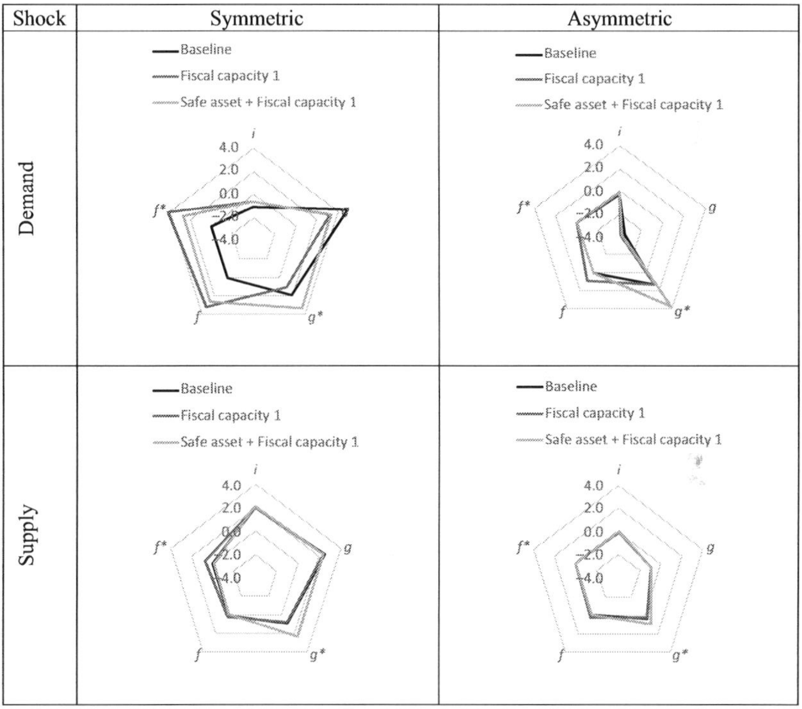

Figure 10.3 Shock responses[a] – baseline, safe asset and fiscal capacity 1[b]

Notes:

a Each diagram shows the shock responses to a specific type of shock (demand or supply, symmetric or asymmetric, see main text). In a situation without shocks all variables are zero.

b Baseline refers to a situation without a safe asset and without fiscal capacity at the centre. Fiscal capacity 1 refers to the situation where fiscal policy at the centre aims to minimise the aggregate output loss.

c The policy instruments shown are the monetary policy rate i, the fiscal stance in the core g, the fiscal stance in the periphery g^*, the stance of the fiscal capacity in the core f, and the stance of the fiscal capacity in the periphery f^*.

Policy objectives[c]

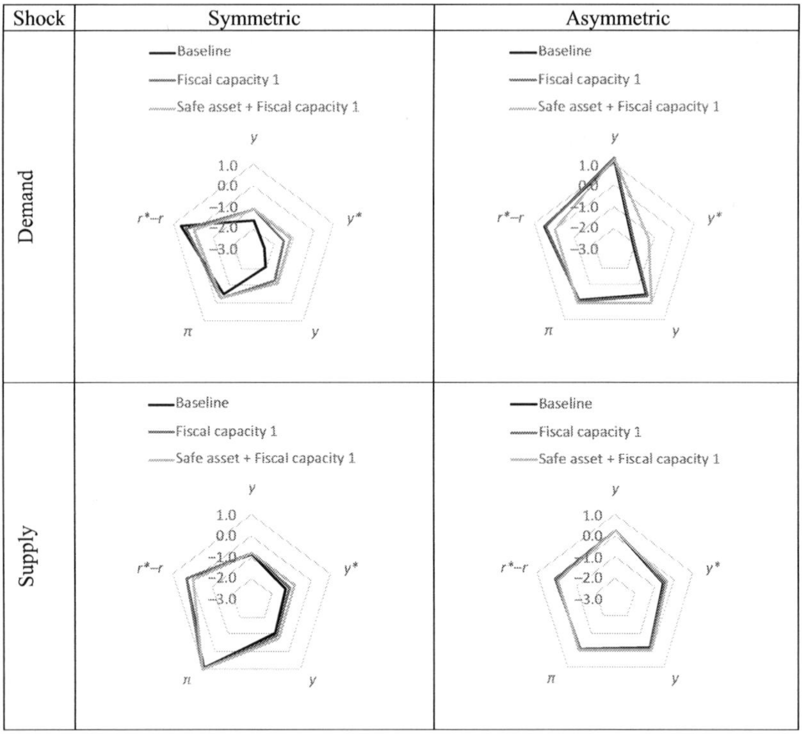

Shock	Symmetric	Asymmetric
Demand		
Supply		

Figure 10.3 (*cntd.*) Shock responses[a] – baseline, safe asset and fiscal capacity 1[b]

Notes:

a Each diagram shows the shock responses to a specific type of shock (demand or supply, symmetric or asymmetric, see main text). In a situation without shocks all variables are zero.

b Baseline refers to a situation without a safe asset and without fiscal capacity at the centre. Fiscal capacity 1 refers to the situation where fiscal policy at the centre aims to minimise the aggregate output loss.

c The policy objectives shown are the levels of output in the core y, in the periphery y^*, and on aggregate $\overline{y}$, the aggregate rate of inflation $\overline{\pi}$, and the spread between the costs of bank credit in the periphery and in the core $r^* - r$.

additional stimulus to both countries, while fiscal stimulus of the national sovereign falls in the periphery (to limit the widening of the rate spread). However, when also a safe asset is introduced, fiscal stimulus in the periphery partly shifts back from the fiscal capacity to the national sovereign, though overall stimulus increases.

2   In the case of supply shocks, be they symmetric or asymmetric, the fiscal capacity is relatively ineffective, even in combination with a safe asset. This is obviously due to the nature of the shocks (demand stimulus is of no help when supply shrinks). When the supply shocks are asymmetric, demand

stimulus at the supra-national level aimed at the aggregate output has no impact at all.

Overall, fiscal capacity aimed at the aggregate cycle (on its own but even more so in combination with a safe asset) provides a relatively powerful stabilisation mechanism in the case of demand shocks but is by comparison of little help in the case of supply shocks, especially when these are asymmetric.

4.5   Fiscal capacity aimed at minimisation of cyclical divergence

In our final set of impulse responses, we look at the case where the fiscal capacity minimises cyclical divergence. Cyclical divergence is absent when shocks are symmetric, and the doom loop neutralised, so in that case, we a priori do not expect fiscal capacity at the centre to be able to make any significant contribution to achieving stabilisation policy goals. Only when the shocks are asymmetric and/ or the doom loop operates would this be different. These priors are confirmed by the impulse responses reported in Figure 10.4:

1   When the demand shock is symmetric, the fiscal capacity makes some difference as it helps to offset the asymmetric output response to the shock resulting from the doom loop. However, addressing the doom loop itself – through the introduction of a safe asset – is much more powerful.
2   When the demand shock is asymmetric, the introduction of fiscal capacity shifts the onus of the overall fiscal expansion from the core to the periphery, with the fiscal capacity running a surplus in the core, which implies a transfer from the core to finance the fiscal capacity's deficit in the periphery. With a safe asset introduced alongside the fiscal capacity also, the periphery sovereign can expand its fiscal policy (relative to baseline) as well.
3   Our conclusion with regard to supply shocks in the previous section – that the fiscal capacity adds little value in that case also holds when the fiscal capacity is aimed at minimising cyclical divergence. Demand stimulus to offset supply shocks is just not a good idea.

The upshot is that combining a safe asset and fiscal capacity aimed at minimising cyclical divergence is a powerful way to address asymmetric demand shocks, but it also implies a cross-country fiscal transfer as the fiscal capacity runs a surplus in the core and a deficit in the periphery.

4.6   Comparing the alternatives

These results indicate different degrees of effectiveness of the various devices depending on the type of shocks.

Specifically, in the case of a symmetric demand shock, without any of the two devices in place, fiscal stimulus in the periphery is held back by the need to contain

Policy instruments[c]

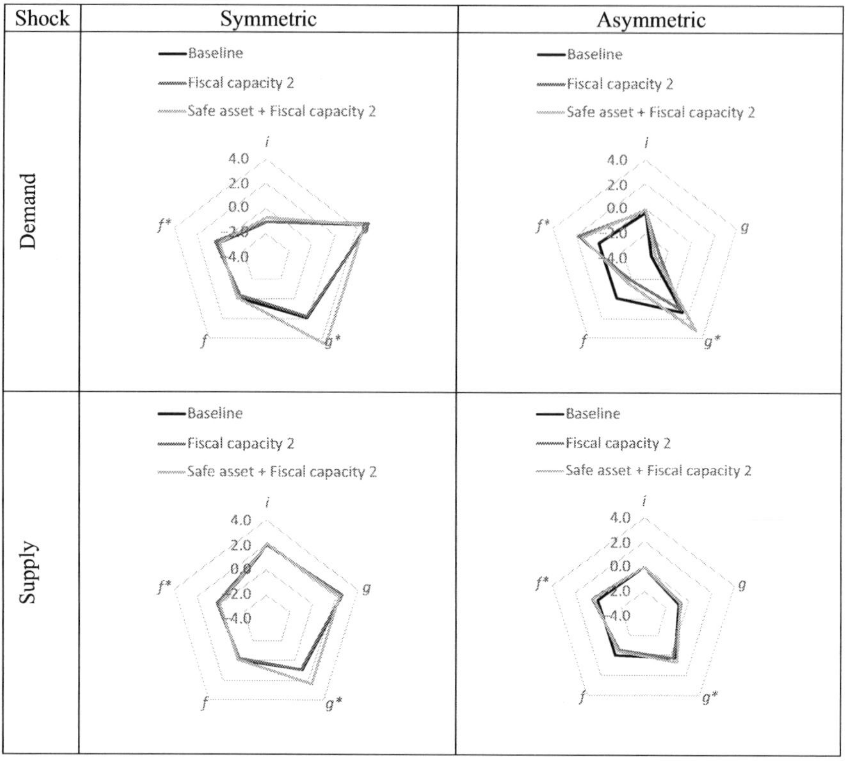

Figure 10.4 Shock responses[a] – baseline, safe asset and fiscal capacity 2[b]

Notes:

a Each diagram shows the shock responses to a specific type of shock (demand or supply, symmetric or asymmetric, see main text). In a situation without shocks all variables are zero.

b Baseline refers to a situation without a safe asset and without fiscal capacity at the centre. Fiscal capacity 2 refers to the situation where fiscal policy at the centre aims to minimise the divergence of output between the core and the periphery.

c The policy instruments shown are the monetary policy rate i, the fiscal stance in the core g, the fiscal stance in the periphery g^*, the stance of the fiscal capacity in the core f, and the stance of the fiscal capacity in the periphery f^*.

the increase in the cost of bank lending. A safe asset would render fiscal stimulus symmetric, with the yield spread on bank loans disappearing. Importantly, both economies would benefit owing to cross-border spill-over demand effects. Fiscal capacity at the centre aimed at minimising the eurozone output gap provides helpful stimulus to both economies, but some asymmetry in economic slack remains. The latter only disappears once fiscal capacity aimed at aggregate stabilisation is combined with a safe asset.

Policy objectives[c]

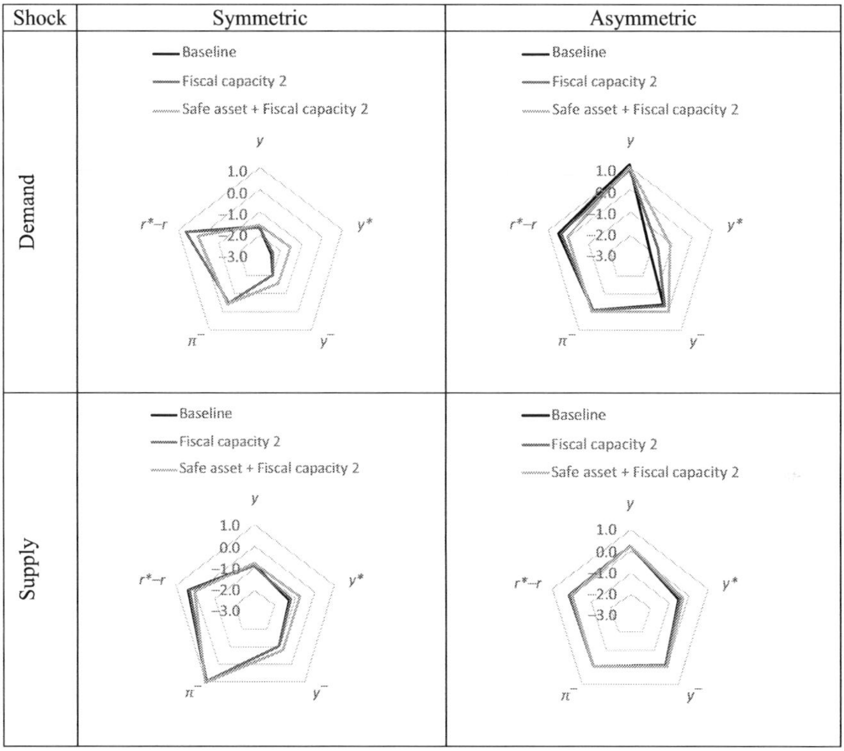

Figure 10.4 (*cntd.*) Shock responses[a] – baseline, safe asset and fiscal capacity 2[b]

Notes:

a Each diagram shows the shock responses to a specific type of shock (demand or supply, symmetric or asymmetric, see main text). In a situation without shocks all variables are zero.

b Baseline refers to a situation without a safe asset and without fiscal capacity at the centre. Fiscal capacity 2 refers to the situation where fiscal policy at the centre aims to minimise the divergence of output between the core and the periphery.

c The policy objectives shown are the levels of output in the core y, in the periphery y^*, and on aggregate $\bar{y}$, the aggregate rate of inflation $\bar{\pi}$, and the spread between the costs of bank credit in the periphery and in the core $r^* - r$.

In the case of a symmetric supply shock inflation kicks in materially and hence monetary policy would be tightened. Its impact is asymmetric, however, because it results in a higher cost of credit and a more muted fiscal expansion in the periphery than in the core. Again, a safe asset would remove this asymmetry, while fiscal capacity at the centre would be comparatively ineffective because it fails to address the cause of instability in this case – which is a lack of aggregate supply rather than a lack of aggregate demand. Generally, when shocks (demand or supply) are symmetric, the effectiveness of fiscal capacity aimed at minimising divergence is very limited if not absent.

In the case of an asymmetric demand shock – favourable for the core but unfavourable for the periphery – fiscal easing in the periphery falls short of the tightening in the core, so on balance the fiscal stance tightens on aggregate. With a safe asset, this asymmetry in the policy response disappears. The introduction of fiscal capacity aimed at minimising cyclical divergence implies a de facto transfer from the core to the periphery over the central budget, providing support to activity in the periphery. With a safe asset introduced alongside the fiscal capacity, the periphery sovereign can expand its fiscal policy (relative to baseline) as well. However, fiscal capacity aimed at aggregate output has little impact in this case. In the case of an asymmetric supply shock, none of the devices is of much help.

5   Conclusions

Addressing structural weaknesses and building up fiscal buffers to enable countercyclical stimulus is a requirement for all countries in the eurozone. Any sharing of risk or liability is not feasible without countries behaving responsibly and, eventually, giving up sovereignty (i.e. unity of liability and control). Without giving up sovereignty completely, moral hazard will always be a risk. It needs to be addressed by strict enforcement of the fiscal rules and allowing countries to default if they do not comply and/or are in case of an ESM adjustment programme.

Against this backdrop, the chapter makes a very simple point: it is welfare enhancing, i.e. good from an economic point of view for all, both for the eurozone periphery and the core, to have a mechanism in place to absorb negative symmetric and asymmetric shocks smoothly. The vulnerability implicit in high debt-to-GDP ratios, the poor quality of bank assets in some countries and the ZLB tend to magnify shocks. The extra stress falls disproportionally on the periphery, but also adversely affects the core. The responsible conduct of policies, while desirable in itself, would still not protect the periphery from being hit disproportionately by shocks in the absence of exchange rate adjustment and the constraints on monetary policy due to the ZLB.

Therefore, purely from an economic point of view, it would be desirable to have a safe asset and fiscal capacity to absorb these shocks. The alternative would be to allow these shocks to play out as a deterrent to misguided policies fully. However, over time, this would undermine social cohesion and political support for integration. A safe asset and fiscal capacity can only come with strict conditionality and with a democratically legitimate transfer of sovereignty to the centre. Rejecting these devices would, however, leave the eurozone exposed to unnecessary stress.

Specifically, our modelling exercise shows that the current situation leaves peripheral countries particularly exposed to symmetric and asymmetric demand shocks. Regardless of the type of shock (demand or supply), the periphery is always worse off due to the banks-sovereign doom loop. The introduction of the safe asset removes the doom loop, makes the impulse responses of both countries perfectly symmetric, while the spread on bank lending rates disappears. The output loss is reduced for both blocks and the stabilisation properties of fiscal policy improve for both blocks as well, especially in the case of symmetric demand shocks. Moreover, the safe asset creates some space for the periphery to expand its fiscal policy more than in the baseline.

The introduction of fiscal capacity aimed at stabilisation of the aggregate business cycle can provide additional fiscal impetus to both blocks. Combined with a safe asset, fiscal stimulus in the periphery can be shared between the fiscal capacity and the national sovereign. Fiscal capacity aimed at smoothing the aggregate cycle, on its own but even more so in combination with a safe asset, thus provides a relatively powerful stabilisation mechanism in the case of demand shocks, although it is by comparison of little help in the case of supply shocks, especially when these are asymmetric.

When fiscal capacity aims at minimising cyclical divergence, it helps to minimise output losses in both blocks in case of asymmetric demand shocks. In combination with a safe asset introduced alongside fiscal capacity, the periphery sovereign can expand its fiscal policy (relative to baseline) as well, and fiscal capacity becomes a powerful way to address asymmetric demand shocks, but it also implies cross-country fiscal transfers. Fiscal capacity adds little value in case of supply shocks, and it would not be a good idea to use it for that purpose.

We repeat that, while the economic rationale for a safe asset and fiscal capacity in the eurozone emerges clearly from our analysis, their introduction needs to be accompanied by a proper democratically legitimate process that leads to centralised control, without weakening the signalling role of financial market discipline or increasing "moral hazard".

Notes

1 See for instance Codogno and Galli (2017).
2 The Euro Summit on 14 December 2018 endorsed the terms of reference on the reform of the European Stability Mechanism and asked the Eurogroup to prepare the necessary amendments to the ESM Treaty by June 2019. In the terms sheet, there is an explicit reference to the need "to improve the existing framework for promoting debt sustainability in the euro area. . . . We also reaffirm the principle that financial assistance should only be granted to countries whose debt is sustainable and whose repayment capacity is confirmed. This will be assessed by the Commission in liaison with the ECB, and the ESM". The principle is "reaffirmed" as some argue it is already explicit in the preamble of the current ESM Treaty: "(12) In accordance with IMF practice, in exceptional cases an adequate and proportionate form of private sector involvement shall be considered in cases where stability support is provided accompanied by conditionality in the form of a macro-economic adjustment programme".
3 On the specifics, see Zettelmeyer and Leandro (2018).
4 See for this proposal Bini Smaghi and Marcussen (2018).
5 There are also some drawbacks. Tranching would reduce liquidity, which may call for higher premia. Moreover, the convex shape of the credit curve may also imply higher average cost of borrowing.
6 This, by the way, raises a huge political problem as, in some circumstances, high-unemployment countries would have to pay benefits to low-unemployment countries even though the unemployment gap remains wide.

7 It could be argued that market discipline would even be strengthened as the part of the debt remaining at national level would be perceived as riskier.

8 The model developed in this section is based on a two-country version of the single-country model developed by Buti et al. (2002) which has similarities with the model developed in Buti et al. (2003), except that we assume here most model parameters to be strictly identical (symmetric) across countries.

9 See note 2.

10 The penalty on bank lending rates applies to the periphery but not to the core. However, bank lending rates may be due to a number of factors not related to the banks-sovereign doom loop described in the paper. Other channels may transfer the rising sovereign risk to bank credit risk, such as the government guarantees on the banking sector. Appropriate policies, i.e. bank resolution framework, supervision, and so on, may mute the effects of these channels. Moreover, for the banks there may be a tradeoff between increasing banking rates and reducing bank loans, i.e. improving the quality of their bank portfolio. Although these two effects may have different impacts on the economy, to maintain the exercise simple we assume that bank loan spreads can also represent other possible transmission mechanisms.

11 In the model, the penalty on the bank lending rate is only applied for national fiscal expansions, which is the identifying assumption and thus crucial to derive the result that centralised expansions are more desirable. Admittedly, there is the possibility that centralised expansions are financed via common debt and thus the high-risk countries are compensated by low-risk countries. However, if the safe asset is de facto back-stopped by the ECB, fiscal expansions at the centre would carry no risk other than the risk of inflation and tighter monetary policy in the future. Without a backstop, indeed, there is sovereign risk that is henceforth shared between the core and the periphery, and therefore yields in the core would end up higher than baseline. The experience of the Outright Monetary Transactions (OMT) seems to suggest that the "insurance" offered to the periphery did not translate into higher rates at the core. Moreover, if the whole point of a safe asset is that it enjoys a central bank backstop, then the yield curve may steepen after fiscal expansion at the centre. However, this would not be different from the baseline case, and thus we have not included it in the model.

12 See for instance Baldacci and Kumar (2010) for the impact of the fiscal deficit on sovereign yields and Hervé et al. (2010) for the fiscal and monetary policy multipliers.

13 After eight quarters the multiplier is 1.1 for the core and −1.0 for the periphery, with slightly larger but still modest differences for shorter and longer time horizons.

References

Baldacci, E. and M. S. Kumar (2010), "Fiscal Deficits, Public Debt, and Sovereign Bond Yields", *IMF Working Paper*, WP/10/184, August.

Ball, L., D. Leigh and P. Loungani (2013), "Okun's Law: Fit at 50?", *IMF Working Paper*, WP/13/10.

Barrell, R., D. Holland and I. Hurst (2012), "Fiscal Multipliers and Prospects for Consolidation", *OECD Journal: Economic Studies*, 2012(1), 71–102.

Baum, A., M. Poplawski-Ribeiro and A. Weber (2012), "Fiscal Multipliers and the State of the Economy", *IMF Working Paper*, WP/12/286.

Bayoumi, T., R. Harmsen and J. Turunen (2011), "Euro Area Export Performance and Competitiveness", *IMF Working Paper*, WP/11/140.

Bini Smaghi, L. and M. Marcussen (2018), "Delivering a Safe Asset for the Euro Area: A Proposal for a Purple Bond Transition", *VOX CEPR Policy Portal*, 19 July.

Buti, M. and N. Carnot (2018), "The Case for a Central Fiscal Capacity in EMU", *VOX CEPR Policy Portal*, 7 December.

Buti, M., C. Martinez-Mongay, K. Sekkat and P. van den Noord (2003), "Macroeconomic Policy and Structural Reform: A Conflict between Stabilisation and Flexibility?", in Buti, M. (ed.), *Monetary and Fiscal Policies in EMU*, Cambridge: Cambridge University Press, pp. 187–213.

Buti, M., W. Roeger and J. in't Veld (2002), "Monetary and Fiscal Policy Interactions under a Stability Pact", in Buti, M. et al. (Eds.), *The Behaviour of Fiscal Authorities: Stabilisation, Growth and Institutions*, London: Palgrave, pp. 241–267.

Clements, B., Z. G. Kontolemis and J. Levy (2001), "Monetary Policy under EMU: Differences in the Transmission Mechanism?", *IMF Working Paper*, WP/01/102.

Codogno, L. and G. Galli (2017), "Can Fiscal Consolidation Be Counterproductive?", *Economia Italiana*, No. 2017/1–2–3, December.

De Grauwe, P. and Y. Ji (2018), "Financial Engineering Will Not Stabilise an Unstable Euro Area", *VOX CEPR Policy Portal*, 19 March.

ECB (2013), "Intra-Euro Area Trade Linkages and External Adjustment", *ECB Monthly Bulletin*, January.

European Commission (2011), *Green Paper on the Feasibility of Introducing Stability Bonds*, 818 final, November.

Girouard, N. and C. André (2005), "Measuring Cyclically-Adjusted Budget Balances for OECD Countries", *OECD Economics Department Working Papers*, No. 434.

Hervé, K., P. Richardson, F. Sédillot and P.-O. Beffy (2010), "The OECD's New Global Model", OECD Economics Department Working Papers, No. 768, OECD Publishing, Paris.

Llaudes, R. (2005), "The Phillips Curve and Long-Term Unemployment", *ECB Working Paper Series*, No. 441, February.

Zettelmeyer, J. and Á. Leandro (2018), "Europe's Search for a Safe Asset", *Policy Brief*, Petersen Institute for International Economics, October.

Part 5

The eurozone

Not just a monetary union?

11 Can the euro succeed without European political union?

The organizational challenges facing a multi-government monetary union in the "managed currency" era

Tim Congdon

European monetary unification has been a unique endeavour. The sharing of one currency by countries which retain fiscal sovereignty and a substantial degree of banking-system autonomy has been attempted nowhere else in the era of managed currencies.[1] What are the conditions for the achievement of monetary and financial stability in a multi-government monetary union of this sort?[2] And how far have these conditions been met since the introduction of the euro in 1999?

This paper will begin by arguing – in its opening sections – that the conditions are of two kinds:

- Those which are much the same as in a traditional monetary jurisdiction
- Those which are specific to Europe's post-1999 exercise in monetary unification

Neither set of conditions has been fully met in practice, although the third section will find that the eurozone's managers came closer to achieving them in the euro's first decade than subsequently. The violation of the conditions for the success of the monetary union has led a conspicuous financial imbalance in the TARGET2 settlement system. This imbalance is manifested in a large, persistent and unresolved nexus of debits and credits between the central banks of member states; it is of great concern to member states partly because of potential defaults and losses, but also because – even if they are eventually honoured – the terms of the debts have significant distributional implications while they are current.[3] Some observers believe that the TARGET2 imbalance is unsustainable and may rupture the monetary union.[4] By specifying the requirements for the avoidance of inter-state transfers via the ECB's balance sheet and hence for the eurozone's constitutional integrity, the paper may help to inform the debate on future policymaking.

1 General conditions for policy success in a monetary union

Now that all the world's currencies have broken the link with a commodity, most economists agree that they have to be managed by the appropriate state-backed authorities, usually a central bank. Given the long-run similarity of the rates of changes of the quantity of money and nominal national income, a well-established point of view is that these authorities should ensure that money growth is held at a low, but positive, rate and that it should be steady over time.[5] A suitably low rate of money growth ought to deliver stability of the price level (or, at any rate, modest inflation in line with an official target), while money growth that is steady at a positive rate can contribute to the avoidance of large cyclical fluctuations in demand, output and employment.

No consensus has emerged on the concept of money that is appropriate in a prescription for currency management, but it is taken for granted here that an all-inclusive (or broadly defined) money aggregate is to be watched and controlled in the eurozone.[6] This is compatible with the tradition of monetary targeting pursued by the Bundesbank when in the 1980s and 1990s it was, by common consent, the most admired central bank in Europe; it is also consistent with the so-called P-star approach to the specification of a money target.[7] Although the correct approach to monetary management is another matter for debate, it is undoubtedly true that bank deposits are the principal constituent of broad money in modern Europe, that deposits are the main liabilities of banking systems and that any increase in banks' total liabilities must be matched by an identical increase in their assets. A desired rate of growth of the quantity of money therefore has implications for the growth of the credit counterparts on the assets side of bank balance sheets and so for policy decisions in the management of those counterparts.

Can these remarks be translated into more specific numbers for monetary control? To set the favoured rate of money growth, guidance is needed on the two components of the nominal growth of gross domestic product (that is, real growth and inflation), and allowance should be made for any likely change in the ratio of money to GDP. The trend rate of growth of real output in the eurozone at present is widely thought to be under 1.5% a year, although a somewhat higher number prevailed before 2008.[8] The European Central Bank's (ECB's) website has for many years given a clear and exact statement about the meaning of the price stability notion. In 1998, its Governing Council advanced a quantitative definition in the following words: "Price stability is defined as a year-on-year increase in the harmonised index of consumer prices (HICP) for the euro area of below 2 per cent". It further elaborated in 2003 that "in the pursuit of price stability [the ECB] aims to maintain inflation rates below, but close to, 2 per cent over the medium term". A reasonable view is that price stability is tantamount to a rise in the price level of 1% a year. On this basis an increase in nominal GDP of about 2.5% a year ought to be consistent with price stability, as the ECB sees the matter.

Quantity-theory economists have long appealed to the "proportionality hypothesis" in their theoretical work. This boils down, in essence, to the claim that changes in the quantity of money and the price level ought to equi-proportional when the quantity of money is subject to a large upward or downward shift and nothing real in the economy is altered.[9] In practice most nations experience a rise in the ratio of broad money to GDP in the course of economic development.[10] The early phases of European monetary unification amounted to a major financial liberalization in many member states, notably those on the eurozone periphery where burdensome official restrictions on banks' asset composition were common before 1999. The single currency therefore boosted the competitiveness of the banking system and enabled banks to grow their balance sheets faster than GDP without adverse macroeconomic consequences. A plausible surmise is that in the eurozone broad money can safely be allowed to expand by 1% or even 2% a year more than nominal GDP. With the aim of a 2.5% a year advance in nominal GDP, the ideal rate of money growth for the eurozone comes out at, say, 3% to 4.5% a year.[11]

Roughly speaking, the implied prescription is that banks' assets ought also to expand at the same rate. But a complication arises from role of banks' equity capital and such non-monetary liabilities as bonds.[12] As capital is a liability of the banking system, large rises and falls in capital may cause bank deposits (and hence broad money) to increase at a different rate from total assets. The procedure in this paper is to suggest that the desired percentage increase in total assets be expressed relative to broad money, which is somewhat lower than banks' balance-sheet totals. If equity and bond capital is taken to be about 20% of liabilities, the policy prescription – the rule that should deliver approximate stability of the price level and output growth – becomes that banks' assets should grow *in any particular year* at between 4% and 6% of the stock of broad money *at the start of that year*. Another difficulty with the approach is that banks can acquire claims on the foreign sector, while money growth is affected by the eurozone's international financial transactions. Although important, this difficulty is ignored here in order to keep the analysis manageable. So the rule applies to banks' domestic assets – that is, the sum of their credit to the public and private sectors.

Figure 11.1 shows the annual sum of bank credit to the public and private sectors as a percentage of the stock of broad money at each year's beginning, in the

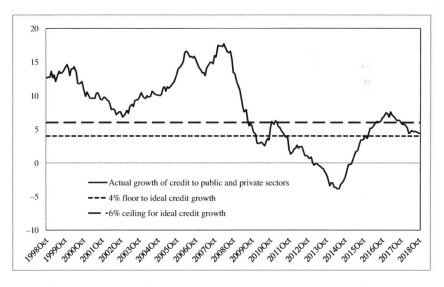

Figure 11.1 Bank credit to the eurozone domestic economy (i.e. to public and private sectors), in 12-month periods, as a percentage of stock of M3 at period start

Source: ECB database and author's estimates.

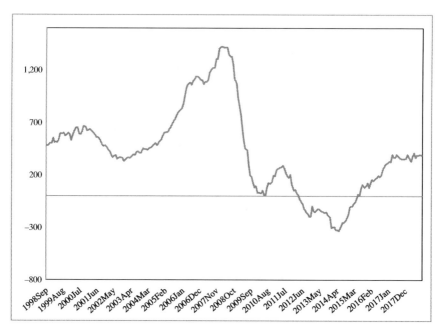

Figure 11.2 Bank credit to the private sector (flow), in the euro's first two decades –
12-month totals, monthly data, in billions of euros

Source: ECB database.

20 years leading up to October 2018, and Figure 11.2 shows the annual value of bank credit to the private sector by itself. (The data are monthly.) If the eurozone's monetary managers had remembered the Bundesbank's commitment to low and stable money growth at a constant rate, and if the prescription of the last few paragraphs had been respected, the line representing credit expansion would have been between the two straight lines horizontal to the x-axis, for the floor and ceiling to the credit growth prescription. It is quickly evident that this was not the case. Credit expansion exhibited much year-by-year volatility and was much more rapid in the eurozone's first decade than in its second.[13]

In the ten years to October 2018 the sum of bank credit to the public and private sectors in one-year periods averaged 12.1% of M3 at the years' starts; in the next ten years it averaged only 3.4%, on the same basis. Perhaps surprisingly, the buoyancy of credit growth in the first decade was consistent with reasonable price stability *of goods and services*. Part of the explanation was a rise in the equilibrium ratio of broad money to GDP, due to financial-liberalization effects, as noted previously; another influence was that banks funded their balance-sheet growth to a significant extent from bond issuance (that is, not by money creation), as securitisation was popular in global financial markets. Overall the first decade was regarded by contemporaries as a success, not least because the credit boom and high money growth were associated with big gains in the prices *of assets* (*notably residential real estate*), and robust advances in output and employment, particularly in 2006 and 2007. (But by late 2007 and early 2008 the ECB was nervous about the spread of inflation to labour and product markets.)[14] The second decade was quite different. For much of it, policymakers were concerned that the price level might fall, with some commentators making conjectures that deflation could become entrenched.[15] Their job was less to restrain inflation, more to prevent deflation.

The macroeconomic experience of the eurozone as a whole is consistent with a monetary account of the determination of national income and wealth; it confirms the importance of suitably low and stable growth of credit and money to the attainment of wider monetary stability. Unhappily, in the euro's first 20 years instability in credit expansion and money growth was accompanied by variations in inflation pressure, and marked cyclical fluctuations in output and employment. A fair comment is that these variations and fluctuations undermined the popularity of European integration.[16] Nevertheless, the price level rose only slowly and in that sense monetary stability was secured.[17]

2   Conditions for policy success specific to a monetary union

What about the second type of conditions for the realization of a multi-government monetary union, namely those that are specific to it and are not applicable in a traditional currency jurisdiction? Has the eurozone performed any better on this front?

The extension of bank credit involves the laying of claims to resources, since the borrower is enabled by a loan to spend money on the acquisition of goods, services and assets that would not otherwise be possible. Since resources are finite and parties excluded from their use may resent the loss, the distribution of a nation's resources between different agents is – at least partly – a political matter.[18] Of course, if the extension of bank credit affects the distribution of control over resources and output between different groups, it is liable to cause tension between them. History provides many examples in which, even within a nation, the selection of a currency standard (gold rather than silver, for example) excites antagonism between sectional interests.[19] But the risk of inter-group (or intergovernmental and international) tension is much greater in a multi-government monetary union.

Of course, many credit decisions are driven by market criteria rather than political considerations. Bank lending to the private sector by privately owned banks – where both the borrower and the lender are motivated by profit and returns – may proceed with no reference to politics whatsoever. However, credit can be extended by the central bank as well as by profit-seeking commercial banks, and nowadays the central bank is invariably state owned. In general, credit extension by the central bank is therefore far more political – and hence much more likely to stir up sectional grievances (or even international sensitivities) – than commercial bank credit to the private sector. The scope of central-bank credit extension is a crucial issue in the design of a multi-government monetary union.

The Maastricht Treaty of 1992, which set in train the process of European monetary union, appeared to limit the availability of bank credit to particular governments and nations. Most fundamentally, the "no bailout" clause (Article 125) was meant to ensure that the responsibility for repaying public debt stayed at the national level. Indeed, a protocol to the Treaty spelt out that nations incurring budget deficits that exceeded certain percentages of GDP could be fined by the EU authorities. The resulting "excessive deficits procedure" had its origins in Articles 121 and 126 of the Maastricht Treaty, but was made more definite in a separate Stability and Growth Pact agreed by eurozone member states in 1997.

Further, by Article 123 the Maastricht Treaty prohibited overdraft finance from the ECB (or any of the national central banks that constituted the so-called eurosystem) to any national government. Article 123 spread to the entire eurozone a principle contained in the 1957 German legislation which created the Bundesbank, that governments must not finance their expenditure by resort to the printing press. According to Wyplosz in a 2010 analysis, the no bailout clause, the excessive deficits procedure and the prohibition on overdrafts to governments were three vital "safeguards" for the eurozone's long-run viability. They would prevent fiscal irresponsibility at the national level undermining the price stability that monetary union was intended to deliver.[20] Governments had to keep deficits and borrowing down, and – if they did have deficits – they were not to finance them from central banks.

Nevertheless, the Maastricht Treaty was far from rigorous and comprehensive in its treatment of the potential problems. Specifically, it failed to spell out in enough detail how the ECB and the national central banks were to operate once the single currency came into being. In a traditional monetary jurisdiction the central bank has two customers, the government and the commercial banking system. It takes deposits from the government and records the government's transactions across this account, and it finances part of the government's activities. A key observation for the present discussion is that finance can be granted by holding securities issued by the government rather than by making direct loans. The central bank also takes deposits from commercial banks, which settle imbalances between each other in its legal-tender cash liabilities. Occasionally it also lends to commercial banks. Such loans may be routine and uncontroversial in nature, or they may be necessary in conditions of financial stress when banks have trouble funding their assets. In stress conditions the central bank loans are typically called "lender of last resort finance" or "emergency liquidity assistance".

The Maastricht Treaty was silent on basic issues which stemmed from these recognised and familiar functions of a central bank. First, while Article 123 stopped overdraft finance from the central bank to the government, the Treaty empowered it to buy and sell marketable securities for monetary policy purposes. Government securities are of course everywhere the most liquid and therefore the most marketable available. By implication, the ECB might hold the government securities of any or all of the eurozone's sovereign states.

Sometimes such holdings might be temporary and technical, as with repurchase operations used to signal interest rate levels. With repo activity in a one-government monetary area, holdings of government securities do not represent a long-term intention to own and constitute only a nominal granting of central bank credit. But sometimes the central bank buys government securities and sits on them for several years or even to redemption. Ownership is then meaningful. It follows that, in a monetary union, the central bank's decisions on government bond purchases could affect the distribution of resources and output between member states. But the Maastricht Treaty did not specify the proportions of its assets – or of its total holdings of government securities – that might be represented by securities issued by the governments of individual nations. Given that central bank finance is usually lower-cost than funding from capital markets, this omission was potentially serious. If the government securities of one nation were over-represented in the ECB's balance sheet (relative, say, to that nation's output share in the eurozone), that might lead to charges of discrimination and unfairness. To offer an extreme example, would it be right for the liabilities of the Portuguese government to exceed half of the ECB's total holdings of government securities? Would that not be hard to justify, in view of Portugal's much lower share (about 2%) of eurozone output?[21]

Secondly, the Maastricht Treaty gave no indication about how the ECB was to act as a lender of last resort. Almost by definition, banking emergencies due to cash runs on deposits are inherently unpredictable. The central bank has to act flexibly, pragmatically and with full discretion. Often there is rough justice in its behaviour. In established nation states – to which political and financial elites have long-standing loyalties – people tolerate the rough justice for the sake of the financial system (and the nation) as a whole.[22] Given the opacity of banking crises, and the dangers of media misrepresentation, the central bank's last-resort loans are likely to be far more controversial in a multi-government monetary union than in nation states with one government, one central bank and one commercial banking system. A refusal by the ECB to lend to cash-short, but solvent, banks in one member country could heavily damage that country's financial system and its economy. At the time of the Maastricht Treaty, a sensible conjecture might have been that the ECB would not antagonise member states in this way, and hence would be liberal and easy-going with lender-of-last-resort assistance. An obvious danger would then be that an accompanying relaxed attitude to banking supervision might lead, over time, to lower credit standards.[23]

The textbook formula for last-resort lending is that, as long as it is collateralised by good security, it should be available on an abundant scale, but at an above-market (or "penal") interest rate.[24] This formula dates back to the mid-Victorian thinker Walter Bagehot, who wrote about the subject in his path-breaking 1873 book *Lombard Street*. The ready availability and amplitude of cash support are vital. Market participants must appreciate that the cash will *not* run out, so that they have no further incentive to convert deposits into cash. It follows that last-resort facilities in a multi-government monetary union must be potentially on a massive scale if they are to work, just as applies in a one-nation currency jurisdiction. But there is an awkward new wrinkle in the eurozone. To the extent that the ECB makes emergency loans disproportionately to the commercial banking system of one member country rather than the commercial banking system(s) of another (or others), the nation's banking system – and so that nation itself – is receiving a privileged form of finance. If the last-resort loans are at a penalty rate, in line with the Bagehot principle, the lending countries are unlikely to be worse off. However, if the last-resort loans are at a beneath-market rate, the borrowing countries may benefit unfairly at the lenders' expense.

To summarise, the Maastricht Treaty contained a no bailout clause intended to clarify a core organizational principle: the introduction of the single currency would not lead to inter-governmental (and hence inter-state) transfers within the eurozone. Monetary union was to promote political union between eurozone members, but it was not to become "a transfer union" between them. Unfortunately, the treaty overlooked a difficulty so fundamental that it amounted to virtual self-contradiction. The very existence of a fully empowered central bank was almost certain to result in significant net cross-border payments. If open market operations had the effect that one government's debt was over-represented in ECB assets, and if last-resort lending were skewed towards the banks of one or a few member states, the ECB's decisions – even if ostensibly technical in nature – could have the same results as inter-state payments in a transfer union.

In other words, by pursuing its understood objectives, and by doing so with long-established methods in accordance with functions and responsibilities blessed by precedent, the ECB would – very probably – affect the inter-governmental distribution of resources and output. If undertaken on a large scale, familiar and seemingly unobjectionable central-banking operations could breach the no bailout clause. The ECB's actions as a central bank might result in bailouts by stealth. A de facto transfer union might emerge, regardless of the precise wording of Article 125 of the Maastricht Treaty.

The risk of these outcomes was greatest in a certain kind of macroeconomic context. The first section of this chapter contrasted the eurozone's first and second decades, with policymakers in the second decade often more worried about deflation than inflation. Some critics of the single currency had remarked in the 1990s that monetary policy might find deflation the harder evil to tackle. In his 2008 book *The Birth of the Euro*, Otmar Issing, the ECB's first chief economist, tried to meet this challenge. In his words, the ECB could respond to "a highly deflationary" environment "just like other central banks". It "could if necessary inject unlimited amounts of central bank money through the purchase of all kinds of debt securities".[25]

The trouble was that the ECB was not – and still is not – "just like other central banks". Whereas they are answerable to just one government and one commercial banking system, the ECB conducts business with a large number of governments and commercial banking systems.[26] If the central bank in a multi-government monetary union has to expand its balance sheet rapidly to counter deflation, it has to decide the quantities of government and other securities it will buy from each and every member state, and the prices at which such purchases will take place. These are vexed and intensely political issues, with immediate distributional consequences akin to those in a transfer union. Indeed, before the euro began in 1999, the various European nations had utterly different intellectual traditions and practices in this area of policymaking. Germany – with the eurozone's largest economy – had virtually no post-war experience of short-term government financing at all.[27] On the other hand, the government of Italy – with the eurozone's third-largest economy – had for decades been reliant on banks to meet its enormous short-term cash needs.[28]

Suppose that the deflation threat is real. Suppose that ECB's Governing Council decides to counter it by large-scale purchases of "all kinds of securities", in line with Issing's remarks in *The Birth of the Euro*. The ECB could buy bonds issued by the private sector, but it thereby takes risk onto its balance sheet and may be charged with favouritism if it buys too much paper from one country's private sector than another's. In practice, purchases of government securities are almost certain to be the dominant element. We come back to the issue raised a few paragraphs ago. By what criteria is the value of purchases of the different governments' debt to be determined? Given that ratios of public debt to GDP vary widely across the eurozone, any set of criteria is likely to be contentious. A policy debate might expose the rift between German (and North European) and Italian (and South European) mind-sets about these matters. Indeed, for the ECB deliberately to buy the debt of a government (or governments) with public debt far in excess of the limits stated in the Maastricht Treaty might appear to reward it (or them) for fiscal profligacy.[29]

3   Policy-making in practice

What does the discussion in the last section imply about the circumstances in which a multi-government monetary union would be a success? Of course, the three crucial rules of fiscal discipline spelt out in the Maastricht Treaty, and identified as essential "safeguards" by Wyplosz in 2010, had to be respected. But, over and above that requirement, our discussion predicts that inter-governmental tensions would be least, and that the monetary union would avoid friction, if

- the dominant form of credit extension is *commercial* bank lending to the private sector, rather than the *central bank* financing of budget deficits;
- the rate of growth of bank credit to the private sector is just right – not too high, not too low – to sustain domestic credit expansion at a level consistent with inflation-target money growth;
- central bank operations are mostly repurchase agreements to signal interest rate intentions rather than operations which result in the long-term granting of credit, perhaps on a differential basis, to the governments and banks of particular nations; and
- banks are profitable, well-capitalised and credit-worthy, since that facilitates the funding of assets from wholesale sources and limits the need for last-resort central bank loans to meet cash runs.

The first two conditions go together. If bank credit to the private sector is too high and results in excessive money creation, the result will be inflation, which will discredit the monetary union; if bank credit to the private sector is too low, inadequate money growth and the deflation peril may have to be avoided by central bank purchases of sovereign bonds that discriminate improperly between governments, which will also discredit the monetary union.

The contrast between the euro's successful first and its unsatisfactory second decade now becomes easier to understand. Figure 11.1 shows that the rate of growth of domestic bank credit fell markedly between 2008 and 2010, and Figure 11.2 highlights that the slump in bank credit to the private sector was far greater than in bank credit to the public sector. Whereas in the peak period (the year to February 2008) new bank credit to the private sector was over €1,420 billion, just two years later (the year to February 2010) it was less than €30 billion. The figure was to remain at under €200 billion until mid-2016. Indeed, for an extended period, the three years to April 2015, the annual change in the stock of bank credit to the private sector was negative.

Unless offset by some other influence on bank balance sheets, weakness in bank credit to the private sector is certain to be associated with low growth in the quantity of money. Outright contractions in the stock of such credit may result even in falls in the quantity of money. Low growth or falls in the quantity of money are likely to lead to recession, rising unemployment and heightened deflation risk. These were indeed the experiences of the eurozone in its first recession (in 2008 and the first two quarters of 2009) and a second milder one (in the two years to the second quarter of 2013). In the first recession budget deficits widened sharply because of the cyclical hits to tax revenues and social security costs, and governments sought bank finance to a greater extent than in previous years. But this was far from being a deliberate policy across the entire eurozone. (Note, however, that banks needed more short-term government securities in order to comply with regulatory demands that they hold more liquid assets.) After the second recession the ECB embarked, amid much publicity and with full self-awareness, on a programme of large-scale asset purchases (or "quantitative easing"), which in fact meant mostly central bank purchases of government securities. Bank credit to the general government sector was €326 billion in the year to January 2016 and €453.5 billion in the year to January 2017. This contributed to an acceleration in broad money growth and a recovery in the real economy.

Figure 11.3 shows the split between bank credit to the private and public sectors in the eurozone's first two decades. The increase in bank credit to the private sector was cumulatively €7,375.6 billion in the decade to October 2008 and a mere €998.4 billion in the decade to October 2018. The behaviour of bank credit to general government sector was completely different. The increase in bank credit to general government was cumulatively a tiny €59.4 billion in the decade to October 2008 and €2,169.5 billion in the decade to October 2018. The first decade of the eurozone was characterised by a surge in the banking system's claims on the private sector, which meant that market criteria became more important in asset-acquisition strategies and could be viewed as a "de-politicisation" of banking. For

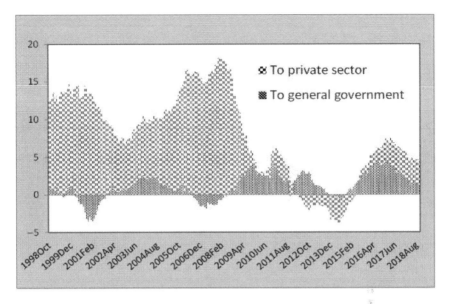

Figure 11.3 Destinations and growth rates of stock of bank credit in the eurozone, 1998–2018, annual totals as a percentage of M3 at period start

much of the time the ECB's holdings of securities were attributable to repo activity, which was virtually neutral in its effects on different member states. By contrast, the second decade saw a clampdown on banks' risk assets and a build-up of their safe claims on the state sector. This would have made banks' asset portfolios more political even in a standard monetary jurisdiction with only one government. In the eurozone it was accompanied by almost constant inter-governmental bickering and an undoubted politicisation of monetary decision-taking.

It was suggested earlier that high-level disagreements, reflecting de facto inter-governmental redistributions of claims on resources, would arise if credit extension were mostly from state-owned central banks (that is, the central banks belonging to the euro-system) rather than from privately owned commercial banks. Such credit extension could take the form of both central bank acquisitions of government debt and of central bank lending to commercial banks. What do the data show about the development of these two forms of central bank credit since 1999?

Figure 11.4 tells the story. In the first four years of the euro's existence the ECB's domestic claims *fell* slightly. The next five years saw the ECB's claims on other eurozone credit institutions (that is, of banks) more than treble, with the bulk of the increase occurring in 2007 and 2008. This reflected the adoption of so-called non-standard measures after August 2007. They were mostly ECB loans to banks to counter the damaging effects of the withdrawal of inter-bank credit lines, and so to ensure that banks could finance their portfolios of loans and securities. The non-standard measures were for the most part were *not* priced at penalty rates and

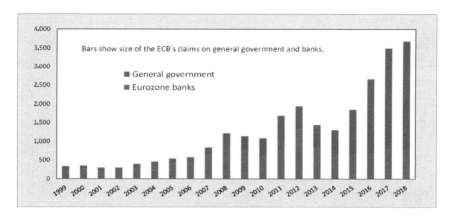

Figure 11.4 Growth and composition of the ECB's domestic claims, 1999–2018, in billions
of euros and related to year-end

represented a low-cost form of last-resort finance. In 2009 and 2010 the ECB tried
to cut back on the non-standard measures, with its chief economist, Jürgen Stark,
anxious that the expansion of the central bank balance sheet foreshadowed a return
to inflation.[30] In the two years to end-2010 the ECB's claims on commercial banks
duly dropped from €917.3 billion to €592.4 billion.

Unhappily, if predictably, the withdrawal of the non-standard measures weakened the ability of banks to fund their assets, particularly in the eurozone periphery (in, for example, Greece, Portugal and Ireland). These banks sold the most
liquid assets they had (that is, securities issued by their governments, the governments of Greece, Portugal, Ireland and so on). The sales drove up yields on
government bonds, giving rise to the eurozone's "sovereign debt crisis" in spring
2010. In April 2010 the yield on ten-year Greek government bonds soared above
30%. The member states were split about how best to respond to this situation,
which might culminate in Greece's departure from the eurozone and massive
harm to the single currency's credibility. On Friday 14 May a sharp confronta-
tion between the French President, Nicolas Sarkozy, and the German Chancellor, Angela Merkel, was widely reported.[31] Sarkozy favoured large-scale and
highly publicised ECB purchases of peripheral government debt, while Merkel
opposed them. Sarkozy's view prevailed, and in the next few weeks the ECB
organised significant purchases of Greek, Portuguese and Irish government debt.
These transactions were largely responsible for the increase in the ECB's total
holdings of government debt from €364.8 billion at end-2009 to €492.4 billion
at end-2010.

For the rest of 2010 and most of 2011 Greece and other vulnerable eurozone
states struggled to bring their public finances and banking systems into better
order. Throughout the period worries about possible eurozone break-up, and
about banks' loan losses and capital strength, weakened banks' ability borrow

from inter-bank markets or to raise long-term capital. Although the crisis was widely perceived as posing an existential threat to the eurozone, the ECB's president, Jean-Claude Trichet, made no effort to restore the non-standard measures. In December 2011, Mario Draghi, shortly after succeeding Trichet at the top of the ECB, changed tack radically. He announced the return of the non-standard measures, but on a larger and more easy-going basis, and emphasised that banks that drew on the over €1,000 billion of available funds (from "long-term refinancing operations") would suffer no reputational stigma. The press gave the return of the non-standard measures the label of "Draghi's bazooka". At the end of 2012 the ECB's loans to commercial banks approached €1,330 billion. With the extra firepower many banks were able to increase their holdings of government securities, which usually offered a yield well above the low cost of the LTRO money. As a result, the pressure on the ECB to buy government bonds was less acute. At end-2014 its holdings of government bonds were €617.0 billion, slightly lower than three years earlier.

Draghi's bazooka was sufficient to keep the eurozone intact, but it did not stop the eurozone entering its second recession in 2012 and 2013. Even in early 2014 growth was sluggish, and deflation later in the year and in 2015 was viewed as a serious possibility. Towards the end of 2014 the ECB's Governing Council decided to copy the asset purchase programmes (or "quantitative easing") that had been adopted successfully in the US and the UK (in 2008 and later) to combat recession. As noted earlier, the ECB's asset purchases were predominantly of government bonds and constituted finance for the governments of the eurozone's member states. The ECB's claims on general government soared from €617.0 billion at end-2014 to €2,923.2 billion at end-2018.

To summarise, in the early years of the single currency, central bank financing of either commercial banks or the eurozone's governments was negligible. But the paralysis in the international wholesale money markets from August 2007 obliged the ECB to lend to commercial banks so that they could continue to finance their assets, and it did so freely and generously. From then until now pressures of various kinds have made it expedient for the ECB to increase its claims on both commercial banks (with finance that is privileged, low-cost and quasi-permanent) and governments. Latterly the increase in claims on governments has been rationalised in macroeconomic-policy terms, in that central bank asset purchases should help economic activity and prevent deflation. An earlier discussion in the paper demonstrated that in a multi-government monetary union the extension of large-scale central bank finance – even if apparently justified as the traditional exercise of central bank responsibilities – could have a differential effect on member nations' command over resources and output. At the end of 2018 the ECB's combined claims on eurozone "credit institutions" and general governments totalled €3,675.3 billion, more than ten times higher than at end-1999 (when the figure was €333.4 billion). If the pattern of net claims on different nations' credit institutions and governments was unbalanced (that is, if the euro-system had a mix of large and persistent net debtors and creditors), the eurozone could be interpreted as in reality a transfer union.

4　Was evolution towards a *de facto* transfer union inevitable?

As is well-known, the pattern of net claims between central banks in the TAR-GET2 settlement system is indeed unbalanced and has been so for over a decade. Germany (that is, the Bundesbank) first became a creditor of the system in 2005, but only since 2009 has it been a significant net creditor to the tune of hundreds of billions of euros. The counterpart debtors have been particularly Italy and Spain. Since early 2012 they have been consistently in the red, also to the tune of hundreds of billions of euros.

The argument of this paper has been that, if the ECB acts – like any central bank – as a claimant on governments and lender to commercial banks, and if its claims are in practice on differential basis to the governments and banks of the various eurozone member states, the result will be a de facto transfer union. An explanation for the TARGET2 nexus of debits and credits is therefore that the ECB has behaved according to its remit as the eurozone's central bank. In the course of open market operations, notably the large-scale asset purchases from early 2015, and of support for commercial bank liquidity through the "non-standard measures" from 2007 to 2010, and again from 2011 to today, it has extended credit to eurozone government and banks to the value of over €3,500 billion. The credit has to some extent been unbalanced, most clearly helping Italian and Spanish banks rather than the banks of other countries, and that is why the TARGET2 debit/credit position has emerged. Figure 11.5 shows the correlation between Germany's TARGET2 credit balance and the growth of the ECB's domestic assets.[32]

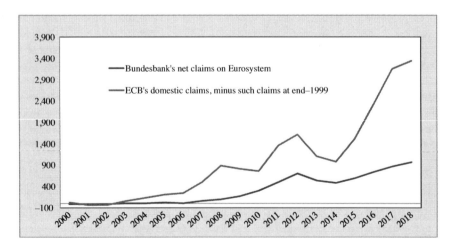

Figure 11.5 The growth of the Bundesbank's claims on the TARGET2 settlement system and the ECB's domestic claims (domestic claims are on governments and banks), in billions of euros and related to year-end

Source: ECB database.

Sure enough, Germany's TARGET2 credit position can also be attributed to the large and apparently chronic current account surplus on Germany balance of payments. But that is not a rival analysis or a wholly compelling answer. A nation's current account surplus can be recorded in a variety of financial channels; it can appear in central banks' accounts or in the accounts that member central banks hold in the settlement system of a multi-government monetary union; it can also appear in trade credit, in commercial bank accounts and in holdings of a plethora of financial securities. If the ECB had not extended so much credit to eurozone governments and banks, and if it had not done so on a differential basis, Germany could not have had a large surplus in the TARGET2 settlement system. The German current account surplus would have been registered in other ways (in trade credit, on commercial bank accounts, etc.).

In conclusion, the Maastricht Treaty overlooked the dangers inherent in giving the ECB the powers of a traditional central bank. As a by-product of standard central bank operations, the eurozone could mutate into a transfer union. The three "safeguards" identified by Wyplosz in 2010, and much emphasised by German commentators throughout the process of currency unification, were necessary conditions for the prevention of a transfer union. But they were not sufficient. A separate and more far-reaching agreement was required to pre-empt the risk of a transfer union. Such an agreement would have specified that the ECB would not hold large claims *of any sort* on any government, and that the task of emergency liquidity assistance to the banking system should be conducted only at the national level (so that no cross-border claims could emerge) and not on the account of a euro-system member.[33]

In June 2012, Angela Merkel, the German Chancellor, said in an interview for Spiegel International, there would no debt mutualisation in the eurozone "as long as I live".[34] But in fact the first two decades of the euro's existence – and particularly the second of those decades – had already seen extensive debt mutualisation in the eurozone. The contrast between the first and second decades further suggested how best to limit the tensions and strains that may be inevitable in a multi-government monetary union with a fully empowered central bank. If money growth arises solely from commercial bank credit to the private sector, if the pace of growth of both money and bank credit are consistent with price stability, and if central bank operations are restricted to repurchase transactions (between it and commercial banks) for the signalling of interest rates, a multi-government monetary union should work easily and with little inter-governmental rancour. In these circumstances there should be little or no inter-state transfers by stealth, and little or no quarrelling between member states' governments. On other hand, if money growth stems from the extension of central bank credit, if the pace of growth of money and credit is volatile and inconsistent with price stability, and if central bank operations result in large and seemingly ineradicable claims on different nations' governments and banking systems, a multi-government monetary union is likely to be fractious and difficult to manage. It might also appear to suffer from centrifugal forces as disadvantaged member states – whether they have a legitimate grievance or not – threaten to break away.

Notes

1 The "era of managed currencies" is understood to be that which has prevailed since the ending of the dollar's convertibility into gold in 1971. In contrast to the gold standard, the value of money is no longer linked to a commodity and must instead be managed by discretionary state action. The only comparable approach (that is, the sharing of a currency by fiscally sovereign states) is small-scale, the Eastern Caribbean Currency Union, where – in any case – monetary policy is not discretionary. It is instead geared to maintaining a fixed exchange rate with the US dollar.

2 In accordance with an emerging consensus, monetary stability is to be understood as the stability of a price index, maintaining the real value of money, while the touchstone of financial stability is deemed to be the convertibility of bank deposits into legal-tender cash, so that deposit money keeps its full nominal value.

3 At present no return is received on TARGET2 credit balances. Given that a reasonable long-return expectation on foreign equity investments might be 5% a year in real terms, Germany suffers (at the time of writing, July 2019) an implicit almost €50-billion-a-year loss on its TARGET2 credit balance, relative to that which would have been achieved if its citizens held equity investment abroad. (The German TARGET2 balance has been positive – at over €900 billion – since early 2018.)

4 See, for example, Ambrose Evans-Pritchard, "German Bundesbank comes clean on euro default risks after Italy's 'parallel currency' decree", *The Daily Telegraph*, 4 June 2019, about a Bundesbank report on the risk of losses to ECB creditors in the event of default by a member state. Analyses by Hans-Werner Sinn of the Ifo Institute have raised the alarm for some years, but Sinn supports the euro, and European monetary and political integration. See, again for example, Hans-Werner Sinn, *The Target Trap* (Oxford: Oxford University Press, 2014).

5 In a large literature the classic statement is perhaps Milton Friedman, *A Program for Monetary Stability* (New York: Fordham University Press, 1960).

6 The author has long argued that the key propositions in monetary theory apply only with a broadly defined money aggregate. See, for example, essays 15 and 16, pp. 330–373, in his 2011 collection *Money in a Free Society* (New York and London: Encounter Books, 2011).

7 Otmar Issing, *The Birth of the Euro* (Cambridge: Cambridge University Press, 2008), pp. 105–8. For international respect of the Bundesbank's role, see Francesco Giavazzi and Alberto Giavannini, "The role of the exchange-rate regime in a disinflation: Empirical evidence on the European Monetary System" pp. 85–107, in Francesco Giavazzi, Stefano Micossi and Marcus Miller (eds.) *The European Monetary System* (Cambridge: Cambridge University Press, 1988), particularly p. 104 on "imported credibility". For an example of Bundesbank interest in the P-star model, see Karl-Heinz Tödter, "Monetary indicators and policy rules in the P-star model" Discussion paper 18/02 (Frankfurt: Economic Research Centre of the Deutsche Bundesbank, 2002).

8 According to the International Monetary Fund, the average growth rate of eurozone output was 1.9% in the last 7 pre-single-currency years from 1992 to 1998 and 2.1% in the first decade of the single currency. It was only 0.7% in the 11 years to 2019 inclusive. In its October 2018 *Economic Outlook*, the IMF expected average growth in the 5-year period 2020–2024 inclusive to be 1.4%.

9 Discussion of the proportionality hypothesis is often subsumed in work on "the neutrality of money". See, for example, Don Patinkin, "Neutrality of money", entry in *The New Palgrave Dictionary of Money & Finance*, pp. 16–24, *The New Palgrave* (London and Basingstoke: Macmillan Press, 1992), vol. 3.

10 In their conclusion (pp. 149–153) to Michael Bordo and Lars Jonung, *The Long-Run Behaviour of the Velocity of Circulation* (Cambridge: Cambridge University Press, 1987), Bordo and Jonung propose that institutional forces such as monetization and

financial development can explain secular declines in the velocity of circulation of broad money in several societies.

11 So, if the rate of money growth is much above 6% a year for an extended period, inflation is likely to exceed target. Conversely, if it is much beneath 2% a year, then the price level may fall for several years, accompanied by disappointing output and employment outcomes.

12 Banks' capital-raising reduced the annual rate of money growth by 1.07% on average in the decade to October 2008 and by 1.13% in the following decade. (The estimate is the author's, using ECB data.) Given that the second decade saw much slower growth of bank balance sheets, this shows how after autumn 2008 the drive for extra bank capital – under the auspices of the Bank for International Settlements – became a more important concern for banks' managements.

13 Using national data from the IMF (which remain available despite the existence of a monetary union meant to supersede the notion of nation-specific monies), Juan Castañeda and the author found in a 2017 paper that rates of money growth varied hugely between eurozone member states. See Juan Castañeda and Tim Congdon, "Have central banks forgotten about money: The case of the European Central Bank, 1999–2014", pp. 101–29, in Tim Congdon (ed.) *Money in the Great Recession* (Cheltenham, UK and Northampton US: Edward Elgar Publishing, 2017). See, particularly, pp. 121–123.

14 In its March 2008 *Monthly Bulletin* the ECB noted that consumer inflation had "stabilised in February after reaching a record level of 3.2 per cent in January, following five consecutive months of sharp increase". It opined, just a few months before the start of the Great Recession, "The risks to the outlook for inflation over the medium term are on the upside". (See March 2008 issue of the ECB's *Monthly Bulletin* [Frankfurt: ECB], p. 58.)

15 See, for example, Ferdinando Giugliano, "Europe: Deflation decoded", *Financial Times*, 9 January 2015.

16 The topic is large, but the rise of Eurosceptic populism in Italy and Greece in the 2010s has been interpreted in these terms. The financial crises in Europe caused the future French president, Emmanuel Macron, to talk in July 2015 of a new "war of religion" in Europe, between the prudent Nordics, Germany and the Netherlands in one camp, and the more financially relaxed France, Italy and Spain on the other. Adam Tooze, *Crashed: How a Decade of Financial Crises Changed the World* (London and New York: Penguin Random House, 2018), p. 531.

17 According to the IMF, the average rate of consumer inflation in the 20 years 1999 to 2018 inclusive was 1.7%, while in the decade 1999 to 2008 inclusive it was 2.2% and in the decade 2009 to 2018 inclusive it was 1.2%.

18 The word "resources" is shorthand. Of course, loan proceeds can be used to acquire factors of production, goods and services recently produced, and existing assets.

19 By his celebrated "cross of gold" speech at the Democratic National Convention in Chicago in 1896, William Jennings Bryan secured his nomination as presidential candidate. Bryan supported bimetallism or "free silver", which he believed would bring the nation prosperity. He condemned the gold standard with his conclusion, "you shall not crucify mankind upon a cross of gold".

20 Charles Wyplosz, "European Stabilisation Mechanism: Promises, realities and principles", 12 May 2010 blog for VoxEU. Wyplosz also said that that the Stability and Growth Pact "never worked", while the two remaining of his three safeguards had "been blown away".

21 The author made this point in a 1992 paper (Tim Congdon, "Problems that were neglected at Maastricht", summer 1992 issue, *Central Banking* [London: Central Banking Publications], pp. 54–62.) in the early debates on European monetary union. "Extremely awkward questions relate to the ECB's holdings of different governments' debts" (p. 57). The Treaty also said nothing about government financing from commercial banks (which can increase money growth) or about deposit insurance.

22 Again, the author made this point in his 1992 paper for *Central Banking*. See the discussion on pp. 61–62 of his "Problems that were neglected at Maastricht". Similar concerns were expressed by two IMF economists, Alessandro Prati and Garry Schinasi, "Will the European Central Bank be the lender of last resort in EMU?", pp. 227–256, in Michael Artis, Axel Weber and Elizabeth Hennessy (eds.) *The Euro: The Challenge and Opportunity for Financial Markets* (London and New York: Routledge, 2000). Even in nation states banking crises can fuel misunderstanding and resentments. Thus, in the US the massive Federal Reserve loans to the banking system in 2008 and 2009 provoked hostile comment. Many members of the public believed that taxpayer dollars would be lost, with rich bankers "bailed-out" at the expense of low-paid government employees. In fact, according to Bernanke, then the Fed's chairman, "although we made thousands of loans to a wide range of borrowers, every penny was repaid, with interest – and the Fed, and thus the taxpayers, profited by billions of dollars". Ben Bernanke, *The Courage to Act* (New York and London: W. W. Norton & Company, 2015), p. 469.

23 The travails of the Banca Monte dei Paschi di Siena, the fifth largest in Italy, illustrate the problem. See B. Mesnard, M. Magnus and A. Margerit, "The precautionary recapitalisation of Monte dei Paschi di Siena", 6 July 2017 briefing for European Parliament. In 2017 the European Commission permitted a state-aid capital injection of over €5 billion, but by early 2019 this was deemed insufficient.

24 See Thomas Humphrey, "Lender of last resort" entry, pp. 571–3, in *The New Palgrave Dictionary of Money & Finance*, pp. 16–24, *The New Palgrave* (London and Basingstoke: Macmillan Press, 1992), vol. 1. Humphrey argued that Henry Thornton in his 1802 *Paper Credit*, not Walter Bagehot, was the first theorist of central bank's last-resort role. Humphrey summarizes Bagehot's contribution as, "lend freely at a high rate".

25 Otmar Issing, *The Birth of the Euro*, p. 124.

26 Initially, at the ECB's establishment in 1999, the Eurozone had 11 members; at the time of writing (July 2018) it has 19.

27 On Germany, see pp. 210–212 of Wolfgang Kitterer, "Public finance and the central bank", pp. 165–217, in Deutsche Bundesbank (ed.) *Fifty Years of the Deutsche Mark* (Oxford: Oxford University Press, 1999). In Germany, between 1949 and 1994, the federal government issued debt only with a maturity longer than one year. It started to issue paper with a maturity of under a year in 1997.

28 On Italy, see pp. 134–141 of Terenzio Cozzi, "Public finance and monetary policy in Italy (1973–83): Trends and problems", pp. 120–45, in Henry Cavanna (ed.) *Public Sector Deficits in OECD Countries* (London and Basingstoke: Macmillan Press, 1988).

29 This would be true even, for example, if the mix of government bond purchases accorded with the ECB's capital key, which reflected member states' share of eurozone GDP.

30 Jürgen Stark's "Economic recovery and exit strategies", speech at the debate on "The post-crisis strategy for growth and jobs" and "Modernisation of the global financial architecture" between the Committee on Economic and Monetary Affairs of the European Parliament and national parliaments, Brussels, 16 March 2010. To quote Stark in that speech, the "phasing-out some of the non-standard measures to avoid risks to price stability at a later stage is fully in line with the ECB's price stability mandate under the current circumstances".

31 Johan van Overtveldt, *The End of the Euro* (Chicago: B2 Books, for Agate Publishing, 2011), p. 99.

32 When the Bundesbank's net claim on the eurosystem is regressed on the ECB's total domestic claims (that is, the sum of its credit to general governments and eurozone credit institutions), the best-fitting equation has a coefficient of determination of 0.9. The t statistic on the regression coefficient (0.31) is 12.3. When the Bundesbank's credit

balance is regressed on either ECB claims on general government or ECB claims on credit institutions (that is, banks), the equation is of lower quality.

33 Banks in a particular nation could capitalize an emergency funding entity that could hold claims only on banks in that nation. The emergency funding entity – which might receive state support or be associated with a deposit insurance fund (financed by insurance premiums from banks, as with the Federal Deposit Insurance Corporation in the US) – would be separate from the central bank.

34 Spiegel International (English site), "Merkel vows 'no Eurobonds as long as I live'", 27 June 2012.

12 Proposals for reforming the eurozone

A critique

Roland Vaubel

1 Introduction

On 6 December 2017, the European Commission published its "roadmap" for reforming the eurozone.[1] The document contained the following proposals:

1 "Investment Stabilisation Function",
2 "Structural Reform Support Programme",
3 "Convergence Facility",
4 using the European Stability Mechanism (ESM) as a "backstop" for the Single Resolution Fund,
5 "European Deposit Insurance Scheme",[2]
6 transforming the ESM into a European Monetary Fund under EU law,
7 incorporating the Fiscal Compact in EU law,
8 appointing a "Finance Minister" of the eurozone.

Subsequently, the Commission revised and detailed some of its proposals.[3] When the Investment Stabilisation Function met with opposition, the French and the German government agreed to examine the possibility of establishing a European Unemployment Insurance Fund in order to stabilise effective demand in the eurozone.[4]

To justify its proposals the Commission argued that "the financial and economic crisis that hit Europe in 2008 . . . laid bare some of its institutional weaknesses". However, only proposals 4 and 5 are motivated by the 2008 crisis. Proposal 1 (the investment stabilisation function) is not related to the financial crisis because the crisis was a symmetric external shock – a panic caused by the collapse of the US subprime mortgage market – whereas the proposed investment stabilisation function is designed for asymmetric shocks. Proposals 4 and 5 are part of the so-called banking union – the common supervision, regulation, recapitalisation, resolution and insurance of banks. They are not inspired by the internal market project as originally defined. Originally, i.e. in the Single European Act of 1987, the internal market was defined as "an area without internal frontiers in which the free movement of goods, persons, services and capital is ensured". International diversity in the supervision, regulation and insurance of banks is perfectly compatible with the free movement of capital. But in 1989 the European Court of Justice changed the meaning of "internal market" to "conditions of competition which are not distorted".[5] Any difference between national regulations may be claimed to distort competition. In the meantime the Court's re-interpretation of "internal market" has been legalised in a protocol attached to the Lisbon Treaty.[6] Banking Union is about the centralisation of economic policy.

Politically, the Commission's proposals were inspired by Emmanuel Macron, who had been elected French president in May 2017. In his election campaign Macron had presented a wide-ranging programme to increase the powers of the European Union. Three reasons seem to explain his initiative:

First, the crisis of the eurozone since 2010 had revealed that the monetary union is problematic, controversial and threatened by exit. Second, even though his campaign has apparently been funded by French banks and big business, Macron claims to be a politician of the centre. He was looking for political issues on which many conservatives, liberals and socialists agree. The euro is one of them. By offering a pro-euro agenda Macron tried to present himself as their common leader against Marie Le Pen. Third, in the European Union a window of opportunity seemed to be opening for a "relance européenne". The political personnel in Berlin is still weak and willing. But Chancellor Merkel will step down in September 2021 at the latest. The British have voted to leave and would be out of the way. In the eurozone France has formed a majority coalition of governments willing to follow her lead on monetary policy and on bailing out banks and governments.

In June 2018, Berlin and Paris agreed on a common response to the Commission's proposals. However, Dutch Prime Minister Mark Rutte and his Finance Minister, Wopke Hoekstra, assembled a group of north European countries (the so-called Hanseatic League) which object to most of the Franco-German demands. Before the European elections and the appointment of the new Commission, few decisions were taken. As these obstacles are out of the way and the next Multi-annual Financial Framework starting in 2021 is being negotiated, the Commission is resuming its efforts to "strengthen the euro" and gain more power. Are these proposals well-founded?

2   A European Investment Stabilisation Function (EISF) or a European Unemployment Insurance Fund?

The Commission has suggested that the countries participating in the euro and in the Exchange Rate Mechanism II should be entitled to receive up to 30 billion euros in subsidised credits "to preserve public investment in the event of large asymmetric shocks". A shock is considered to be large if the country's unemployment rate rises by at least one percentage point and exceeds its five-year moving average. The Commission wants to finance these loans by borrowing in the capital market on behalf of the eurozone. According to the Commission, "the ESM or its legal successor could provide further support in addition to support under EISF". The proposed stabilisation function is problematic for a number of reasons.

First, at the most basic level, it is doubtful that EU or eurozone interference with public investment in a member state is compatible with the subsidiarity principle.

Second, the mutualisation of debt creates incentive problems. The Commission rather than the government that is investing would borrow in the capital market. The eurozone as a whole would be liable for repayment. Joint liability weakens the incentive to make efficient use of the credit and repay it.

Third, the absorption of asymmetric shocks does not require subsidised credits from the Commission. The shocks would also be absorbed if the recession-hit country borrowed in the capital market on its own. Capital would flow in from abroad and offset the shock. Indeed, borrowing by the investing government in the world capital market at the market rate of interest is more efficient than borrowing from the Commission at a subsidised rate of interest. The subsidy distorts incentives. However, the Commission is bound to offer a subsidy. If it did not, governments would not prefer borrowing from the Commission to borrowing directly in the capital market.

Fourth, the proposed indicator of asymmetric shocks is inadequate. A high and increasing unemployment rate is not a sign of an asymmetric shock. It may be due to a symmetric shock or no shock at all. A shock is an unanticipated change. However, an increase in unemployment may be fully anticipated. If so, the economy has already adjusted to the expected change, and there is no need to stabilise demand. Moreover, the increasing and high unemployment may be entirely of the country's own making. It is likely to be caused by excessive wage increases, new labour market regulations, the introduction of additional social transfers or rising taxes. In all these cases, responsibility rests with the member state, and international subsidies are neither required nor incentive-compatible.

Fifth, the prospect of receiving subsidised credits from the Commission in a recession would weaken the incentive to stay away from the 3% deficit limit of the Stability and Growth Pact. Budget deficits would increase.

Finally, the Commission wants to base EISF on Art. 175 para. 3 TFEU which permits "specific actions outside the Funds".[7] But this article comes under the title "Economic, Social and Territorial Cohesion". It is about structural policy – not about stabilisation policy. Moreover, Art. 175 concerns the EU as a whole – it does not belong to the title covering the eurozone. Finally, subsidised credits to finance public investment in the eurozone are not likely to benefit cohesion of the EU as a whole because the poorest countries of the eurozone are better off than the poorest countries in the EU which are outside the eurozone. For all these reasons, the legal base chosen by the Commission is inappropriate.[8] The Investment Stabilisation Function would require a (unanimous) amendment of the treaty or a (unanimous) agreement of eurozone governments separate from the European treaties.

In June 2018, Berlin and Paris agreed on "a eurozone budget within the framework of the European Union to promote competitiveness, convergence and stabilisation in the euro area, starting in 2021" (Meseberg Declaration). On 19 November 2018, the two governments submitted a joint proposal to the eurogroup, i.e. the finance ministers of the countries of the eurozone: "The eurozone budget would

... support relevant investments ... in euro area member states. ... The eurozone budget could also play a stabilising function in the eurozone, especially as investments are prone to be shed in case of pressure on national public finances". Thus, the stabilising impact of the investment subsidies would be a mere side effect. Contributions to the eurozone budget would be "transferred to the EU budget on the basis of an intergovernmental agreement". This means that each signatory state could unilaterally withdraw from the eurozone budget. The Franco-German proposal maintained Art. 175 para. 3 TFEU as the legal base. The Euro Summit of 14 December 2018 "mandates the Eurogroup to work on the design, modalities of implementation and timing of a budgetary instrument for convergence and competitiveness". The stabilisation function was not mentioned any further. According to press reports, this was due to resistance from the Dutch government and its "Hanseatic League".

Instead, stabilisation is now to be pursued by a European Unemployment Insurance Fund. The project has been agreed in Meseberg and proposed to the eurogroup. The fund would not be part of the EU budget. It would be based on an intergovernmental agreement of the eurozone countries. If a country experienced high and rising unemployment and if its cyclically adjusted budget was balanced, its unemployment insurance would be entitled to obtain a subsidised credit from the eurozone fund. The size of the credit and the interest rate would be determined by the ministers of the eurozone. The credit would have to be repaid within five years. The fund would be financed from insurance contributions paid by all workers in the eurozone.

The German Minister of Finance, Olaf Scholz, a Social Democrat, justifies his proposal by the need to maintain unemployment benefits in a recession. This has been a famous bone of contention in German history. In 1930, a German grand coalition collapsed over this issue. Unemployment benefits were cut, and the Social Democrats left the government in protest. It was the beginning of the end of the Weimar Republic. What followed were minority governments ruling by presidential decree until Adolf Hitler was appointed chancellor at the head of a right-wing majority coalition of NSDAP and Deutsch-Nationale Volkspartei.

Scholz rings a bell with his fellow Social Democrats but his argument is misleading. Nowadays no German or eurozone government would cut unemployment benefits in a recession. There is general agreement that the unemployment insurance serves as a built-in stabiliser of the demand for goods and services. If the reserves of the national insurance fund are depleted, the government borrows in the capital market. Obviously, the world capital market is a more efficient shock absorber than a common Unemployment Insurance Fund confined to the eurozone.

Moreover, to repeat, borrowing at the market rate of interest is more efficient than borrowing at a subsidised interest rate from a eurozone fund which is eager to attract customers and demonstrate European solidarity. The subsidy would be inefficient for two reasons. First, it would enable the fund to crowd out borrowing from the capital market which is the broader shock absorber. Second, the subsidy would distort the incentives of those responsible for the unemployment – typically the government or the unions or the employers of the country concerned.

Is the market solution feasible despite the deficit limit of the Stability and Growth Pact? Yes, the 3% limit has been set on the basis of simulations with the explicit aim of leaving enough leeway for recession-induced deficits provided that the government is balancing its budget over the cycle.

If the subsidised credits from the European Unemployment Insurance Fund do not count as part of the deficit, which is to be expected, they, too, weaken the governments' incentive to stay away from the 3% limit in normal times because, in the event of a recession, they could get along without borrowing in the market and, therefore, would not approach the 3% limit. Scholz wants to avoid this unwelcome incentive effect by confining the subsidised credits to governments whose cyclically adjusted budget is balanced. But cyclical adjustment is a matter of discretion. Economists may not even agree on the cyclically neutral position of the economy. The Scholz proposal is bound to provoke conflicts. It is not compatible with the EU's solemn aim of fostering mutual understanding among the peoples of Europe. Moreover, in the end, most finance ministers on the board of the fund are likely to be too lenient about the deficit – especially if a colleague from a large country is asking for a cheap credit.

Dolls (2019) has simulated the working of the Scholz fund in the period 2000–2016. In both of his variants, Germany would have been the principal lender to the fund while Spain and Greece would have been the main borrowers (his Figure 2). In the meantime, Scholz's German coalition partners, the Christian Democratic Union party (CDU) and the Christian Social Union party (CSU) have rejected all plans for a European unemployment insurance in their manifesto for the European elections. The Dutch government is also opposed. The eurogroup, after its meeting in December 2018, reported to the Euro Summit: "We did not reach a common view on the need and design of . . . the unemployment insurance scheme. Technical discussions continue".

The stabilisation function receives support from the European Central Bank (ECB). In a report published as part of the ECB Economic Bulletin the authors conclude that "setting up a well-governed common macroeconomic stabilisation function at the centre of EMU [European Monetary Union] . . . would help to contain the procyclicality of fiscal rules at the country level" (Leininger-Killinger and Nerlich 2019, abstract and p. 38). However, a much better solution is shock absorption and stabilisation through the world capital market – i.e. budget rules like the original Stability and Growth Pact and the sixpack, which leave enough room for deficit spending in a recession. Politically, a central stabilisation fund run by governments is a device by which politicians try to protect themselves against being judged by the market – especially before elections. By charging low and uniform interest rates, it insures them against the electoral damage which a visibly poor credit standing might otherwise cause.[9]

Since sovereign debt problems tend to arise in recessions, the European Stability Mechanism (ESM) does already serve as a stabilisation function. However, for the reasons given, market borrowing by individual eurozone governments seems to be more efficient than any fund, facility, mechanism or fiscal capacity financed by collective borrowing of the eurozone.

3   A Structural Reform Support Programme or Budgetary Instrument for Reform and Convergence?

The purpose of this programme is "to support reform commitment packages agreed with the Member States". The reforms would be agreed with the Commission and relate to its country-specific recommendations under the European Semester procedure. In the past, only about 10% of these recommendations have been adopted (Deroose and Griesse 2014). The Commission wants to spend up to 22 billion euros on such grants. They would be available to eurozone and European Exchange Rate Mechanism (ERM II) countries in proportion to their population size. The money is to come from the EU budget and possibly, later on, from the proposed successor to the ESM.

In February 2019, Berlin and Paris agreed that the reform support grants would have to be co-financed by the recipient states and that they would not be disbursed before the reforms have been completed. In the eurogroup meeting of April 2019, the finance ministers of the Netherlands, Austria, Finland and Ireland insisted that the Structural Reform Support Programme and the whole eurozone budget would have to be based on EU law rather than an intergovernmental agreement as French Finance Minister Bruno LeMaire had suggested.[10]

In the meantime, the Structural Reform Support Programme has been transformed to a "Budgetary Instrument for Convergence and Competitiveness". In June 2019, the eurogroup decided that this instrument should "support both structural reforms and public investment . . . within the euro area". The grants are to be paid in instalments, "subject to the fulfillment of agreed milestones". The instrument is to be part of the EU budget but its governance framework is to be codified in an additional act.

The Budgetary Instrument for Convergence and Competitiveness is objectionable for several reasons.

First, it creates an incentive to reject the recommendations of the Commission unless and until the latter offers money in exchange. Thus, the grants would mainly be paid for reforms which the governments would have implemented anyway.

Second, the money would mainly go to governments which have shied away from structural reforms in the past. This point has been made by Dutch Prime Minister Mark Rutte who said: "We in the Netherlands have implemented many reforms without help from abroad – and now we are asked to give money to those who have failed to undertake reforms in the past?"[11] By rewarding inaction in the past, the Budgetary Instrument for Reform and Convergence would weaken the incentive to adopt reforms in time.

Third, the European Commission would compete for customers with the International Monetary Fund (IMF). The EU Commissioners would be more partial in judging the merits of eurozone governments than the more broadly-based IMF Board of Executive Directors. For both reasons, the Budgetary Instrument for Reform and Convergence would lower standards and compliance.

4   A Convergence Facility?

The Convergence Facility is designed "for Member States on their way to joining the euro", notably Bulgaria, Croatia and Romania. The facility is to make it easier for these countries to satisfy the convergence criteria for admission to the monetary union. The Commission wants to spend up to 2.16 billion euros on subsidised credits and 840 million euros on "technical support".

Has it been too difficult to join the monetary union? Probably, the opposite is the case. Should Greece have been admitted – quite apart from its fudging the relevant statistics?[12] The fast growing east European countries are not optimal members of the eurozone either because the Balassa-Samuelson effect forces them to suffer from much higher inflation rates than the rest. Their currencies are bound to appreciate in real terms, and the most efficient way to bring this about is nominal exchange-rate appreciation vis-à-vis the euro – possibly under a pre-announced crawling peg.

The Convergence Facility would also be incompatible with Art. 140 TFEU, which stipulates that, for accession the euro, the convergence has to be "sustainable". This means that it must not be due to temporary measures. The transfers from the Convergence Facility would be temporary.

In view of these problems, the Meseberg Declaration has dropped the aim of facilitating entry to the monetary union. Berlin and Paris suggest that a eurozone budget for convergence should be set up within the existing EU structural funds devoted to economic convergence. But why does the eurozone need a special convergence budget of its own?

5   The ESM as a backstop to the Single Resolution Fund?

The Commission suggests in its "roadmap" that the ESM ought to become a "backstop" to the Single Resolution Fund (SRF) and that "any funds used would be recovered from the banking sectors in the Member States participating in the Banking Union". The SRF would have the right to borrow up to 60 billion euros from the ESM, and the Board of Governors of the ESM could "flexibly" increase this amount as they think fit. The ESM has 500 billion euros at its disposal. Up to now it has granted its subsidised credits exclusively to eurozone governments. It finances its credits by borrowing in the world capital market. The taxpayers of the eurozone countries are jointly liable for the repayment of what the ESM has borrowed from the capital market.

The Commission's proposal draws on a decision which the eurogroup took on 18 December 2013 in the context of its Banking Union agreement:

> A common backstop will be developed during the transition period. Such a backstop will facilitate borrowings by the SRF. The banking sector will ultimately be liable for repayment by means of levies in all participating Member States, including ex post. The backstop will be operational at the latest after ten years.

In the Meseberg Declaration, Berlin and Paris agreed on (1) the size of the back-stop, (2) the time table for its introduction and (3) the speed of recovery from the banks:

> The size of the backstop should be close to but not bigger than the size of the SRF. The backstop should replace the direct recapitalisation instrument [of the ESM]. . . . The entry into force of the backstop should be brought forward before 2024. In 2020, the relevant authorities will provide a report on the trend of non-performing loans (NPLs) and the building up of subordinated bail-in buffers. On that basis and if risk reduction is satisfactory, the final decision on an accelerated entry into force of the backstop should be taken.

According to the Meseberg Declaration, the backstop loan from the ESM should be repaid by the banks within three years with a possible extension of two years.

The eurogroup in its December 2018 meeting accepted the Franco-German proposal. It added the following decisions:

- First, the maximum amount available for each participating state would be proportional to its SRF contribution.
- Second, the backstop would also be available for banks with liquidity rather than solvency problems.
- Third, each credit line to the SRF would have to be approved by unanimous agreement of the ESM Board of Governors (and, to the extent required under national law, by their parliaments).
- Fourth, the ESM Board of Governors would be entitled to unanimously raise the initial cap on the size of the backstop.
- Fifth, the interest subsidy would be 35 basis points during the first three years and 15 basis points in the fourth and fifth year.
- Finally, the risk assessment in 2020 will focus on the "risk reduction" and, in particular, on the "trend of NPLs" and "be made against the aim of 5 % gross NPLs and 2.5 % net NPLs or adequate provisioning".[13]

This method of risk assessment is inadequate. The main problem of the back-stop mechanism is the cross-subsidisation among banks. The additional or "ex post" contributions which the banks would have to pay to the SRF would hold the well-managed banks liable for the losses of the badly managed banks. This would weaken the banks' incentive to avoid excessive risk in the future.[14] Thus, the risk assessment in 2020 should not focus on the "reduction" or "trend" or share of total NPLs in the eurozone but on the dispersion of these shares among banks or countries. The same applies to the banks' holdings of government debt.

When the availability of subsidised credits from the ESM and ultimately from foreign banks depends on the NPL statistics, the weak banks and their national supervisors have an incentive to underreport NPLs. Whether a loan is likely to be serviced or not is a discretionary decision and difficult to control. Thus, the risk assessment in 2020 will be highly unreliable.

Apart from the cross-subsidisation, the backup scheme would have three major effects.

First, by substituting the backstop for the recapitalisation instrument, the ESM would obtain claims against the SRF rather than against a national government. This is in the interest of the ESM because an ESM loan to the SRF will be recovered from all banks in the eurozone while an ESM loan to a national government is subject to a substantial risk of not being repaid.

Second, by substituting the backstop for the recapitalisation instrument, the SRF would be enabled to raise the contributions to be paid by eurozone banks in line with the credit which the ESM had granted. This is in the interest of the SRF.

Third, by extending the role of the ESM from bailing out overindebted governments to bailing out illiquid or insolvent banks, the architects of the ESM would protect their work against those who want to restore the no-bailout rule of the Maastricht Treaty, i.e. abolish the ESM. The ESM is based on an international treaty. Each signatory state may give notice on the grounds that circumstances have changed fundamentally, e.g. that the sovereign debt crisis is over. Each signatory state may leave the ESM without leaving the euro or the EU at the same time.

If the backstop enters into force between 2021 and 2024 as announced by the eurogroup, it encourages national supervisory authorities to postpone action on non-performing loans in their own countries because, under the backstop, losses will be shared with the banks of the other ESM countries.

There remains a final question. If a national minister of finance on the Board of Governors of the ESM realises that any backstop loan granted to the SRF to recapitalise the banks of other eurozone countries will ultimately have to be repaid in large part by the banks of his own country with adverse effects on their customers, will he or she nevertheless agree to the backstop loan? Agreement has to be unanimous.

In June 2019, the eurogroup published the draft of a revised ESM Treaty which incorporates the ESM's new role of serving as a backstop to the Single Resolution Fund. In December 2019, it set an "absolute limit to the amount that the ESM could lend to the SRB" amounting to 68 billion euro.

6   A common deposit insurance scheme for the eurozone?

The Commission's first proposal for a European Deposit Insurance Scheme (EDIS) dates from November 2015.[15] In October 2017, the Commission modified its proposal and suggested that, initially, EDIS would provide only credits to national deposit insurance schemes whose reserves are depleted.[16] Both proposals assume that deposits would be guaranteed up to 100,000 euros. This guarantee is currently provided by the national deposit insurance schemes in accordance with the Deposit Guarantee Scheme Directive covering all EU member states.[17] Under EDIS each bank would have to pay an ex ante contribution and, if necessary, ex post contributions in accordance with its share in total covered deposits and with its individual risk multiplier. Both schemes are to be introduced in stages. Both documents plead for EDIS on the grounds that it would provide uniform insurance coverage independent of the depositor's geographical location. However, this aim can also be attained by approximating the national deposit insurance schemes as the Deposit Guarantee Scheme Directive has done.

In December 2018, the eurogroup appointed a "High-level Working Group" chaired by Hans Vijlbrief, the Dutch Treasurer General, with a mandate to draft a roadmap for political negotiations on EDIS by June 2019. The working group has appointed a "Technical Group" chaired by the German state secretary Joerg Kukies. The German Bundesbank has declared that "a European deposit insurance is neither helpful nor necessary to stabilise the monetary union in its current shape"[18] and that "in this setting, a European deposit insurance scheme would ultimately mutualise fiscal risk and run counter to the principle of liability".[19] The scheme is fiercely opposed by the German savings banks and cooperative banks, which have their own well-functioning support systems. But the German Banking Federation, which is dominated by the large banks, fell into silence on this issue in 2014 when the large banks came under the supervision of the European Central Bank.[20]

The ECB has devoted a major study to the problem of cross-subsidisation in a European deposit insurance (Carmassi et al. 2018). The authors assume that contributions to EDIS would be calculated according to one of the methods which the guidelines of the European Banking Authority (EBA) recommend for the national deposit insurance schemes in the EU member states under the Deposit Guarantee Directive. However, this method is quite different from the method which the eurozone itself has adopted to calculate contributions to its Single Resolution Fund. As the authors of the ECB study concede (p. 27), the SRF method is less fair than the EBA method. Since EDIS would be a eurozone institution while EBA is an EU institution, political preferences in the eurozone rather than the whole EU matter for EDIS. They favour the SRF method. Thus, EDIS is very likely to be based on the SRF method.

Why is the SRF method not actuarily fair? Why does it not sufficiently allow for the differences in financial risk – both within countries and between countries?

First, the 12 risk indicators used by the SRF[21] do not include the share of non-performing loans (NPLs), nor are they strongly affected by it. However, according to the Commission's most recent "Progress Report on the Reduction of Non-performing Loans and Further Risk Reduction in the Banking Union",[22] the share of gross non-performing loans and advances (in total gross bank loans and advances) differs considerably among the eurozone countries. It is 44.9% in Greece, 28.1% in Cyprus, 11.7% in Portugal and 10.0% in Italy but only 0.6% in Luxembourg, 1.1% in Finland, 1.7% in Germany and 1.8% in Estonia. Moreover, according to the report, loss provisions as a share of total doubtful and non-performing loans amount to 83.6% in Germany but only 52.2% in Greece and 48.6% in Cyprus, for example. The ECB study (Carmassi et al. 2018, Table 1) presents econometric evidence that the share of NPLs significantly raises the probability that a bank will get into difficulties.

Second, the 12 risk indicators used by the SRF do not include the banks' claims on the domestic government (as a share of total bank assets), nor are they affected by this share. In 2017, according to the Basle Committee on Banking Supervision (2017), bank claims on domestic government debt as a share of total bank assets differed widely in the eurozone. They amounted to 18% in Italy, 13% in Spain and 12% in Portugal but only 6% in France, for example. Similarly, in February 2019, bank claims on all governments in the eurozone as a share of total bank assets ranged from 14% in Portugal to less than 2% in Estonia, Finland and France (Gehringer 2019, Figure 1). Bank claims on governments are treated as riskless in the risk management of banks despite the Greek haircut of 2011. Since many are risky, the wide differences among them imply that there are large differences in risk among banks which are not reflected in contributions.

Third, to calculate a bank's contributions the SRF does not take the (normalised) value of each risk indicator but the bank's rank with regard to the indicator. Obviously, this procedure favours outliers like Greece and the other southern member states at the expense of the others which are closer to the mean.

Fourth, the range of the risk multiplier is artificially restricted. A bank's risk multiplier is a weighted average of its ranks with regard to the 12 risk indicators scaled to a multiplier range from 0.8 (smallest risk) to 1.5 (largest risk). This means that the risk multiplier of the weakest bank is restricted to be less than double the risk multiplier of the safest bank. In other words, the maximum ratio of the highest to the lowest risk multiplier is less than 2:1 in the SRF. In the US deposit insurance FDIC the maximum ratio for large banks is 37,5:1.

If the ex ante contributions are far from fair, they encourage the banks to take excessive risks. A poorly designed insurance can make things worse, and a larger insurance is not necessarily better than a smaller one.

When insurance contributions do not adequately allow for differences in risk, national deposit insurance schemes are likely to be fairer and more efficient because financial risk tends to be more uniform within countries than within the whole eurozone. For example, as the ECB study (Carmassi et al. 2018, Table 1) shows, financial risk is significantly affected by country-specific factors like unemployment (+), inflation (+) and housing prices (−), none of which are used as risk indicators under the SRF method of calculating contributions.

The safest way to arrive at actuarily fair insurance contributions is, of course, to leave the problem to the banks themselves, i.e. to let them set up their own mutual support systems.

The prospect of EDIS, like the prospect of the ESM backstop, encourages the weak banks and their national supervisors to postpone the declaration and clearance of non-performing loans until EDIS is in force. The prospect of EDIS aggravates financial risk.

The Dutch government and its "Hanseatic League" are opposed to establishing a common deposit insurance for the eurozone.

7   Transforming the ESM into a European Monetary Fund under EU law?

The so-called European Stability Mechanism[23] is based on a separate international treaty. It is not an EU body. As has been mentioned, each participating state is entitled to withdraw from the ESM without leaving the monetary union or the

European Union. To prevent withdrawal and expand its own power, the Commission has proposed to incorporate the ESM in EU law, rename it European Monetary Fund (EMF) and give it additional competences.

The demand for a European Monetary Fund is an old French idea. It goes back to Raymond Barre in 1968, Valéry Giscard d'Estaing in 1978 and Nicolas Sarkozy in 2011. However, as the ESM finances itself by borrowing in the capital market it resembles the World Bank rather than the International Monetary Fund. The ESM is not a "monetary fund".

As an EU body, in the words of the Commission, the ESM/EMF would be dependent on "endorsement" from the Council, "accountable" to the European Parliament and obliged to "cooperate" with the Commission. "Urgent decisions" would merely require a qualified majority so that individual member states – including their parliaments – could be outvoted.

According to the Commission, the ESM/EMF would not only become a backstop for the SRF (as has been discussed in section 5). It would also gain more control over its programmes and could "develop new financial instruments. . . . Over time, such instruments could supplement or support other EU financial instruments and programmes . . ., particularly . . . in support to a possible stabilisation function in the future".

The Commission's proposals for expanding ESM power were a direct reaction to suggestions from German Finance Minister Wolfgang Schaeuble and the German Bundesbank. Schaeuble wanted to give the ESM two additional powers:[24] (1) monitoring compliance with ESM conditionality (in place of the "Troika" of Commission, ECB and IMF) and (2) budgetary surveillance of eurozone governments under the "sixpack" procedure (in place of the Commission).[25]

As the Commission does not want to cede these powers to the ESM it has proposed another way to prevent the ESM from being abolished: making it a Union body.

The German Bundesbank has suggested that the ESM should be in charge of sovereign debt rescheduling in the eurozone[26] even though the ESM is one of the creditors. The Bundesbank also recommends that the ESM rather than the Commission should assess the economic prospects, debt sustainability and financial needs of applicant countries and later monitor their compliance with policy conditions.[27]

In the Meseberg Declaration, Berlin and Paris agreed that "the ESM could be renamed" and that it "should have an enhanced role in designing and monitoring programmes in close cooperation with the Commission and in liaison with the ECB", i.e. without the IMF. But the German government insisted that incorporation in EU law should merely be considered "in a second step". The two governments also agreed that the Precautionary Credit Line of the ESM "could be used in case of risk of liquidity shortages where ESM Members are facing a gradual loss of market access, without the need for a full programme" (i.e. without policy conditions). This mirrors the decision on the backstop, i.e. that the ESM should lend to the SRF regardless of whether the banks in trouble are insolvent or merely illiquid.

In November 2018, the Commission and the ESM proposed that they would jointly assess applications for ESM credits and design and negotiate policy conditions, getting rid of IMF and ECB. The eurogroup in December 2019 accepted this proposal and easier access to the Precautionary Credit Line. They also decided that, by 2022, all governments participating in the ESM would commit themselves to introduce single-limb collective action clauses in their debt contracts. Watering down the Bundesbank's proposal on rescheduling, the eurogroup concluded that "the ESM may facilitate dialogue between its Members and private investors" (in a sovereign debt crisis). According to the draft of the revised ESM Treaty, the ESM may also "follow and assess the macroeconomic and financial situation of its Members" (Art. 3). The eurogroup did not take up the Commission's proposals to rename the ESM, make it a Union body or give it a stabilisation function. Nor is the ESM to monitor the budgetary policies of eurozone governments under the "sixpack" procedure as suggested by Schaeuble. Probably, all these proposals were rejected by the Dutch-led "Hanseatic League".

Thus, except for the backstop agreed in principle in 2013, the Commission's ESM-related proposals have all been discarded. However, the new unconditional access to precautionary ESM credits "in case of risk of liquidity shortages" is likely to be abused. Probably, in the future, most ESM credits will be granted without policy conditions.

8   Incorporating the Fiscal Compact in EU law?

Like the ESM Treaty, the Treaty on Stability, Coordination and Governance (2012) – generally known under the name "Fiscal Compact" – is to be incorporated in EU law if the Commission has its way. The treaty obliges the eurozone countries to introduce debt brakes into national law. Art. 16 foresees incorporation in EU law "within a defined time frame". By unionising the compact the Commissioners hope to protect it against being revoked and expand their own power. However, since the compact concerns only the eurozone countries, it is difficult to see why the whole EU should be in charge. This incentive problem has also been emphasised by the Dutch prime minister. Neither the Meseberg Declaration nor the eurogroup report of December 2019 mention the Fiscal Compact.

9   A minister of finance for the eurozone?

The same is true for the idea of appointing a Minister of Finance of the eurozone. The Commission took it from French President Macron. According to the Commission, the minister would be "a Commissioner, possibly a vice-president of the Commission", and, at the same time, president of the eurogroup. More precisely, "the role of the Minister as Vice-President of the Commission could be established as part of the appointment of the next Commission as from November 2019. For him or her to chair the Eurogroup, the latter could informally agree to elect the Minister President". This means that the Minister of Finance of the eurozone would be selected and appointed by the president of the Commission. According to the Commission, the minister would "oversee the use of EU and euro-area budget-ary instruments" and "strengthen policy coordination".

In Germany, both the Minister of Finance (Schaeuble) and the President of the Bundesbank (Weidmann) have expressed support for a European Minister of Finance.[28] Schaeuble even suggested that the managing director of the ESM – currently a German whose name is Klaus Regling – should get the position. In a manifesto signed by 154 German professors of economics and published in May 2018,[29] the proposal of a European minister of finance was rejected on the grounds that it would politicise monetary policy because the Minister of Finance of the eurozone would become the direct counterpart of the European Central Bank. Moreover, as with the Fiscal Compact and the ESM, for the reasons given, EU involvement in eurozone affairs is not incentive compatible.

The Franco-German Meseberg Declaration did not mention the European minister of finance even though, shortly before the meeting, the French Minister of Finance Bruno LeMaire had insisted that the proposal would be taken up "at the end of the process".[30] The eurogroup has not commented on the idea. The German CDU and its Bavarian sister party CSU, in their joint programme for the election of the European Parliament, expressly rejected the European Minister of Finance.

10   Conclusion: an alternative agenda

The proposals of the Commission, and what has become of them, may be contrasted with the recommendations which the 154 German professors of economics have made in their manifesto:

1   Government bonds should no longer be privileged in the risk management of banks.
2   The eurozone needs an orderly insolvency procedure for governments.
3   The eurozone needs an orderly exit procedure.
4   The capital market union ought to be completed.
5   In the ECB, liability and voting rights should be linked.
6   TARGET balances ought to be settled at regular intervals.
7   The ECB's purchases of government bonds should soon be stopped.

A few comments are in order.

As government debt is not riskless, this risk ought to be taken into account in the risk management of banks and their contributions to the SRF. By reducing their holdings of domestic government debt, they would mitigate the so-called doom loop by which debt problems of the government lead to debt problems of the banks (and vice versa). The risk multiplier of a bank ought to reflect (1) its holdings of government debt, (2) the risk premia which the various governments have to pay in the capital market, (3) their net debt to GDP ratios and possibly other fiscal indicators. As the Basle Committee are dragging their feet on this issue, the European Union or the eurozone should take the lead.

For an orderly government insolvency procedure, collective action clauses are essential. As mentioned, the eurogroup is committed to this reform. Moreover, the no bailout rule has to be restored. That requires the abolition of the ESM.

As for an orderly exit procedure, a first step was taken in June 2015 when several members of the eurogroup agreed that Greece should leave the eurozone. The European Council, a few days later, rejected the idea but the case may arise again. An orderly exit procedure could define "divergence criteria" of whether a country may or must leave the monetary union. For example, a country may be entitled or obliged to leave if it violated one of the "convergence criteria" for accession to the monetary union over an extended period of time.

In the ECB Governing Board three tiny member states (Cyprus, Luxembourg and Malta) together have more votes than each of the other countries – even the most populous like Germany, France, Italy or Spain. As the ECB's monetary policy affects more people in Germany than in Cyprus, Luxembourg and Malta, the ECB's legitimacy would benefit if national voting rights were in line with capital subscriptions or population.

The TARGET2 balances between the ECB and national central banks in the eurozone are much larger than anticipated. In 2019, for example, the Bundesbank's claims on the ECB were close to one trillion euros. If a member state left the eurozone without settling its TARGET debt to the ECB, the loss to the other central banks would be enormous. To reverse these unintended consequences of the TARGET2 system, the balances ought to be settled at regular intervals as required in the equivalent Fedwire's US Federal Reserve System.

Under its public sector assets purchase programme the ECB has bought more than 2.1 trillions of government bonds on a net basis. By doing so it has provided cheap and easy finance to eurozone governments and encouraged excessive government spending. Purchases of government bonds may be justified as an instrument of monetary policy in an emergency provided that the central bank does not discriminate between borrowers and buys a representative market portfolio. But the crisis is over. The ECB should return to normal and sell its holdings of government bonds. In this way it would induce the governments of the eurozone to return to budgetary discipline and sound methods of financing their expenditure.

Notes

1 COM(2017)821.
2 The Commission reiterated its proposals of November 2015 (COM[2015]586) and October 2017 (COM[2017]592).
3 COM(2018)387 concerning the Investment Stabilisation Function and COM(2018)391 concerning the Reform Support Programme.
4 Meseberg Declaration, 19 June 2018.
5 This was the Titandioxide decision (C-300/89, nr. 4).
6 This is the "Protocol on the Internal Market and Competition".
7 COM(2018)387.
8 This is also the conclusion of the detailed juridical analysis of Horn (2019).
9 I have made this point with regard to the International Monetary Fund (Vaubel 1991, p. 212). Dreher and Vaubel (2004, Table 3) show that net borrowing from the IMF is significantly

larger before elections. It does not come as a surprise that there are also researchers at the IMF who advocate a "rainy day fund" for the eurozone (Arnold et al. 2018).

10 *Financial Times*, 9 April 2019.
11 Euro-intelligence, 7 October 2014.
12 See Schmidt and Vaubel (2015). Greece (2001) violated the deficit limit and the criterion of sustainable price-level stability. The deficit limit was also exceeded by Italy (1999) and Malta (2008). The convergence criterion of sustainable price-level stability was not satisfied by the five east European entrants (Slovenia 2007; Slovakia 2009; Estonia 2011; Latvia 2014; Lithuania 2015).
13 Net non-performing loans are net of reserves set aside for this purpose.
14 For these reasons the European Constitutional Group (2018) concludes: "We do not believe that more mandatory risk-sharing among banks in the euro area is necessary or desirable". Juergen Stark (2019), the former German ECB Board member who resigned in protest at the end of 2011 adds: "The proliferation of backstops not only prevents risk mitigation, but actually invites even more risk. . . . The assumption is that the more risks are shared, the more stable the eurozone will be. But this is a fallacy".
15 COM(2015)586.
16 COM(2017)592.
17 Directive (2014/49/EU).
18 Monatsbericht, July 2013, p. 24 (my translation).
19 Annual Report for 2018, p. 22.
20 For a critique of the Single Supervisory Mechanism see Vaubel (2013).
21 In the SRF, the following risk indicators enter the risk multiplier (weights in parentheses): own funds and eligible liabilities held by the institution in excess of MREL (12.5%), leverage ratio (12.5%), common equity tier 1 capital ratio (12.5%), total risk exposure divided by total assets (12.5%), net stable funding ratio (10%), liquidity coverage ratio (10%), share of inter-bank loans and deposits in the EU (10%), trading activities (3%), off-balance sheet exposure (3%), derivatives (3%), membership in an institutional protection scheme (9%), extent of previous extraordinary public financial support (2%). Sources: Directive 2014/59/EU and Delegated Regulation (EU)2015/63 of the Commission.
22 COM(2018)766.
23 To the extent to which the ESM weakens the incentive to avoid excessive debt, it leads to instability instead of stability.
24 Stuttgarter Zeitung, 15 October 2016.
25 The German Bundesbank supports this proposal (Monatsbericht, April 2019, p. 81) even though the ESM Board of Governors consists precisely of the Ministers of Finance who are responsible for the budget deficits.
26 Monatsbericht, July 2016, p. 64.
27 Monatsbericht, July 2016, p. 57.
28 Schaeuble in Stuttgarter Zeitung (15 October 2016), Weidmann in Sueddeutsche Zeitung (8 February 2016).
29 "Der Euro darf nicht in die Haftungsunion führen" (The euro must not lead to shared liability), Frankfurter Allgemeine Zeitung, 22 May 2018.
30 Der Spiegel, 16 June 2018.

References

Arnold, Nathaniel G., Bergljot B. Barkbu, H. Elif Ture, Hou Wang, and Jiaxiong Yao (2018), "A Central Fiscal Stabilization Capacity for the Euro Area", *IMF Staff Discussion Notes*, Nr. 18/03, Washington, D.C.

Basle Committee on Banking Supervision (2017), *The Regulatory Treatment of Sovereign Exposures*, Discussion Paper, December (online), Basle.

Carmassi, Jacopo, Sonja, Dobkowitz, Johanne Evrard, Laura Parisi, André Silva, and Michael Wedow (2018), *Completing the Banking Union with a European Deposit Insurance Scheme: Who Is Afraid of Cross-Subsidisation?*, European Central Bank, Occasional Paper 208, April (online), Frankfurt.

Deroose, Servaas, and Joern Griesse (2014), *Implementing Economic Reforms: Are EU Member States Responding to European Semester Recommendations?*, European Commission, ECFIN Economic Brief 37, October (online), Brussels.

Dolls, Mathias (2019), *An Unemployment Re-Insurance Scheme for the Eurozone?*, EconPol Policy Report, Ifo Institut, Muenchen, January (online).

Dreher, Axel, and Roland Vaubel (2004), "Do IMF and IBRD Cause Moral Hazard and Political Business Cycles? Evidence from Panel Data", *Open Economies Review 15*, No. 1, 5–22.

European Constitutional Group (2018), *Open Letter to the President of the European Commission*, 5 April, wirtschaftlichefreiheit.de

Gehringer, Agniezka (2019), *Das Gespenst des europäischen Staaten-Banken-Nexus*, Flossbach von Storch Research Institute, Köln, Studien, 16 April (online).

Horn, Hans-Detlef (2019), *Zur Rechtsgrundlage einer Europäischen,* Marburg. *Investitionsstabilisierungsfunktion (EISF)*, Legal Opinion for the European Conservatives and Reformists Group in the European Parliament, Universitaet Marburg.

Leininger-Killinger, Nadine, and Carolin Nerlich (2019), "Fiscal Rules in the Euro Area and Lessons from Other Monetary Unions", *ECB Economic Bulletin*, No. 3, Frankfurt.

Schmidt, Linda, and Roland Vaubel (2015), *Der Missbrauch der Konvergenzkriterien 2001–2015*, Oekonomenstimme 828, 16 April (online), Zurich.

Stark, Juergen (2019), "The Risk-Sharing Fallacy", *The International Economy*, Winter, 58–59.

Vaubel, Roland (1991), "The Political Economy of the International Monetary Fund: A Public Choice Analysis", in Thomas D. Willett and Roland Vaubel (eds.), *The Political Economy of International Organizations: A Public Choice Analysis*. Boulder, CO: Westview Press, 204–244.

Vaubel, Roland (2013), "Probleme der Bankenunion: Falsche Lehren aus der Krise", *Credit and Capital Markets 46*, No. 3, 281–302.

Index